LLOYD D. NEWELL

Come,
LISTEN TO A
Prophet's
VOICE

**DAILY COUNSEL AND INSPIRATION
FROM LATTER-DAY PROPHETS**

DESERET
BOOK

SALT LAKE CITY, UTAH

To my father,
Neil O. Newell

© 2006 Lloyd D. Newell

All rights reserved. No part of this book may be reproduced in any form or by any means without permission in writing from the publisher, Deseret Book Company, P. O. Box 30178, Salt Lake City, Utah 84130. This work is not an official publication of The Church of Jesus Christ of Latter-day Saints. The views expressed herein are the responsibility of the author and do not necessarily represent the position of the Church or of Deseret Book Company.

DESERET BOOK is a registered trademark of Deseret Book Company.

Visit us at deseretbook.com

Library of Congress Cataloging-in-Publication Data

Newell, Lloyd D., 1956-
    Come, listen to a prophet's voice : daily counsel and inspiration from Latter-day prophets / Lloyd D. Newell.
        p.   cm.
    Includes bibliographical references.
    ISBN-13: 978-1-59038-621-7 (hardbound : alk. paper)
    ISBN-10: 1-59038-621-3 (hardbound : alk. paper)
    1. Mormon Church—Prayer-books and devotions—English.
2. Church of Jesus Christ of Latter-day Saints—Prayer-books and devotions—English   3. Devotional calendars.   I. Title.
    BX8656.N483 2006
    242'.2—dc22
                                                    2006021431

Printed in the United States of America
Inland Press, Menomonee Falls, WI

10   9   8   7   6   5   4   3   2   1

PREFACE

On the day the Church was organized in this dispensation, the Lord revealed his law regarding the prophets: "Wherefore, meaning the church, thou shalt give heed unto all [the prophet's] words and commandments which he shall give unto you as he receiveth them, walking in all holiness before me; for his word ye shall receive, as if from mine own mouth, in all patience and faith. For by doing these things the gates of hell shall not prevail against you; yea, and the Lord God will disperse the powers of darkness from before you, and cause the heavens to shake for your good, and his name's glory" (D&C 21:4–6). We need divine guidance and heaven's blessings more than ever. The inspired words of latter-day prophets are vital for us in these days "when dark clouds of trouble hang o'er us." Truly, we thank God for prophets.

In the preparation of this volume, I gratefully acknowledge several who have made it possible: Jana

Erickson, for her enthusiastic support and encouraging counsel; Jay Parry, for his keen editorial eye and professionalism, assisted by Lisa Mangum; Richard Erickson and Sheryl Smith for the layout and design; Tonya Facemyer for the typesetting; and especially, my wife, Karmel, who heartens my efforts and makes my writing and my life so much better.

Finally, this book is dedicated to my dear father, who passed away in 1986. One of my clearest memories is of my father at general conference time. He recorded each session on his worn, but trusted tape recorder and then carefully labeled each tape with detailed information. Over the next six months, as he commuted to and from work in his old truck (which didn't have a tape player in it), he would position the tape recorder on the seat next to him and listen to the tapes. I still have many of those tapes that he recorded and, more than twenty years later, cannot bring myself to throw them away. They symbolize for me so much of what my father was about: humility, obedience, and goodness. It was my father who taught me to love and sustain the prophets of God.

JANUARY

~

*God does not begin by asking us about
our ability, but only about our availability,
and if we then prove our dependability,
he will increase our capability!*

NEAL A. MAXWELL

*You must begin with the first, and go on until
you learn all the principles of exaltation.*

JOSEPH SMITH
TEACHINGS, 348

The gospel is the new and everlasting covenant that
will lead faithful followers of Jesus Christ to "peace in
this world and eternal life in the world to come"
(D&C 59:23). It is the plan of happiness, a marvelous
work and wonder to the inhabitants of the earth
who accept the gospel and keep their covenants. Cul-
minating in exaltation, or the endowment of celestial
glory, the panoramic plan of salvation offers us hope
and perspective that gives meaning to the here and
now. Each of the principles of exaltation leads us to
the perfection that is found only in Christ. Referring
to the principles of exaltation, the Prophet Joseph
Smith said, "But it will be a great while after you have
passed through the veil before you will have learned
them. It is not all to be comprehended in this world;
it will be a great work to learn our salvation and exaltation even beyond the grave" (*Teachings,* 348). Line
upon line, little by little, we progress into eternity.

The course of our lives is seldom determined by great, life-altering decisions. Our direction is often set by the small, day-to-day choices that chart the track on which we run. This is the substance of our lives—making choices.

GORDON B. HINCKLEY
STAND A LITTLE TALLER, 13

All of life is a series of choices. We exercised our agency in the premortal council in heaven and kept our first estates by rising up in favor of God's plan of happiness. Adam and Eve were told, "nevertheless, thou mayest choose for thyself" (Moses 3:17). Joshua exhorted the people of his day, "choose you this day whom ye will serve" (Joshua 24:15). In the meridian dispensation, Jesus taught that "no man can serve two masters" (Matthew 6:24). And to the ancient inhabitants of the Americas came the eternal truth: "Ye are free; ye are permitted to act for yourselves" (Helaman 14:30). The small, daily decisions we make each day determine our happiness here and our destiny hereafter. They accumulate to influence for good or ill the great, life-altering decisions we make. Indeed, wrong decisions are rarely made about those big issues when righteous decisions are made in daily living.

We do not lack a prophet; what we lack is a listening ear by the people and a determination to live as God has commanded. That is all we need. The way has been made perfectly clear.

J. REUBEN CLARK JR.
CONFERENCE REPORT, OCTOBER 1948, 80

In every dispensation, the Lord has spoken clearly to the people through prophets (Amos 3:7). The prophet is the Lord's authorized spokesman on the earth, and what he says is what the Lord would say (D&C 1:38; 68:4); he is the only man on earth who possesses and exercises all of the keys of the priesthood (D&C 132:7). Now, as in times past, we need the steady and reassuring voice of the Lord's anointed apostles and prophets who will show us the pathway to happiness and spiritual safety. The responsibility and opportunity is ours. All we need is to *listen* and *do.* If we wish to have the influence of the Spirit of the Lord in our lives we must humbly hearken to the counsel of the prophets, we must do what God commands, and we must be steadfast and immovable in following the oracles of the Lord. Truly, we thank God "for a prophet to guide us in these latter days" (*Hymns,* no. 19).

*The closer we keep our lives in harmony with
the direction the Lord has given us to guide our lives,
the more we will be in tune with His Spirit.*

L. TOM PERRY
ENSIGN, NOVEMBER 2003, 86

Those who enter into a covenant relationship with Jesus Christ and then continue to keep those covenants sacred are entitled to the promptings of the Holy Ghost. Elder L. Tom Perry wrote, "A person who petitions the Lord for guidance must be worthy to receive it. His life must be in harmony and in keeping with the standards the Lord has prescribed for His children. His life must be in good standing before God and His people. It must be in harmony with the teachings of the scriptures, the prophets, and the order of the Church" (*Ensign,* November 2003, 86). The Spirit will not inspire those who are lazy and lackadaisical, those who are lustful and licentious, those who are duplicitous and dishonest. And though we are all less than perfect, the Lord knows our hearts and minds, and will abundantly bestow his Spirit upon those who are humble and obedient. If we wish to receive inspiration, we must strive to live worthy of the Spirit.

To hear the laughter of children, to witness the expression of love by parents, and to feel the embrace of brothers and sisters provide a preview of heaven and the eternal joy to be found there.

THOMAS S. MONSON
ENSIGN, NOVEMBER 2003, 57

Family joys are the sweetest and most sublime of all earthly delights—everything else pales in comparison. Family joy is like the dye that seeps deep down into the fabric of the home. The world's pleasures, conversely, are like a veneer painted on the surface. We may get transitory pleasure and momentary enjoyment from them, but enduring happiness that lifts, even in times of trouble, comes from family. Of course, no family is immune from heartache, stress, and sorrow; but rising above it all is the knowledge that God himself lives in the family unit, and he has placed us in families and given us each other for a reason—a reason with eternal implications. Love and laughter, compassion and caring, kindness and kinship are best developed and expressed in the loving embrace of family.

*We are commanded to seek learning by study,
the way of reason, and by faith, the way that relies on
revelation. Both are pleasing to God.*

DALLIN H. OAKS
THE LORD'S WAY, 72

The Lord gave us important guidance regarding revelation: "Yea, behold, I will tell you in your mind and in your heart, by the Holy Ghost" (D&C 8:2). We are to use both reason (mind) and revelation (heart), both study (mind) and faith (heart) in all the pursuits of life. So, whether teaching a Primary class, performing surgery as a physician, or dealing with a difficult familial issue, we are to think it through and study it out, all the while pondering and seeking heaven's help. Reason and revelation are complementary associates, not enemies. Elder Dallin H. Oaks observed, "[The Lord] uses both ways to reveal light and knowledge to his children. But when it comes to a knowledge of God and the principles of his gospel, we must give primacy to revelation because that is the Lord's way" (*The Lord's Way,* 72). We cannot know the things of God without the Spirit of God (see 1 Corinthians 2:11).

There is comfort and strength in the knowledge that God is our Heavenly Father, that he is not a distant, indefinable abstraction, but a loving and understanding parent so near that we can have daily communication with him.

MARION G. ROMNEY
ENSIGN, AUGUST 1976, 4

Our Father in Heaven is not a disembodied presence or abstraction who mysteriously fills the immensity of space. He is our Father. We were not made from nothing, nor are we a product of chance occurrences. We are his beloved sons and daughters, his great and final creation, with a direct connection to heaven and the heavenly. As we begin to understand who our Father is we begin to comprehend our inherent worth and infinite potential. We come to know our Father through sincere fasting and prayer, through study and pondering, through humbly doing the will of the Father, through service and sacrifice for the kingdom. May we have the desire, courage, and meekness to gain knowledge of the Father and enjoy his strengthening and protecting power by communicating with him daily.

The Lord works from the inside out.
The world works from the outside in.

EZRA TAFT BENSON
A WITNESS AND A WARNING, 64

We're all familiar with the terms *self-esteem, self-concept,* and *self-image.* The world teaches that worth comes from success, that behavior is changed through sheer willpower, that the social mirror has the greatest power to shape our lives. Prophets of the Lord teach otherwise. "The world would take people out of the slums. Christ takes the slums out of people, and then they take themselves out of the slums," President Ezra Taft Benson taught. "The world would mold men by changing their environment. Christ changes men, who then change their environment. The world would shape human behavior, but Christ can change human nature" (*A Witness and a Warning,* 64). Meaningful and lasting change comes from turning our lives over to Christ, from believing and trusting him, from being "born of God, changed from [our] carnal and fallen state, to a state of righteousness, and thus [we] become new creatures" (Mosiah 27:25–26).

JANUARY 9

If there is a chink in your integrity,
that is where the devil concentrates his attack.

SPENCER W. KIMBALL
TEACHINGS, 192

The apostle Paul exhorted the Saints to test themselves as to righteousness, "Examine yourselves. Know ye not your own selves?" (2 Corinthians 13:5). We all have blind spots, Achilles' heels that we may not recognize in ourselves. These shortcomings can be revealed to us, either by the gentle entreaty of loved ones or by the whisperings of the Spirit, when we humbly seek for truth. In order to withstand the wiles of the adversary, we need to see ourselves truthfully—without self-deception or rationalization. Then we can face those susceptibilities and foibles, and because of the Atonement, "make weak things become strong" (Ether 12:27). This process establishes integrity. President Spencer W. Kimball observed, "Integrity . . . is one of the foundation stones of good character, and without good character one cannot hope to enjoy the presence of God here or in the eternities" (*Teachings,* 192).

Human beings are expected by their Creator to be actively employed in doing good every day of their lives, either in improving their own mental and physical condition or that of their neighbors.

BRIGHAM YOUNG
DISCOURSES, 88

Prophets of God have always believed in the gospel of work. They know that the work of the Lord is done by ordinary men and women who are willing to exert themselves to build Zion. We do not build Zion, others, or even ourselves by pontificating and conceptualizing the mysteries of godliness. The Lord expects us to go about *doing* good—whether by being a faithful home or visiting teacher, a kind neighbor, a generous friend, or a loyal family member. We can help build Zion by sharing the gospel and exemplifying righteousness in our daily walk and talk. Some have compared this process to a wagon wheel: Sometimes we're on the top lifting others and sometimes we're on the bottom being lifted; but as long as most of us are pressing forward, the cause of righteousness is advanced. As the hymn so aptly expresses, "Put your shoulder to the wheel; push along, / Do your duty with a heart full of song" (*Hymns*, no. 252).

The Lord's tender mercies are the very personal and individual-
ized blessings, strength, protection, assurances, guidance, loving-
kindnesses, consolation, support, and spiritual gifts which we
receive from and because of and through the Lord Jesus Christ.

DAVID A. BEDNAR
ENSIGN, MAY 2005, 99

Great are thy tender mercies, O Lord" (Psalm 119:156). Indeed, through study, pondering, prayer, and keen observation, we can come to better understand that the Lord lovingly extends to each of us his tender mercies and abundant blessings. We know that the Lord suits "his mercies according to the conditions of the children of men" (D&C 46:15), and we know that "the tender mercies of the Lord are over all" (1 Nephi 1:20). We also have the sweet assurance that the Lord knows us individually and knows what we need in order to develop the attributes of godliness and reach our potential. The Lord's tender mercies are given in the wisdom of him who is omniscient and omniloving. This we gratefully acknowledge: "The Lord is good to all: and his tender mercies are over all his works" (Psalm 145:9).

I know of no easy formula to success.
Persist, persist, PERSIST; work, work, WORK—
is what counts in the battle of life.

HEBER J. GRANT
TEACHINGS OF PRESIDENTS OF THE CHURCH, 36

Heber J. Grant is well known for his hard work and uncommon persistence. Whether learning to play baseball or practicing penmanship, he believed that success would come if he invested the time needed to become proficient. He said, "It is by exercise and by practice that we become proficient in any of the vocations or avocations of life, whether it be of a religious or of a secular character." He also admonished: "Stick-to-it-iveness and determination are the qualities that will help you to win the battle of life" (*Teachings of Presidents of the Church,* 36). Our battles may not be with a baseball or a pen, but with more weighty matters—pride, slothfulness, or any of a host of things that prevent the Spirit of the Lord from influencing our lives. We grow spiritually as we pray humbly, as we ponder deeply, as we feast daily upon holy writ and reach out to others in love. Real success is never quick or easy. Steadfast persistence and earnest work are ultimately what make the difference.

JANUARY 13

*For anyone seeking the courage to repent and change,
I remind you that the Church is not a monastery for the isolation
of perfect people. It is more like a hospital provided
for those who wish to get well.*

JEFFREY R. HOLLAND
TRUSTING JESUS, 66

We all have in common the need to repent and become more alive in Christ. A feeling of divine discontent imbues us with humility and prompts us to make changes, both big and small, that bring us closer to Christ. We all need the "hospital" of the Church, where we can learn of the Lord and participate in gospel ordinances, seek healing and fellowship, serve one another, and develop spiritually. Elder Jeffrey R. Holland has said: "Do whatever you have to do to come into the fold and be blessed. For some of you that is simply to live with greater faith, to believe more. For some of you it does mean to repent—right here. Today. For some of you it means to be baptized and come into the body and fellowship of Christ. For virtually all of us it means to live more by the promptings and promises of the Holy Ghost" (*Trusting Jesus,* 66). The Church is a place where each of us can come to get well and stay well.

*You can make a little heaven right here among yourselves,
if you want to; and you need not go anywhere else for it. Live your
religion, and you will be blessed in time and all eternity.*

JOHN TAYLOR
JOURNAL OF DISCOURSES, 22:321

We've all heard the expression "Bloom where you're planted." That has relevance for us today as we find ourselves in a range of circumstances with customized challenges and opportunities. Wherever we are right now, whatever the past or present, we can begin to build upon a hopeful future and make today a little heaven in our lives. We don't need to travel abroad to find goodness; we don't need to yearn for the Great Beyond to find joy. Alma taught: "For that same spirit which doth possess your bodies at the time that ye go out of this life, that same spirit will have power to possess your body in that eternal world" (Alma 34:34). If we do our best and strive to live the gospel with full purpose of heart, we will receive a portion of the promised blessings. Some of heaven's peace and joy can be felt right now: "He who doeth the works of righteousness shall receive his reward, even peace in this world, and eternal life in the world to come" (D&C 59:23).

*Developing Christlike attributes in our
lives is not an easy task, especially when we move away from
generalities and abstractions and begin to deal with real life.
The test comes in practicing what we proclaim.*

DIETER F. UCHTDORF
ENSIGN, NOVEMBER 2005, 102

Developing Christlike attributes is a lifelong process. Elder Dieter F. Uchtdorf said: "The reality check comes when Christlike attributes need to become visible in our lives. . . . We can recognize our growth, as can those around us, as we gradually increase our capacity to 'act in all holiness before [Him]' (D&C 43:9). . . . The Savior invites us to learn His gospel by living His teachings. To follow Him is to apply correct principles and then witness for ourselves the blessings that follow. This process is very complex and very simple at the same time. Ancient and modern prophets described it with three words: 'Keep the commandments'" (*Ensign,* November 2005, 102). Those who keep the commandments of God "are blessed in all things . . . ; and if they hold out faithful to the end they are received into heaven, that thereby they may dwell with God in a state of never-ending happiness" (Mosiah 2:41).

*We are not here to while away the hours of this
life and then pass to a sphere of exaltation; but we are here to
qualify ourselves day by day for the positions that our
Father expects us to fill hereafter.*

GEORGE ALBERT SMITH
TEACHINGS, 17

We are here to be anxiously engaged in primary causes: keeping commandments, resisting temptations, mastering appetites, creating and strengthening families, learning and working with our eyes single to God. Secondary causes, just like empty calories, fill our lives for a moment but then leave us unfilled and wanting. President George Albert Smith taught us to make good use of the time we have: "We have been placed here for a purpose. That purpose is that we may overcome the evil temptations that are placed in our way, that we may learn to be charitable to one another, that we may overcome the passions with which we are beset, so that when the time comes for us to go to the other side we may be worthy, by reason of the effort we have put forth, to enjoy the blessings that our Father has in store for the faithful" (*Teachings*, 17). Wonderful blessings and opportunities are ahead for those anxiously engaged in righteousness.

*As we look into the eyes of our children . . . , we see the
doubt and fear of our times. They hear about unemployment,
poverty, war, immorality, and crime. They wonder,
"How can we cope with these problems?"*

ROBERT D. HALES
ENSIGN, MAY 2003, 16

We live in perilous times of uncertainty and fear. Sometimes we may worry what the world in which our children and grandchildren live will be like. But this is not the time for the fainthearted and weak-kneed. If we are prepared, we need not fear (D&C 38:30); if we are clothed in the armour of righteousness, we need not be afraid (Ephesians 6:10–18); if we strive to live with virtue and charity, our faith will grow (D&C 121:45). Parents can manifest a quiet confidence in the promises of the Lord. Elder Robert D. Hales said, "[Our children] need to see us continuing to pray and study the scriptures together, to hold family home evening and family councils, to serve faithfully in our Church callings, to attend the temple regularly, and to be obedient to our covenants. When they see our steadfastness in keeping the commandments, their fears will subside and their confidence in the Lord will increase" (*Ensign,* May 2003, 17).

*Because of [Jesus'] Atonement, our Father's plan
of happiness will succeed. Satan's plan is doomed to failure.*

RICHARD G. SCOTT
ENSIGN, JUNE 2002, 37

With Jesus Christ as our Savior and Anchor, we cannot fail. Because of our Redeemer's infinite and intimate Atonement, we each can have power in the present and hope in the future. That *power* is manifest in faithfulness and righteousness; that *hope* is reflected in a sweet assurance of a coming day of peace and rest. Elder Jeffrey R. Holland testified of Christ's saving power in our world today: "In a world of unrest and fear, political turmoil and moral drift, I testify that Jesus is the Christ—that He is the living Bread and living Water—still, yet, and always the great Shield of safety in our lives, the mighty Stone of Israel, the Anchor of this His living Church. I testify of His prophets . . . and bear witness that . . . such oracles are at work now, under the guidance of the Savior of us all, in and for our very needful day" (*Ensign,* November 2004, 9). With Christ, we will not fail.

Happiness comes from unselfish service.
And happy homes are only those where there is a daily striving
to make sacrifices for each other's happiness.

HAROLD B. LEE
TEACHINGS, 296

Home is a laboratory of love, a sacred place where we make sacrifices for one another. If we wish to create happy homes, we learn to give up things of lesser value for those of lasting value. We offer our time, talents, and all the blessings we've been given to help others, especially those near and dear to us. By giving of our hearts to those we love—especially those who can be difficult to love—we create lasting bonds. When a mother stays up all night to care for a sick child, her sacrifice of sleep enlarges her heart. When a father turns off a ballgame to participate in a family activity, he lets his family know how important they are to him. When spouses make time for each other, they grow closer together—and to the Lord. All these sacrifices, large and small, are a similitude of the sacrifice of the Son of God, who unselfishly gave his all that we might have a fulness of joy.

The time has come when members of the Church
need to speak out and join with the many other concerned people
in opposition to the offensive, destructive, and mean-spirited
media influence that is sweeping over the earth.

M. RUSSELL BALLARD
ENSIGN, NOVEMBER 2003, 17

The world needs our voices of morality and virtue. Too often the quiet majority, those who truly love God and family and principles of truth, sit silently by while the world sinks ever deeper into lasciviousness and carnality. We may be too occupied with our own lives to even notice the slow stain of sinfulness. Or we may be apathetic or feel powerless to change anything. But our voices of honesty and integrity, of righteousness and decency, must be raised. Elder M. Russell Ballard noted: "The new morality preached from the media's pulpit is nothing more than the old immorality. It attacks religion. It undermines the family. It turns virtue into vice and vice into virtue. It assaults the senses and batters the soul with messages and images that are neither virtuous, nor lovely, nor of good report, nor praiseworthy" (*Ensign,* November 2003, 17). In civil and appropriate ways, let our voices of virtue and morality be heard.

*If two people love the Lord more than their own lives
and then love each other more than their own lives, working
together in total harmony with the gospel program as their basic
structure, they are sure to have this great happiness.*

SPENCER W. KIMBALL
TEACHINGS, 309

It has been said that marriage is a marathon, not a sprint. As such, a happy, healthy, and lasting marriage is a full-time commitment that, like anything we cherish, must be nurtured, nourished, and supported. President Spencer W. Kimball prescribed a recipe for marital success: "When a husband and wife go frequently to the holy temple, kneel in prayer together in their home with their family, go hand in hand to their religious meetings, keep their lives wholly chaste, mentally and physically, so that their whole thoughts and desires and love are all centered in one being, their companion, and both are working together for the upbuilding of the kingdom of God, then happiness is at its pinnacle" (*Teachings,* 309). By following the prophet's counsel, marriages can stay strong, and together, husbands and wives can withstand the buffetings of modern life.

*Our challenges are like yours. We are all subject to
sorrow and suffering, to disease and death. Through times good
and bad, the Lord expects each of us to endure to the end.*

RUSSELL M. NELSON
ENSIGN, NOVEMBER 2005, 85

Apostles and prophets are not immune from life's
realities. They have experienced their share of life's
many sorrows and vicissitudes, including the loss of
loved ones, familial heartache, and health problems.
Observing how they endure challenges and difficulties can give us a model of faith to follow. Elder Russell
M. Nelson observed, "On occasion some of our most
fervent prayers may seem to go unanswered. We wonder, 'Why?' I know that feeling! I know the fears and
tears of such moments. But I also know that our
prayers are never ignored. Our faith is never unappre-
ciated. I know that an all-wise Heavenly Father's perspective is much broader than is ours. While we know
of our mortal problems and pain, He knows of our
immortal progress and potential. If we pray to know
His will and submit ourselves to it with patience and
courage, heavenly healing can take place in His own
way and time" (*Ensign,* November 2005, 86).

*It is truly good to . . . hear the word of
the Lord, and it is truly a good thing to believe in it,
but it is still better to practice it.*

WILFORD WOODRUFF
TEACHINGS OF PRESIDENTS OF THE CHURCH, 154

Our belief is manifest in our actions. *Believing,* for most of us, is the easy part; *doing* demands real devotion. If we hear the word of the Lord without hearkening unto it, we may as well not have listened. Hearing is a first step; but hearkening impels a change of heart, a sincere and willful effort. Spirituality is evident in the way we talk, treat, and even think about others. Discipleship is developed over time as we hear and study the word of the Lord and then sincerely strive to put it into practice. For what doth gospel truth profit us if we believe and hear but don't do? True disciples signify devotion to the Lord not just by what they believe and think, but by what they do—and by who they are becoming.

*Make a commitment that the next time you are taught
by one of the servants of God, you will heed any prompting, even
the faintest prompting, to act, to do better.*

HENRY B. EYRING
TO DRAW CLOSER TO GOD, 18

We live in a day when we desperately need divine
guidance. So much of life is confusing, stressful, and
complex. But comfort and direction are available. If
we are striving to live in harmony with the teachings
of the prophets and humbly seeking for righteousness,
the Lord will distill upon us revelation as the dews of
heaven. The Lord, as Elijah learned so long ago, speaks
not in the wind, nor the earthquake, nor the fire, but
in a still small voice (1 Kings 19:11–12). Revelation
whispers gently to the heart. It does not shout or compel but invites with a still, small voice. Promptings will
come as we sincerely seek for answers and listen for
inspiration. If we feast upon the good word of God, if
we hold still and really ponder, we can receive spiritual guidance. The more we act upon such promptings, the more we will receive.

If you wish to go where God is, you must be like God,
or possess the principles which God possesses, for if we are not
drawing towards God in principle, we are going from
Him and drawing towards the devil.

JOSEPH SMITH
HISTORY OF THE CHURCH, 4:588

On Sunday, April 10, 1842, the Prophet Joseph Smith preached a sermon in a grove in Nauvoo at which he reproved the wicked and exhorted the Saints to become like God: "Search your hearts, and see if you are like God. I have searched mine, and feel to repent of all my sins. . . . If God should speak from heaven, he would command you not to steal, not to commit adultery, not to covet, nor deceive, but be faithful over a few things. As far as we degenerate from God, we descend to the devil and lose knowledge, and without knowledge we cannot be saved, and while our hearts are filled with evil, and we are studying evil, there is no room in our hearts for good, or studying good. Is not God good? Then you be good; if He is faithful, then you be faithful. Add to your faith virtue, to virtue knowledge, and seek for every good thing" (*History of the Church,* 4:588). Our mortal quest is to learn of God and strive to become more like him.

*God does not begin by asking us about our ability,
but only about our availability, and if we then prove our
dependability, he will increase our capability!*

NEAL A. MAXWELL
QUOTE BOOK, I

God is our Father and, as such, knows full well our
strengths and weaknesses. He knows in what ways we
must be stretched and molded to achieve the greatest
good and to become, as the Prophet Joseph described,
"a smooth and polished shaft in the quiver of the
Almighty" (*History of the Church,* 5:401). The gospel of
Jesus Christ is a call to become more than we otherwise would. In this second estate, God wants us to
develop willing hearts. He wants us to make earnest
efforts in moving forward the kingdom of God on the
earth. As we do, he enhances our abilities and capacities. Opportunities to teach and serve will come to
every one of us. How well we seize those opportunities determines how abundantly the Lord can bless us.
"I the Lord am bound when ye do what I say; but
when ye do not what I say, ye have no promise" (D&C
82:10). As we willingly and wholeheartedly serve, he
will bless us to be able to do all that he requires.

The Lord has given to man his agency.
That is a divine principle [that] is inherent, born with us.
We have it because the Lord gave it to us in the spirit world.

JOSEPH FIELDING SMITH
CONFERENCE REPORT, OCTOBER 1936, 59

Every soul always has been and will ever be free to choose. "Ye are free; ye are permitted to act for yourselves; for behold, God hath given unto you a knowledge and he hath made you free" (Helaman 14:30). Elder Joseph Fielding Smith taught: "That is a divine principle upon which exaltation can come. It is the only principle upon which rewards can be given in righteousness. Satan's plan in the beginning was to compel. He said he would save all men and not one soul should be lost. He would do it if the Father would give him the honor and the glory. But who wants salvation when it comes through compulsion, if we have not the power within ourselves to choose and to act according to the dictates of conscience? What would salvation mean to you if you were compelled?" (*Doctrines of Salvation*, 1:70). The devil cannot force us to do evil, and the Lord will not coerce righteousness. Thanks be to the Lord for the divine endowment of agency.

All human beings—male and female—are created in the image of God. Each is a beloved spirit son or daughter of heavenly parents, and, as such, each has a divine nature and destiny.

THE FIRST PRESIDENCY AND QUORUM
OF THE TWELVE APOSTLES
ENSIGN, NOVEMBER 1995, 102

With undaunted clarity, prophets and apostles proclaim to the world that each of us is a child of heavenly parents. We literally have a Heavenly Father and a Heavenly Mother who love us, their sons and daughters, with a perfect, encompassing love. The proclamation on the family gives us an enlightened perspective of our divine nature and destiny. We are created in the image of God and thus have something of divinity within us—an inherent worth as children of heavenly parents. We know who we are and *whose* we are. Understanding this deep doctrine can powerfully change the way we see ourselves, our family and loved ones, and others around us and across the world. This knowledge gives us a greater sense of humility and compassion toward other struggling, imperfect people; it helps us see the divine in each individual—and in humanity in general.

*What does repentance mean? A change of life,
a change of thought, a change of action.*

DAVID O. MCKAY
GOSPEL IDEALS, 328

Repentance is *soul* change, not merely behavioral change. Repentance involves feeling godly sorrow (2 Corinthians 7:10); ceasing to do evil; confessing our sins; and changing attitudes, beliefs and behaviors—all of which manifest a change of heart. Jesus is the author of our repentance, the enabler of real change. Without him, lasting change is not possible; without him, forgiveness is unattainable; without him, "the peace of God, which passeth all understanding" is out of reach (Philippians 4:7). But repentance is possible because of the enabling power of the Lord's infinite Atonement. We signify our acceptance of his grace-filled invitation to become sanctified by humbly submitting and yielding our hearts to God (Helaman 3:35).

The time has come for us to stand a little taller, to lift our eyes and stretch our minds to a greater comprehension and understanding of the grand millennial mission of [the Church].

GORDON B. HINCKLEY
STAND A LITTLE TALLER, 2

To stand for something and make a difference in the world, we must stand taller—a *little* taller. We are not expected to be perfect, to stand towering over all people and things. We just need to be a little better, a little kinder, and move a little closer to the Lord each day. Over time, these small but earnest efforts will add up to make us true men and women of Christ. President Gordon B. Hinckley has said, "This is a season to be strong. It is a time to move forward without hesitation, knowing well the meaning, the breadth, and the importance of our mission. It is a time to do what is right regardless of the consequences that might follow. We have nothing to fear. God is at the helm. He will overrule for the good of the work" (*Stand a Little Taller,* 2). Let us be strong and "stand fast in the faith" (1 Corinthians 16:13).

*Attend the temple on a regular basis. . . . I promise you
that your personal spirituality, relationship with your husband
or wife, and family relationships will be blessed and
strengthened as you regularly attend the temple.*

HOWARD W. HUNTER
TEACHINGS, 241

Temple work has accelerated over the years as these
holy edifices are being constructed across the earth to
bless the lives of countless numbers on both sides of
the veil. In preparation for the final winding-up scenes
of this last and greatest of dispensations, we will find
joy, peace, and refuge in serving in the house of the
Lord. We can claim promised blessings as we attend
the temple. President Howard W. Hunter observed,
"Many of our temples are still underused, except on
weekends. Much work remains to be done, and we
continue to encourage you to attend the temple as
often as is feasible. Stronger marriages, more attentive
parents, and more faithful children will come as a
result of following this counsel" (*Teachings,* 241). Of
course our lives are busy and the demands on our time
many, but we will be richly blessed as we go to the
temple as often as personal circumstances allow.

FEBRUARY

*This principle of love is the basic
essence of the gospel of Jesus Christ.
Without love of God and love of neighbor
there is little else to commend the
gospel to us as a way of life.*

GORDON B. HINCKLEY

God is more merciful than man is,
he possesses more sympathies with human nature than
man does or ever did, one with another.

JOHN TAYLOR
JOURNAL OF DISCOURSES, 19:155–56

While God's children contend and find fault with each other, God himself is long-suffering, patient, and understanding. While we sometimes struggle to extend mercy and forgiveness, God is everlastingly compassionate. He, as a perfect and loving Father, wants us to become even as he is, to develop his attributes, to receive a prophet's reward by inheriting his everlasting glory (Matthew 10:41). He is perfect in mercy, perfect in knowledge, perfect in his awareness of our challenges and capacities. His magnanimous gift is immortality to all; his inestimable gift is eternal life to those who endure righteously (D&C 14:7). As God himself said, "For behold, this is my work and my glory—to bring to pass the immortality and eternal life of man" (Moses 1:39). Our work is to "love mercy, and to walk humbly with thy God" (Micah 6:8), keeping the commandments with all our might, mind, and strength (D&C 11:20).

There is no necessity for Latter-day Saints
to worry over the things of this world. They will all pass
away. Our heart should be set on things above.

LORENZO SNOW
TEACHINGS, 38

Central to our present happiness and everlasting joy
are the Lord's exhortations for eternal perspective: "Lay
not up for yourselves treasures upon earth, where moth
and rust doth corrupt . . . : But lay up for yourselves
treasures in heaven, where neither moth nor rust doth
corrupt . . . : For where your treasure is, there will your
heart be also" (Matthew 6:19–21). The Lord revealed a
related truth in our dispensation: "I say unto thee that
thou shalt lay aside the things of this world, and seek for
the things of a better" (D&C 25:10). Although the
world crowds upon us, tantalizing us with its allurements, the things that matter to the Lord are the things
that should matter to us. What can possessions or
power or prestige possibly mean to the Master of the
Universe? If we step out of the worldly mainstream,
seek for that which is of everlasting worth, and set our
hearts upon righteousness, we will steadfastly move
toward Zion and its inestimable treasures.

*I teach them correct principles
and they govern themselves.*

JOSEPH SMITH
ENCYCLOPEDIA OF JOSEPH SMITH'S TEACHINGS, 30

The gospel of Jesus Christ and the teachings of the prophets give us true principles we can apply to our individual circumstances. President John Taylor gave us some context for the Prophet Joseph's well-known statement about governance: "Some years ago, in Nauvoo, a gentleman in my hearing, a member of the Legislature, asked Joseph Smith how it was that he was enabled to govern so many people, and to preserve such perfect order; remarking at the same time that it was impossible for them to do it anywhere else. Mr. Smith remarked that it was very easy to do that. 'How?' responded the gentleman; 'to us it is very difficult.' Mr. Smith replied, 'I teach them correct principles, and they govern themselves'" (*Encyclopedia of Joseph Smith's Teachings,* 30). With a few words, the Prophet gave us an inspired doctrine of leadership that has profound implications for all of us involved with helping others reach their potential.

"Are you a 'Mormon'?"
And the answer came straight, "Yes, siree; dyed in
the wool; true blue, through and through."

JOSEPH F. SMITH
GOSPEL DOCTRINE, 518

In the fall of 1857, while in his late teens and having just returned from his mission to the Hawaiian Islands, Joseph F. Smith encountered some anti-Mormon thugs who came upon his little wagon train camp in southern California. Upon seeing the ruffians, the young man wondered if he should flee. Instead, he thought, "Why should I fear them?" and he faced them boldly. One of the assailants raised his pistol to Joseph F. Smith, cursed and threatened, and put the faith of the future prophet to the test: "Are you a Mormon?" Joseph could have made excuses or rationalized his way to safety. Instead he was valiant in the cause of Christ. In response to his courage and integrity, "the ruffian grasped him by the hand and said: 'Well, you are the . . . pleasantest man I ever met! Shake, young fellow, I am glad to see a man that stands up for his convictions'" (*Gospel Doctrine,* 518). Let us not be ashamed of the gospel of Christ (Romans 1:16).

COMPLETE *and* CONSTANT
*integrity is a great law of human conduct. There
need to be some absolutes in life.*

JAMES E. FAUST
IN THE STRENGTH OF THE LORD, 348

Living a life of integrity means that we live truthfully. What we believe is reflected in who we are—how we think, act, and interact. Integrity of heart fuses right actions with pure motives and invites deep trust, abiding love, and inner peace. When we have integrity of heart we act out of love rather than outward appearance. We show our loved ones the same courtesy and respect we show others. We uphold sacred truths regardless of setting or circumstance. Elder James E. Faust said, "Natural, inherent integrity is manifested almost every hour of every day of our lives. . . . There are some things that should not ever be done, some lines that should never be crossed, vows that should never be broken, words that should never be spoken, and thoughts that should never be entertained" (*In the Strength of the Lord,* 348). Those with integrity find the humility to change, ask forgiveness, cleave to truth, and "[love] that which is right" (D&C 124:15).

The witness does not come by seeking after signs. It will not yield itself to pressure or to force. It comes through fasting and prayer, through activity and testing, through obedience. It comes through sustaining the servants of the Lord and following them.

BOYD K. PACKER
THINGS OF THE SOUL, 57

John the Revelator taught that "the testimony of Jesus is the spirit of prophecy" (Revelation 19:10). If we humbly seek a witness, the Holy Ghost will reveal to us that Jesus is, indeed, the Savior. That witness, and all revelatory confirmations concerning the Lord, the gospel, his prophets, and his Church, comes to meek followers of Christ who strive to keep his commandments and seek for divine guidance. Because such witnesses are sacred gifts, they are to be kept close to the heart. Elder Boyd K. Packer further explained, "Dreams and visions and visitations are not uncommon in the Church and are a part of all that the Lord has revealed in this dispensation. Thus a worthy Church member may be the recipient of a marvelous spiritual experience. I have come to know that these experiences are personal and are to be kept private. Recipients should ponder them in their heart and not talk lightly about them" (*Things of the Soul*, 56).

FEBRUARY 7

There is rejoicing when the spirit of a Saint
of the Living God enters into the spirit world and meets
with the Saints who have gone before.

WILFORD WOODRUFF
TEACHINGS OF PRESIDENTS OF THE CHURCH, 81

How glorious it will be for the righteous to pass to the other side of the veil and be greeted by loved ones and the faithful from previous generations! The spirit world is an actual place where spirits reside and "where they converse together the same as we do on the earth" (*Teachings of the Prophet Joseph Smith,* 353). To associate with those who have gone before will be inexpressibly joyous. Those happy reunions give way to the business of the spirit world—working together for the salvation of souls. Wilford Woodruff said, "Some labor this side of the veil, others on the other side of the veil. If we tarry here we expect to labor in the cause of salvation, and if we go hence we expect to continue our work until the coming of the Son of Man" (*Teachings of Presidents of the Church,* 81). We do not sit around strumming harps in the spirit world. It is a place of purposeful work, a place of continued preparation and learning, a place of preaching the gospel.

I testify to you this day that the time will come when every man, woman, and child will look into the Savior's loving eyes. On that day, we will know with a surety the worth of our decision to straightway follow Him.

JOSEPH B. WIRTHLIN
ENSIGN, MAY 2002, 17

As Jesus walked by the Sea of Galilee, he called forth two fishermen: "And he saith unto them, Follow me, and I will make you fishers of men. And they straightway left their nets, and followed him" (Matthew 4:19–20). Then, two other fishermen who were mending their nets were also called by the Lord, "And they immediately left the ship and their father and followed him" (Matthew 4:21). Note how these four apostles instantly left what they were doing to follow the Lord. They didn't worry about inconvenient timing, or the scorn of the world, or other temporal matters. They felt of the power of the Lord and without delay left everything behind for him. Today, we too have nets that keep us from fully following the Lord. Some ensnaring nets may be excessive focus on money, career, or Church callings; they may be materialism and the pride of the world; they may be our own laziness or selfishness. Each, in its own way, can keep us from straightway following the Lord.

I may have my own ideas and opinions, I may set up my own judgment with reference to things, but I know that when my judgment conflicts with the teachings of those that the Lord has given to us to point the way, I should change my course.

GEORGE ALBERT SMITH
TEACHINGS, 69

Safety and peace come to those who follow the Lord's anointed leaders. Of course, we are entitled to our own views and opinions on a variety of subjects as long as they don't conflict with the fundamental doctrines of the gospel. This is a religion of free thinking and self-governance. But it is also a religion of order, of doctrine, and of principle. On the day the Church was organized in this dispensation, the Lord commanded us to take counsel from the prophet: "Wherefore, meaning the church, thou shalt give heed unto all his words and commandments which he shall give unto you as he receiveth them, walking in all holiness before me; For his word ye shall receive, as if from mine own mouth, in all patience and faith" (D&C 21:4–5). A true test of our conversion is our willingness to change our course on an idea or opinion if it runs contrary to the words of the prophets.

*We want to live so as to have the Spirit every day,
every hour of the day, every minute of the day, and every
Latter-day Saint is entitled to the Spirit of God, to the power of
the Holy Ghost, to lead him in his individual duties.*

BRIGHAM YOUNG
DISCOURSES, 82

We live in an ever-darkening world, a world weighed down with sin, secularism, and sensuality. More than ever, we need the light of the Holy Ghost to illuminate our path and reassure us that faithfulness and devotion to truth is both possible and desirable in this alluring, wicked world. The Holy Ghost is a gift of God to all those who diligently seek him (1 Nephi 10:17). It is the power by which the mysteries of God are unfolded (1 Nephi 10:19), and the power by which we may know the truth of all things (Moroni 10:4–5). The Holy Ghost is a comforter and revelator, the means by which the Lord will speak to our minds and hearts (D&C 8:2–3). The Holy Ghost is a testator to the humble seeker, witnessing the reality of the Father and Son and the truthfulness of the great plan of happiness. As we strive to walk righteously before God, we can enjoy the companionship of the Holy Ghost each day.

*The flame of family can warm us and at the same
time be a perpetual pilot light to rekindle us.*

NEAL A. MAXWELL
QUOTE BOOK, 120

All of us face the "mighty winds" and "shafts in the whirlwind" of a nasty and negative world (Helaman 5:12). We seem to encounter the lascivious and alluring each day as we strive to hold back the devil's influence. How comforting and reassuring to have family and home to go to—a place of refuge from the billowing storms about us, a haven of happiness in a darkening world, a shelter of security in a time of uneasiness and confusion. A cohesive and loving family is the surest bastion of strength against the wiles of the adversary; it is a foundation upon which to recommit ourselves to everlasting things. Children can carry the strength of a happy home with them as they launch into the world and face its challenges with testimony and confidence. And when we face difficulties and temptations, the love and joy of a happy and harmonious family can buoy us up and give us strength to carry on.

As in the world so in the Church, we have two classes:
we have the builders, and we have the murmurers. Let each ask
himself in which class shall I be placed?

DAVID O. MCKAY
GOSPEL IDEALS, 142

It has ever been the case that there are builders and murmurers among us. The scriptures teach us of Abel and Cain, Nephi and Laman. One seeks to build and bless, to support and sustain. The other wants to tear down and destroy, find fault and grumble. Always there are naysayers and complainers who look for failure, who don't think it's worth the effort, who refuse to see the hand of God abiding over his work and his people. Zion, whether in our homes or stakes, is built by the pure in heart who desire righteousness with all their hearts. It is created by willing hands and hearts who do their part, who seek the welfare of others, who "do all things without murmurings and disputings" (Philippians 2:14). Let us pray for strength to put off the natural man/murmurer and become a saint/builder: "Let your hearts be full, drawn out in prayer unto [God] continually for your welfare, and also for the welfare of those who are around you" (Alma 34:27).

We are children of God, our Eternal Father. We are eternal beings, at the present time passing through an earthly estate, one of the several successive estates of a continuing eternal existence.

HOWARD W. HUNTER
TEACHINGS, 15

This life has been described as a way station, a temporary stop on a never-ending journey. We all lived for a long, long time as spirit offspring of Heavenly Father in a premortal realm, where we were endowed with agency and given opportunities to learn and progress. Elder Howard W. Hunter said, "Life did not begin with birth into this mortal sphere nor does it end with death. As children of God we lived with him in a premortal state, and there we were taught and prepared to come to earth where we would receive bodies and be given the opportunity for spiritual growth" (*Teachings,* 15). Those faithful in this *first estate* were "added upon" and given a *second estate,* or mortality, in which to be tried and tested to prove themselves worthy of eternal life. Those who by obedience and righteousness "keep their second estate shall have glory added upon their heads for ever and ever" (Abraham 3:26). That is the purpose of our mortal quest.

*This principle of love is the basic essence of the gospel of
Jesus Christ. Without love of God and love of neighbor there is
little else to commend the gospel to us as a way of life.*

GORDON B. HINCKLEY
TEACHINGS, 317

Love's power to transform is one of life's sweetest miracles. Have you noticed that love *for* a person generates more love *within* that person? And that love works a mighty change. When there is love, hope replaces discouragement and faith removes fear. When there is love, there is more kindness in the home and forgiveness in the heart. President Gordon B. Hinckley said, "Love is of the very essence of life. . . . Love is the security for which children weep, the yearning of youth, the adhesive that binds marriage, and the lubricant that prevents devastating friction in the home; it is the peace of old age, the sunlight of hope shining through death. How rich are those who enjoy it in their associations with family, friends, church, and neighbors. I am one who believes that love, like faith, is a gift of God" (*Teachings,* 317). All love comes from God. The more we seek him, the more we will feel his love working a mighty change in our hearts—and in the hearts of those we love.

FEBRUARY 15

We can choose to humble ourselves
by loving God, submitting our will to His, and
putting Him first in our lives.

EZRA TAFT BENSON
SERMONS AND WRITINGS, 337

In President Ezra Taft Benson's classic April 1989 conference address, "Beware of Pride," he shed light on the universal sin of pride and exhorted us to humble ourselves: "Pride is a sin that can readily be seen in others but is rarely admitted in ourselves. Most of us consider pride to be a sin of those on the top, such as the rich, and the learned, looking down at the rest of us. There is, however, a far more common ailment among us—and that is pride from the bottom looking up. It is manifest in so many ways, such as faultfinding, gossiping, backbiting, murmuring, living beyond our means, envying, coveting, withholding gratitude and praise that might lift another, and being unforgiving and jealous" (*Sermons and Writings,* 333). Over and over again in this talk, President Benson said we must choose to humble ourselves, choose to conquer enmity, choose to repent and extend forgiveness. Truly, we come unto Christ by cleansing the inner vessel and purging ourselves of pride.

FEBRUARY 16

The language of the Spirit comes to him who seeks with all his heart to know God and keep His divine commandments. Proficiency in this language permits one to breach barriers, overcome obstacles, and touch the human heart.

THOMAS S. MONSON
LIVE THE GOOD LIFE, 58

Those who desire to follow the Lord act earnestly, promptly, and frequently. "Our opportunities to give of ourselves are indeed limitless, but they are also perishable," President Thomas S. Monson said. "There are hearts to gladden. There are kind words to say. There are gifts to be given. There are deeds to be done" (*Ensign,* November 2001, 60). "Don't postpone a prompting. . . . Rather, act on it, and the Lord will open the way" (*Ensign,* May 2003, 56). The urgings of the Spirit will come as we live worthy of inspiration and as we continually ask, "Lord, make me an instrument to bless and lift another." When we sincerely comfort others, the Lord will send the Comforter to us. Our constant and sincere prayer can be to open our hearts to the whisperings of the Spirit, which will lead us to those in need. Such promptings from the Lord lead us to good works, charitable thoughts, and abundant living.

Always keep good company. Never waste an hour
with anyone who doesn't lift you up and encourage you.

SPENCER W. KIMBALL
TEACHINGS, 262

Life is too short to waste time being negative, tearing down others, belittling, gossiping, or denigrating. Our mortal journey can so easily be sidetracked by negative influences. Instead of getting mired in pessimistic mud, we can seek the higher ground of positive and inspiring associates. Indeed, we believe in keeping company with those who are honest, true, chaste, benevolent, virtuous, and those who do good to all peoples; we seek to spend time with that which is virtuous, lovely, praiseworthy, and of good report (Article of Faith 13). If we strive to emulate those ideals in our own lives, we will attract like individuals. Good and righteous people seek and find good and righteous friends. Of course, we are kind and courteous to all people, but we spend precious time with those who uplift and inspire, who encourage spirituality, and who want for us eternal joy.

The Lord does not desire that the people should suffer.
He is pained when a man does wrong and needs to be punished
and fails to receive the crown or reward that is offered
to those who are faithful and true.

JOSEPH FIELDING SMITH
DOCTRINES OF SALVATION, 2:43

How comforting to know that the same Lord who gives us commandments also gives us the plan of happiness, complete with the Atonement and the Resurrection. The Lord would so much rather exalt than condemn. He stands ready to bless and forgive; we need only repent. If we do, he will bless us with all that he has. Elder Joseph Fielding Smith taught, "Every soul has the right to choose for himself that which he will do. This is the gospel of merit. Every man shall receive that which he is entitled to receive. Every soul shall be blessed according to the diligence, willingness, and integrity put forth in the service of the Lord. The man who will not keep his commandments, the Lord will not exalt. The woman who rejects the light and refuses to abide by the doctrines of our Redeemer shall not be exalted. Those who will be exalted shall be crowned with glory, immortality, and eternal life in the presence of our Father" (*Doctrines of Salvation,* 2:43).

The more we are blessed with means, the more we are
blessed with responsibility; the more we are blessed with wisdom
and ability, the more we are placed under the necessity of using
that wisdom and ability in the spread of righteousness.

BRIGHAM YOUNG
DISCOURSES, 315

Truly, where much is given much is expected. "For of him unto whom much is given much is required; and he who sins against the greater light shall receive the greater condemnation" (D&C 82:3). We are judged according to our awareness and understanding of gospel truths—and according to the opportunities we've been given to accept and obey the gospel law. The Lord knows precisely what went in to shaping us as individuals; he knows our background and potential, our abilities and susceptibilities. It is remarkable that some are able to contribute much at all; and others could certainly be doing so much more. The Lord knows what we have been given and of what we are capable. What we do with what we have—not how much we started with—is what matters to the Lord.

*The people are under obligation to obey the
counsel that is given. . . . No man can be more happy than
by obeying the living prophet's counsel.*

LORENZO SNOW
TEACHINGS, 86

Obtaining a personal witness that a prophet's
words are inspired of God is vital. However, even if we
have not yet received that reassuring witness, we must
remember that a prophet's counsel will always be
timely and beneficial (see, for example, D&C 108:1).
The best way to receive a spiritual witness is to obey.
In fact, it's difficult to receive a witness without obeying. Elder Lorenzo Snow observed, "You may go from
east to west, from north to south, and tread this foot-
stool of the Lord all over, and you cannot find a man
that can make himself happy in this Church, only by
applying the counsel of the living prophet in this life; it
is a matter of impossibility for a man to receive a fulness who is not susceptible of receiving and carrying
out the living prophet's counsel" (*Teachings,* 86). Saints
who are true to the faith are willingly governed by the
counsel of the Lord's anointed servants.

*God bless us that we shall be ready
for the day of inspection. It is going to come—
whether you are ready for it or not.*

MELVIN J. BALLARD
CONFERENCE REPORT, OCTOBER 1937, 24

With all the affection of a tender prophet, Alma exhorted the people of his day: "I wish from the inmost part of my heart, yea, with great anxiety even unto pain, that ye would hearken unto my words, and cast off your sins, and not procrastinate the day of your repentance" (Alma 13:27). Those words echo down the centuries. We must prepare for our "day of inspection." Elder Melvin J. Ballard said: "Thank God for life. God bless us to utilize it to the greatest and the holiest purpose and so live that if tomorrow our summons comes we do not feel to say, 'I wish I had another day or another week or another year to live.' Instead, calm and sure let us be ready as we go to the death couch, like him who wraps the drapery about him and lies down in pleasant dreams. That is the way to go. God help us to live so that we may ever be prepared to leave this life" (*Crusader for Righteousness,* 284).

We may sometimes find satisfaction in sharing our material wealth with others. But far greater satisfaction comes from sharing ourselves, our time, our energy, our affection, and particularly in imparting to others our testimony of God.

HENRY D. MOYLE
CONFERENCE REPORT, APRIL 1957, 32

Apostle Henry D. Moyle lived a remarkable life filled with success as a soldier, attorney, businessman, and public servant. Without hesitation, he left behind his vast business affairs to devote his full strength to building the kingdom and serving the Church as a member of the Quorum of the Twelve Apostles and later as a counselor in the First Presidency to David O. McKay. He was known for his intellect, kindness, generosity, and for his unshakeable testimony of the gospel of Jesus Christ. As do all true disciples of the Lord, he understood that the meaning of life is found in service to others and to God. It's one thing to open our pocketbooks; it's quite another to open our hearts to others, to give of our time and energy, to be willing to be inconvenienced, to unashamedly share our testimony of the gospel of Jesus Christ.

You young men of the priesthood, resolve to live the way you should. Don't be caught up in some of the silly things that are going on in the world, but bear in mind what has been given to you.

DAVID B. HAIGHT
ENSIGN, MAY 2003, 45

Priesthood is the power and authority delegated to man by God, enabling the salvation of his children. Along with the laying on of hands by those who are in authority, personal righteousness allows priesthood bearers—and all who seek for priesthood blessings—to access the privileges of the holy priesthood. Elder David B. Haight admonished, "To all of you priesthood leaders, live as you should. We are different. . . . You hold the priesthood of God, with those great promises and blessings and expectations of you" (*Ensign,* May 2003, 45). All priesthood holders should understand the Lord's exhortation on priesthood power: "The rights of the priesthood are inseparably connected with the powers of heaven. . . . No power or influence can or ought to be maintained by virtue of the priesthood, only by persuasion, by long-suffering, by gentleness and meekness, and by love unfeigned; by kindness, and pure knowledge" (D&C 121:34–36).

Perhaps the greatest charity comes when we are kind to each other, when we don't judge or categorize someone else, when we simply give each other the benefit of the doubt or remain quiet.

MARVIN J. ASHTON
ENSIGN, MAY 1992, 19

The Prophet Joseph called Doctrine and Covenants 88 the "olive leaf . . . , the Lord's message of peace to us" (D&C 88, section heading). In it, the Lord admonishes us: "Clothe yourselves with the bond of charity" (D&C 88:125). But how do we do that, in our day-to-day life? Marvin J. Ashton wisely counseled, "Charity is accepting someone's differences, weaknesses, and shortcomings; having patience with someone who has let us down; or resisting the impulse to become offended when someone doesn't handle something the way we might have hoped. Charity is refusing to take advantage of another's weakness and being willing to forgive someone who has hurt us. Charity is expecting the best of each other" (*Ensign,* May 1992, 19). Charity is our love for the Lord, shown through our love for others. Those who manifest such charity will come to know inexpressible peace and joy.

*Get down on your knees and pray to God
to guide you in all you do.*

HEBER J. GRANT
TEACHINGS OF PRESIDENTS OF THE CHURCH, 174

Prayer is the way we build a relationship with Heavenly Father. "The minute a man stops supplicating God for his spirit and directions . . . he starts out to become a stranger to him and his works," stated President Heber J. Grant. "When men stop praying for God's spirit, they place confidence in their own unaided reason, and they gradually lose the spirit of God, just the same as near and dear friends, by never writing to or visiting with each other, will become strangers. We should all pray that God may never leave us alone for a moment without his Spirit to aid and assist us in withstanding sin and temptation" (*Teachings of Presidents of the Church,* 174). Alma similarly exhorted: "Counsel with the Lord in all thy doings, and he will direct thee for good; yea, when thou liest down at night lie down unto the Lord . . . ; and when thou riseth in the morning let thy heart be full of thanks unto God" (Alma 37:37).

*The most important of the Lord's work you will
ever do will be within the walls of your own homes.*

HAROLD B. LEE
TEACHINGS, 280

No work we do on earth is more important to the
Lord than building happy, strong, and lasting marriages and families. The other things we spend so
much time on fade away and wither in time. But family is forever and is worthy of our best, most diligent
efforts. President Harold B. Lee repeatedly counseled
the brethren not to use their business and Church
assignments as excuses for neglecting their families:
"Our youth are in danger. Keep your home ties strong.
. . . Don't neglect your wives. . . . Don't neglect your
children. Take time for family home evening. Draw
your children around about you. Teach them, guide
them, and guard them. There was never a time when
we needed so much the strength and the solidarity of
the home" (*Teachings,* 294). Our families must be our
primary cause and calling in life and must not be given
secondary efforts.

A prophet is a teacher of known truth; a seer is a perceiver of hidden truth, a revelator is a bearer of new truth.

JOHN A. WIDTSOE
EVIDENCES AND RECONCILIATIONS, 258

Several times each year we have the blessing and opportunity to sustain the First Presidency and Quorum of the Twelve Apostles as prophets, seers, and revelators. Their call is to bear witness of Christ; their commission is to teach truth and testify against evil. A prophet is one who knows by the power of the Holy Ghost that Jesus is the Christ (1 Corinthians 12:3; Revelation 19:10); he is a preacher of righteousness, a spokesman for the Lord. A seer is one who sees with spiritual eyes the past, present, and future; he is an interpreter and clarifier of eternal truth; he can behold things not visible to the natural eye (Mosiah 8:15–17). A revelator makes known to the people something before unknown (D&C 100:11). Elder John A. Widtsoe said, "In the widest sense, . . . the title, prophet, includes the other titles and makes of the prophet, a teacher, perceiver, and bearer of truth" (*Evidences and Reconciliations*, 258). How blessed we are to have watchmen on the tower.

FEBRUARY 28

*I regard patience as one of the finest of all Christian virtues.
It contemplates sympathy, charity, forbearance, suspension of
judgment, and, perhaps, most of all, the ability to wait.*

STEPHEN L RICHARDS
WHERE IS WISDOM? 411–12

We live in a day of instant gratification. We want
things, and we want them now! How difficult it is to
wait, to hold off, to be patient. The things of God take
time and are comprehended only by the Spirit of God
(1 Corinthians 2:11–16). It takes time to be holy, time
to serve others, time to search the scriptures, to ponder and to pray. Shortcuts to discipleship cannot be
found. True Saints of God patiently wait upon the Lord
and his timetable, trusting that his ways are higher than
ours (Isaiah 55:8–9). They seek to become as little children: submissive, meek, humble, patient, full of love,
long-suffering, and diligent in keeping the commandments of God at all times (Mosiah 3:19; Alma 7:23).
Elder Stephen L Richards said, "In the face of many
problems I am not discouraged—the truth will prevail.
We must be patient in all things, but we must also be
vigilant. Patience and vigilance and integrity will see us
out" (*Where Is Wisdom?* 402).

MARCH

A pure testimony is a tower of strength through all time.

JOSEPH F. SMITH

*The Gospel of Christ requires
faith all the day long.*

WILFORD WOODRUFF
TEACHINGS OF PRESIDENTS OF THE CHURCH, 154

Wilford Woodruff, fourth President of the Church, was born on this day in Farmington, Connecticut, in 1807. Twenty-six years later he heard the restored gospel and was baptized. He traveled with Zion's Camp to the state of Missouri; he served a full-time mission to Arkansas and Tennessee and later in the Fox Islands. In 1838 he was called to the Quorum of the Twelve Apostles by a revelation to the Prophet Joseph (D&C 118). As a "special witness of the name of Christ in all the world" (D&C 107:23) he served missions in the United States and Great Britain and became known as one of the greatest missionaries in the history of the Church. Also revered for his journal writing, Wilford Woodruff kept a detailed record of Church history for sixty-three years, making his final entry on August 31, 1898, two days before he died at age ninety-one. His life of faith and commitment was devoted to the cause of truth and righteousness.

*I pray that your example may be such that your
children will live the gospel of Jesus Christ, because that is of
more value that anything else in the world.*

HEBER J. GRANT
GOSPEL STANDARDS, 156

Two faithful grandfathers, late in life, were discussing their families, their children and grandchildren. Having endured some of life's realities and garnered the wisdom of maturity, they chatted about what mattered most to them as grandfathers, what they hoped for their posterity, what they wished they had done differently. For them, the professional success and educational and career attainments of their posterity were all well and good, but what they longed for above all else was that their children and grandchildren would be true to the faith, strong in their testimonies of Jesus Christ, and steadfast and immovable in righteousness (Mosiah 5:15). They both understood that the family is the most important unit in time and in eternity, and that we will have no greater joy than to know that our children walk in truth (3 John 1:4).

*Except a man be born again, he cannot see the kingdom of God.
. . . A man may be saved, . . . but he can never see the celestial
kingdom of God, without being born of water and the Spirit.*

JOSEPH SMITH
TEACHINGS, 12

We often learn best by seeing the contrast between light and darkness, sweet and sour, good and evil. Alma the Younger was a wicked man who went among Church members attempting to destroy the work of his father. During Alma's rebellion, an angel rebuked him, bearing witness of God's purposes. Alma was so shaken by the visitation that for a time he was unable to move or speak. Finally, he stood upon his feet and declared, "I have . . . been redeemed of the Lord; behold I am born of the Spirit" (Mosiah 27:24). Our spiritual rebirth will probably not take the same dramatic form as Alma's, but the results can be similar. Being born again is a continual process of putting off the natural man (Mosiah 3:19; Alma 5:14–31). We must be born again, changed from our fallen state, and receive the baptism of fire to receive salvation in the celestial kingdom (Mosiah 27:24–29). To be born again is to be quickened by the Spirit and receive a change of heart (Mosiah 5:2, 5–7).

*People who study the scriptures get a dimension
to their life that nobody else gets and that can't be gained in any
way except by studying the scriptures.*

BRUCE R. McCONKIE
CHURCH NEWS, JANUARY 24, 1976, 4

As thousands of the faithful can attest, scripture
study brings unnumbered blessings into our lives.
"There's an increase in faith and a desire to do what's
right and a feeling of inspiration and understanding
that comes to people who study the gospel—meaning
particularly the Standard Works—and who ponder
the principles, that can't come in any other way," said
Elder Bruce R. McConkie (*Church News,* January 24,
1976, 4). As we read and ponder, as we study and
reflect, as we daily feast on the good word of God, we
will gain spiritual confidence and receive guidance.
Scripture study educates and softens the heart as we
prepare for eternity. Additionally, family scripture
study unites families and brings a peaceful influence
into the home that, together with family prayer, can
come in no other way. Daily immersion in the scriptures has the power to change lives.

*It is possible to make home a bit of heaven; indeed,
I picture heaven to be a continuation of the ideal home.*

DAVID O. MCKAY
GOSPEL IDEALS, 490

Home is a place filled with joyful noise and tremendous opportunity. In the home, our greatest happiness—and heartache—can be found. In no other place can we more fully develop the attributes of godliness and become true followers of Christ. Each day, we have opportunities to exemplify love and kindness—or contention; to respond in patience and compassion—or otherwise; to draw nearer to the Lord and our loved ones—or further away. We can do our best to establish homes that are full of the Spirit of the Lord, of happiness and contentment, of laughter and love. No place on earth is more important. President David O. McKay was well known for practicing what he preached regarding happy home life: "One should make it his highest ambition to build an ideal home. Make home your hobby, for, if anyone makes a loving home with all his heart, he can never miss heaven" (Conference Report, April 1935, 115–16).

Plead with the Lord for the power to overcome.

EZRA TAFT BENSON
TEACHINGS, 284

It doesn't take much living to know that we all need heaven's help. Amulek told the people of his day to "exercise your faith unto repentance, that ye begin to call upon his holy name. . . . Yea, cry unto him for mercy for he is mighty to save. Yea, humble yourselves, and continue in prayer unto him" (Alma 34:17–19). And in our day, President Ezra Taft Benson has said, "One of Satan's most effective strategies with those whom he has lured into sin is to whisper in their ears that they are not worthy to pray. He will tell you that Heavenly Father is so displeased with you that He will never hear your prayers. This is a lie, and he says it to deceive us. The power of sin is great. If we are to extricate ourselves from it, especially serious sin, we must have a power greater than ourselves. No one is more anxious to help you flee from sin than your Heavenly Father. Go to Him. . . . He has the power to help you triumph" (*Sermons and Writings*, 313).

Brethren and sisters, don't have [gospel] hobbies.
Hobbies are dangerous in the Church of Christ.

JOSEPH F. SMITH
GOSPEL DOCTRINE, 116

Aperson who plays only one or two keys on a piano misses out on the whole range of the magnificent instrument. Likewise, one with a gospel hobby can create disharmony and distort his perception of the beautiful gospel plan. President Joseph F. Smith said, "[Gospel hobbies] are dangerous because they give undue prominence to certain principles or ideas to the detriment and dwarfing of others just as important, just as binding, just as saving as the favored doctrines or commandments. . . . Saints with hobbies are prone to judge and condemn their brethren and sisters who are not so zealous in the one particular direction of their pet theory as they are. . . . The man with a hobby is apt to assume an 'I am holier than thou' position, to feel puffed up and conceited, and to look with distrust . . . on his brethren and sisters who do not so perfectly live that one particular law" (*Gospel Doctrine*, 116–17). The mainstream of the Church is the spiritually safe place to be.

*We are too fond of catering to the world, and too much of the
world has crept into our hearts; the spirit of covetousness and
greed, and . . . dishonesty has spread itself like a plague.*

JOHN TAYLOR
TEACHINGS OF PRESIDENTS OF THE CHURCH, 60

Perhaps the greatest challenge for seekers of righteousness is to live and be actively engaged in the world but not become *of* the world. We all live *in* the world, and yet we must hold back the world's influence. The stain of worldliness penetrates slowly, subtly, and insidiously. If we aren't intentional and clear about the path we're on, we can easily end up in a different place than we intended. As opposed to the meandering and easily accessed path of the world, the path of discipleship is strait and narrow (1 Nephi 8:20). The gospel path is paved with sincere prayer and scripture study, with service and sacrifice for the kingdom, with the ordinances of the gospel and keeping sacred covenants, with conscientious efforts to emulate the more excellent way of the Savior. Although the world beckons with its ephemeral enticements, the Lord's way is the path to peace and joy.

*Are we willing to become totally
obedient to God's law? There comes a time in our lives
when a definite decision must be made.*

HOWARD W. HUNTER
TEACHINGS, 24

At some point in life, a decision must be made to be
on the Lord's side—or not; unless, of course, we choose
by not choosing, or by being apathetic. Some suppose
they can live out their days on the proverbial fence,
watching the world and its ways pass by but never
being fully engaged in building the kingdom of God.
Oftentimes, the apathetic know what is expected of
them but are too caught up in the cares of the world,
too lazy to do what is required to become alive in
Christ. Spiritual strength and commitment are tested
by standing firm against sin. Elder Howard W. Hunter
said, "Obedience is not tested when life is calm and
pleasant and when we are deriving spiritual satisfaction
from doing good; but when thoughts or pressures persuade us to act in a way contrary to God's commandments, then obedience is put to the test" (*Teachings*, 24).
Our life is comprised of daily decisions—either for or
against the Lord and his righteousness.

You parents of the willful and the wayward! Don't give them up.
Don't cast them off. They are not utterly lost. The Shepherd will
find his sheep. They were his before they were yours—
long before he entrusted them to your care.

ORSON F. WHITNEY
CONFERENCE REPORT, APRIL 1929, 110

The love we have for our children can approach the perfect love the Lord has for each of us. This love is unfeigned and focuses on inherent worth and potential. Those possessed of such love patiently forbear and forgive. Of course, all will be held accountable for sins, and none will be forced back into the presence of God. But we must never give up on the sinner. God, who knows us perfectly, will judge us perfectly. Elder Orson F. Whitney said of the wayward: "They have but strayed in ignorance from the Path of Right, and God is merciful to ignorance. Only the fulness of knowledge brings the fulness of accountability. Our Heavenly Father is far more merciful, infinitely more charitable, than even the best of his servants, and the Everlasting Gospel is mightier in power to save than our narrow finite minds can comprehend" (Conference Report, April 1929, 110). We thank the Lord for his loving watch care.

The most vital thing we can do is to express our testimonies through service, which will, in turn, produce spiritual growth, greater commitment, and a greater capacity to keep the commandments.

SPENCER W. KIMBALL
TEACHINGS, 254

We have all heard the expression "Don't *tell* me what you know; *show* me what you know." We best express our testimonies of the Lord and this great latter-day work by reaching out to others in service. It is much easier to ponder and pontificate about gospel truth than it is to *live* it. The "living" of the gospel is done primarily in relation to other people. We grow in righteousness mostly in relation to others, not by moving to the mountaintop and reading scriptures in isolation. It's one thing to memorize scriptures, it's another to have those scriptures *live in our hearts* as manifested by how we treat and help others. It is one thing to know the Church is true, it is another to demonstrate that knowledge by how we act and interact with others. We show our testimonies of this work by what we *do.* As we sincerely serve others, our spiritual growth will deepen, our testimonies will enlarge, and our commitment to truth will expand.

*I go to bed every night and make sure I get up the next morning.
I just keep going. . . . You get your lift from the people. They give
me the energy to keep going. I love being among the Saints.*

GORDON B. HINCKLEY
GO FORWARD WITH FAITH, 554–55

What an extraordinary example of the believers is found in the life of Gordon B. Hinckley, fifteenth President of the Church (1 Timothy 4:12)! Full of wit and wisdom, faith and determination, President Hinckley has tirelessly traveled the world, lifting the Saints, building the kingdom, and testifying as a special witness of Jesus Christ. His example is proof that those who are anxiously engaged in service and righteousness are energized by the Spirit of the Lord, no matter what their age. They are passionate about advancing the cause of Zion. They follow the Lord's exhortation: "Cease to be idle; . . . cease to sleep longer than is needful; retire to thy bed early, that ye may not be weary; arise early, that your bodies and your minds may be invigorated" (D&C 88:124). Truly, those who serve "the Lord shall renew their strength; they shall mount up with wings as eagles; they shall run, and not be weary; and they shall walk, and not faint" (Isaiah 40:31).

*The matter of teaching is one of the greatest importance. We can-
not estimate its value when it is properly done; neither do we know
the extent of the evil that may result if it is improperly done.*

JOSEPH FIELDING SMITH
DOCTRINES OF SALVATION, 1:311

No greater calling can be found in the kingdom of
God than that of teaching. Teachers are called as agents
of God to do his work. The teacher is the herald of
divine truth, the messenger of righteousness. As students, we are not converted to truth because of smooth
rhetoric or impressive credentials, but rather by the
Spirit of the Lord. When teachers align their lives to
the will of the Lord, they, as spokespersons, may deliver
the message that the Spirit dictates. They are able to
speak by the power of the Holy Ghost and thereby
become a means for God's Spirit to communicate
directly to the spirits of others. A teacher needs a
humble heart, a willing mind always growing in gospel
understanding (D&C 84:85; 121:35), a clear purpose,
and a sincere desire to spiritually strengthen those who
will be taught. If we are spiritually prepared, the Spirit
will be with us in the classroom and at home where we
are *always* teaching, day in and day out.

As man now is, God once was;
as God now is, man may be.

LORENZO SNOW
TEACHINGS, 2

Lorenzo Snow spoke of receiving the inspiration for his oft-quoted couplet: "Now I will say what I received in vision, which was as clear as the sun ever shone. The knowledge that was communicated to me I embraced in this couplet: 'As man now is, God once was. As God now is, man may be.' That is a very wonderful thing. It was to me. I did not know but that I had come into possession of knowledge that I had no business with; but I knew it was true. Nothing of this kind had ever reached my ears before. It was preached a few years after that; at least, the Prophet Joseph taught this idea to the Twelve Apostles. Now, however, it is common property; but I do not know how many there are here that have got a real knowledge of these things in their hearts. If you have, I will tell you what its effects will be. As John said, 'Every man that hath this hope in him purifieth himself, even as [God] is pure' (1 John 3:3)" (*Teachings*, 2).

The witness of the Spirit to you, my brethren and sisters, is that you are the offspring of the Lord, that the spirits which inhabit your bodies are immortal, and that in due time, if you are faithful, you will go back to the presence of that God who gave you life.

GEORGE ALBERT SMITH
TEACHINGS, 14

The apostle Paul testified of an immutable truth: "The Spirit itself beareth witness with our spirit that we are the children of God: And if children, then heirs; heirs of God, and joint-heirs with Christ" (Romans 8:16–17). In our day, apostles and prophets have likewise declared that "All human beings—male and female—are created in the image of God. Each is a beloved spirit son or daughter of heavenly parents, and, as such, each has a divine nature and destiny" (*Ensign,* November 1995, 102). As children of heavenly parents, we have "divine power . . . given unto us" that we might be "partakers of the divine nature" (2 Peter 1:3–4). That divine power—the seeds of Godhood within us—includes access to the spiritual gifts that each of us has been given to help us, and others, return "home to that God who gave [us] life" (Alma 40:11; D&C 46:11–12).

*If you will not respond to the so-called insignificant
or menial tasks which need to be performed in the Church and
kingdom, there will be no opportunity for service in
the so-called greater challenges.*

BOYD K. PACKER
THAT ALL MAY BE EDIFIED, 238

Some may be willing to serve in exotic lands as important leaders of vast congregations but somewhat reluctant to serve in the so-called mundane tasks in the kingdom—as a home teacher or visiting teacher, an usher or Cub Scout leader, and so forth. But the Lord needs us to be anxiously engaged in the many less noticeable callings that require our dedicated efforts. We demonstrate our capacity and willingness by how and why we serve. To the Lord, *how* we serve matters much more than *where* we serve. Surely, to him, doing our very best to prepare and then teach with the Spirit a class of ten-year-olds is no less important than serving as Primary president; being a conscientious home teacher is no less vital than serving the Lord in a far-flung foreign land. The Lord cares a great deal about how and why we serve—not what our calling may be.

Let there be no uncertainty in the minds of our Latter-day Saint women as to the Relief Society's being the greatest of all women's organizations. There is no greater organization on the face of the earth for the Latter-day Saint woman.

HAROLD B. LEE
TEACHINGS, 320

On this day in 1842, at Nauvoo, Illinois, twenty women gathered in the room above Joseph Smith's Red Brick Store to organize the Female Relief Society of Nauvoo. The Prophet Joseph organized this notable benevolent society under the direction of the priesthood with Emma Smith as its first president. The Relief Society, a counterpart and complement to the Church's priesthood quorums, has grown into a remarkable worldwide organization, with charitable and humanitarian service fundamental to its identity and mission. Millions around the world—both within and outside the Church—have been richly blessed because of the work of the Relief Society. The lives of countless Relief Society members have been enriched by its programs, fellowship, and camaraderie. No other group, association, or society is more deserving of the time, interest, and involvement of Latter-day Saint women than the Relief Society, organized by a prophet of God.

*The second advent of the Son of God is . . . something that
will not be done in a small portion of the earth . . . and seen only
by a few; but it will be an event that will be seen by all.*

ORSON PRATT
JOURNAL OF DISCOURSES, 18:171

To the apostles in the meridian dispensation, two
heavenly messengers in white apparel declared, "Ye men
of Galilee, why stand ye gazing up into heaven? this
same Jesus, which is taken up from you into heaven,
shall so come in like manner as ye have seen him go into
heaven" (Acts 1:11). The Savior will return as promised
to cleanse the earth of wickedness and to reign with his
covenant people for a thousand years. The coming of
the Lord is near, and "it overtaketh the world as a thief
in the night" (D&C 106:4); it will cause the wicked to
weep, wail, gnash their teeth, and wish that the mountains would fall on them (D&C 29:15; Alma 12:14). The
glory of the Savior's presence will consume the wicked
(D&C 133:41; 5:19); and faithful Saints, both living and
dead, will be caught up to meet Christ at his coming
(D&C 88:96–98; 45:45). These events will be hailed by
the righteous in all ages with excitement and joy. Those
who are prepared need not fear (D&C 38:30).

*The idea is not to do good because
of the praise of men, but to do good because in doing
good we develop godliness within us.*

LORENZO SNOW
TEACHINGS, 7

This life is a time of spiritual development. It is not a time to become as "whited sepulchres, which indeed appear beautiful outward, but are within full of dead men's bones, and of all uncleanness" (Matthew 23:27). It is a time for us to become "new creatures in Christ," to develop his attributes, as we do right things for the *right reasons*—to glorify the Lord and bless his children. When our hearts are riveted on the Lawgiver, and not just the law, we are more apt to be unselfish and strive to bless others. Rather than chasing after the world's applause, we must seek for the quiet peace that comes from living with integrity. If we truly strive to be righteous, if we love the Lord with all our heart, soul, and mind (Matthew 22:37), we will develop godliness within us and have confidence as we are privileged to be in his presence (D&C 121:45).

The object with me is to obey and teach others to
obey God in just what He tells us to do. It mattereth not whether
the principle is popular or unpopular, I will always maintain
a true principle, even if I stand alone in it.

JOSEPH SMITH
TEACHINGS, 332

Staying devout in the face of disbelief and opposition is a true test of faith. The sunshine-believers, who are faithful only when all is well or convenient, don't know the spiritual maturity that comes of enduring trials of faith. Sometimes the steadily faithful are not popular with the world; they are, in a sense, peculiar, and that makes them vulnerable to ridicule and attack. Our test of conversion is if we will remain unwavering even during seasons of discontent and hostility. Of his first vision, the Prophet Joseph Smith said: "Why persecute me for telling the truth? Who am I that I can withstand God, or why does the world think to make me deny what I have actually seen? For I had seen a vision; I knew it, and I knew that God knew it, and I could not deny it; at least I knew that by so doing I would offend God, and come under condemnation" (JS–H 1:25). We stand for truth and righteousness even if we stand alone.

*We should be strictly honest, one with another,
and with all men; let our word always be as good as our
bond; . . . be full of integrity and honor.*

JOHN TAYLOR
GOSPEL KINGDOM, 343

We believe in being honest," says an article of our faith (Article of Faith 13). Living truthfully is the quest of a lifetime. We are promised that as we come to know the truth, the truth will make us free (John 8:32; D&C 98:8)—free from falsehood and hypocrisy; free from corrupt influences and the bondage of deception; free from the worry that our lies will be discovered; and free from the nagging awareness that God knows the truth. The honest in heart don't have to fudge facts or twist truth. Because their hearts are honest, their words and deeds are honest. Each day, they strive to live with integrity. They are also honest enough with themselves to know they aren't perfect. They make mistakes. Truth stands the test of time and will not fade with new fashions and old lies. Real freedom comes as we meekly align our desires and actions with everlasting truth. Real joy comes as we *know* truth—and then *live* it.

We are not only to avoid evil, not only to do good, but, most importantly, to do the things of greatest worth. We are to focus on the inward things of the heart, which we know and value intuitively but often neglect for that which is trivial, superficial, or prideful.

JAMES E. FAUST
IN THE STRENGTH OF THE LORD, 399

The Lord has chastised certain people for their failure to serve diligently: "But your mind has been on the things of the earth more than on the things of me, your Maker . . . ; and you have not given heed unto my Spirit" (D&C 30:2). Indeed, this life is the time for us to learn to "lay aside the things of this world, and seek for the things of a better" (D&C 25:10). Choosing the better part is not only avoiding evil in all its varieties, it is focusing our precious time and energy on the things of greatest worth—not on fleeting possessions, money, and fame. President James E. Faust counseled, "Members of the Church are to seek after loveliness. We do not seek a veneer painted on by a worldly brush but the pure, innate beauty that God has planted in our souls. . . . We should seek after those things that endow higher thoughts and finer impulses" (*In the Strength of the Lord*, 258). We are to center our hearts on the things that matter most.

MARCH 23

*Life itself is a miracle, and surely that we shall live
always is no greater miracle than that we live at all; and surely
that we shall come forth from the grave is no greater
miracle than that we first came forth by birth.*

RICHARD L. EVANS
MESSAGES FROM MUSIC AND THE SPOKEN WORD, 85

Richard L. Evans was born on this date in 1906. He
served for many decades as a member of the First
Quorum of the Seventy and of the Quorum of the
Twelve Apostles. For more than forty years, he was
well known as the writer, producer, and announcer for
the Mormon Tabernacle Choir's weekly broadcast,
Music and the Spoken Word. Many of his words are still
used on the broadcast today, such as: "Again we leave
you from within the shadows of the everlasting hills.
May peace be with you this day and always." His timeless sermonettes attest to his insight and inspiration, as well as his uncommon wisdom and simple
eloquence. Each week he addressed an audience of
millions and spoke to them of universal truths, of the
blessing of life, of the goodness of God and the everlasting things. As a special witness of Jesus Christ he
testified of the miracle of the Resurrection and the
redemption wrought by the Son of God.

*A pure testimony is a tower of
strength through all time.*

JOSEPH F. SMITH
TEACHINGS OF PRESIDENTS OF THE CHURCH, 207

A young man, once a prodigal, repented of his sins and came home to the faith of his father. He spoke of how he gained his testimony: "I testify unto you that I do know that these things . . . are true. And how do ye suppose that I know of their surety? . . . Behold, I have fasted and prayed many days that I might know these things of myself. And now I do know of myself that they are true; for the Lord God hath made them manifest unto me by his Holy Spirit; and this is the spirit of revelation" (Alma 5:45–46). Alma the Younger bore strong testimony, born of the Spirit after having paid the price to know. We, too, can know the truth of all things by the witness of the Holy Ghost (Moroni 10:4–5). We can have the strength of a sure conviction that God lives and loves us, that Jesus is his Son, that they appeared to the boy Joseph, that the Book of Mormon is the word of God, and that priesthood keys and powers have been restored. Our testimonies will lift and fortify us this day and always.

*I believe in the gospel of work. There is no substitute
under the heavens for productive labor.*

GORDON B. HINCKLEY
TEACHINGS, 705

President Gordon B. Hinckley's approach has always
been one of "roll up your sleeves and get to work." His
concept of spirituality does not involve idly pontificating
and conceptualizing; his is a gospel of work, of productive labor, of putting your shoulder to the wheel. He
said, "[Work] is the process by which dreams become
reality. It is the process by which idle visions become
dynamic achievements. We are all inherently lazy. We
would rather play than work. We would rather loaf than
work. A little play and a little loafing are good—that is
one of the reasons you are here. But it is work that spells
the difference in the life of a man or woman. It is
stretching our minds and utilizing the skills of our hands
that lifts us from the stagnation of mediocrity"
(*Teachings,* 705). President Hinckley exemplifies an
admirable model of work. He has always followed the
Lord's command, "You should go forth and not tarry,
neither be idle but labor with your might" (D&C 75:3).

*There is nothing more strikingly plain
and explicit in all the Holy Scriptures than that God is
just and his paths are "mercy and truth."*

MATTHIAS F. COWLEY
COWLEY'S TALKS ON DOCTRINE, 156

Truly, as Nephi acknowledged, "the tender mercies of the Lord are over all" (1 Nephi 1:20). When we deeply consider the Lord's goodness and compassion, we feel to "live in thanksgiving daily, for the many mercies and blessings which he doth bestow upon [us]" (Alma 34:38). Elder Matthias F. Cowley said, "God is just, holy and righteous, wondrously tender, loving, gentle and kind. Eternal rewards are the blessings we receive from God for our faithfulness and fealty to His laws. Eternal punishments are the inflictions which He imposes for our violation of His righteous commands. Our rewards we merit; our punishments we justly deserve. The Lord has said, 'I will never leave thee; I will never forsake thee,' therefore, we are assured that 'His mercy endureth forever'" (*Cowley's Talks on Doctrine*, 159). We steadfastly affirm, as did the psalmist, "I trust in the mercy of God for ever and ever" (Psalm 52:8).

*Live close to your children, that you have
their love and confidence, that you are not harsh, that you are
not cross, that you are understanding. Be firm in the
right—yes, in a kindly, sweet way.*

EZRA TAFT BENSON
TEACHINGS, 502

Every parent knows how challenging it can be to nurture children in light and truth when surrounded by sin and temptation. But it has ever been thus. From the beginning, parenthood has been a challenge. President Ezra Taft Benson gave parents sound advice: "Praise your children more than you correct them. Praise them for even their smallest achievement. Encourage your children to come to you for counsel with their problems and questions by listening to them every day. . . . Treat your children with respect and kindness—just as you would when guests are present. They are, after all, more meaningful to you than guests. Teach your children never to speak unkindly to others regarding members of the family. . . . Implant within children a desire to serve others. Teach them to be thoughtful to the aged, the sick, and the lonely" (*Teachings,* 499). As parents, our calling is to love our children, teach them, respect them, and regard them as our greatest treasures.

[The Lord] has given us the plan of temporal salvation in the Church-wide welfare program, where everyone is to give in labor, money, or service to the full extent of his ability and then receive from out of the bounties, . . . according to his need.

HAROLD B. LEE
TEACHINGS, 307

Harold B. Lee, eleventh President of the Church, was born on this day in 1899 in Clifton, Idaho. Harold B. Lee began a teaching career at the age of seventeen and served as a school principal at eighteen. He is lovingly remembered for his more than thirty years as an apostle and seventeen months as Church President. Among his many contributions to building the kingdom was his visionary leadership with regard to the Church welfare program, extending its services worldwide. The objectives of the inspired welfare program of the Church are to assist the needy both temporally and spiritually, to teach principles of "pure religion" (James 1:27), to build character in givers and receivers, to do away with the curse of idleness, and to strengthen every member in the values of industry, independence, and self-reliance. Church welfare is built on principles of work and service, compassion and self-respect.

The Gods . . . decreed freedom, not tyranny; persuasion, not compulsion; charity, not intolerance. . . . There is no room in all the Government of God for the exercise of unrighteous dominion.

ORSON F. WHITNEY
SATURDAY NIGHT THOUGHTS, 220—21

An angel taught King Benjamin that "the natural man is an enemy to God" (Mosiah 3:19). Fallen (unredeemed) man is self-seeking, self-serving, and, in the end, self-destructive. Not having surrendered his heart unto God, he seeks to impose his will and desires upon others—any means justifies the end. Such a person is power- and possession-hungry, eager to get ahead and to have more than his neighbor. How easily that person can descend to the adversary's modus operandi: unrighteous dominion. The Lord's more excellent way is the path for us to follow: gentle persuasion, long-suffering, charity, and love unfeigned (D&C 121:39—46). When we have surrendered our will to the Lord and are washed clean in the blood of the Lamb, we will live the abundant life—enjoying the refining influence of the Holy Spirit, looking for the good in others, reaching out to lift those who have fallen, and finding great happiness in the joy and success of another.

*The place of woman in the Church is to walk beside
the man, not in front of him nor behind him. In the Church
there is full equality between man and woman.*

JOHN A. WIDTSOE
EVIDENCES AND RECONCILIATIONS, 305

The Lord, whose love is constant and perfect, loves
his daughters as well as he loves his sons. The privileges, expectations, and blessings of the gospel are fun-
damentally alike for both men and women.
Righteousness is the key, not gender. As such, the Lord
set the pattern for the marital partnership when he
indicated that "they twain shall be one flesh" (D&C
49:16). The scriptures teach us that Eve was figura-
tively taken from Adam's rib. This signifies that they
were united, side by side, as equal partners. The one—
male or female—is no more important than the other.
In their sacred stewardships, there is difference without hierarchy, distinctiveness without inequality.
Husbands and wives are to stand as equal partners in
their homes. United in the common goals of celestial
marriage and the rearing of righteous children, they
can be equally yoked for eternity.

*The things of God are of deep import; and time,
and experience, and careful and ponderous and solemn
thoughts can only find them out.*

JOSEPH SMITH
HISTORY OF THE CHURCH, 3:295

Shortly before his martyrdom, the Prophet Joseph Smith gave the King Follett Discourse in which he expounded many doctrines. Among them, he taught the importance of understanding our eternal potential. He said, "If a man learns nothing more than to eat, drink and sleep, and does not comprehend any of the designs of God, the beast comprehends the same things. It eats, drinks, sleeps, and knows nothing more about God; yet it knows as much as we, unless we are able to comprehend by the inspiration of Almighty God. If men do not comprehend the character of God, they do not comprehend themselves" (*History of the Church,* 6:303). We come to know who we truly are by taking time to sincerely study the doctrine, by praying, by humbly listening to our leaders, and by deeply pondering. Revelation is for every faithful follower of the Lord who has received the gift of the Holy Ghost. To find out the things of God, we must cultivate the spirit of revelation.

APRIL

⁓

*The Standard of Truth has been
erected; no unhallowed hand can stop the
work from progressing.*

JOSEPH SMITH

*We meet together often in the Church in conferences
to worship the Lord, to feast upon the word of Christ,
and to be built up in faith and testimony.*

SPENCER W. KIMBALL
TEACHINGS, 521

The first conference of the Church in this dispensation was held June 9, 1830, just two months after the Church was organized. Since then we have been greatly blessed to have regular Church conferences to sustain and be instructed by our leaders, to learn more of the gospel, and to meet in fellowship with the Saints. President Kimball said, "The purpose of . . . conference is that we may refresh our faith, strengthen our testimonies, and learn the ways of the Lord from his duly appointed and authorized servants. May we take this opportunity, then, to remind each other of our covenants and promises and commitments" (*Teachings,* 521). On another occasion, President Kimball encouraged us to listen actively in meetings: "You have heard so many good things tonight. . . . I hope you make copious notes. I wish you would get in the habit of making notes in every meeting you attend" (*Teachings,* 522–23). Conference is a time of spiritual preparation and renewal.

*We are here to learn and not to remain
in ignorance, to keep the commandments, to conquer
ourselves, to learn to live together.*

RICHARD L. EVANS
MESSAGES FROM MUSIC AND THE SPOKEN WORD, 91

We are here in mortality for a brief season as part of a great plan of happiness—a grand design from our Father in Heaven for the eternal destiny of his beloved sons and daughters. It is a plan filled with hope and promise. As Elder Richard L. Evans wisely stated: "When we fumble and fall short, which all of us do, there is always the comforting thought that we were sent here by a loving Father, who sent us not to fail but to succeed. He understands our hearts, our problems, our possibilities. He does not expect of us a presently impossible perfection—but He does expect of us an honest and sincere performance. And with our willingness, He will help us to return to Him with the purpose of this life completed, and with everlasting opportunities with those we love. And despite discouragement and sometimes weariness along the way, the hope, the promise, the certainty of things to come makes all the effort infinitely worthwhile" (*Messages from Music and the Spoken Word*, 91).

We will have our bodies glorified, made free from every sickness and distress, and rendered most beautiful. There is nothing more beautiful to look upon than a resurrected man or woman.

LORENZO SNOW
TEACHINGS, 99

Lorenzo Snow, fifth President of the Church, was born on this day in 1814 in Mantua, Ohio. He joined the Church on June 23, 1836, more than a year after his sister Eliza R. Snow did. Lorenzo arrived in the Salt Lake Valley with his family in the summer of 1848, and on February 12, 1849, he was called to the Quorum of the Twelve Apostles. He served as President of the Church from 1898 until his death from pneumonia four days after general conference on October 10, 1901. Ever true to the truth, President Snow emphasized tithing, missionary work, and faithfulness in keeping the commandments of God. He proclaimed the divinity of Jesus Christ and the divinity within each of us throughout his apostolic ministry. How wonderful it will be for the faithful of all generations to meet those beautiful and glorified prophets, and other righteous men and women, who have worn out their lives in moving forward the cause of Zion.

*I would not knowingly wound the feelings of any,
not even one who may have wronged me, but would seek to
do him good and make him my friend.*

GEORGE ALBERT SMITH
TEACHINGS, 139

George Albert Smith, beloved eighth President of the Church, was born on this day in 1870 and passed into immortality on the same day in 1951. This was his creed: "I would be a friend to the friendless and find joy in ministering to the needs of the poor. I would visit the sick and afflicted and inspire in them a desire for faith to be healed. I would teach the truth to the understanding and blessing of all mankind. I would seek out the erring one and try to win him back to a righteous and a happy life. I would not seek to force people to live up to my ideals, but rather love them into doing the thing that is right. I would live with the masses and help to solve their problems that their earth life may be happy. I would avoid the publicity of high positions and discourage flattery of thoughtless friends. . . . I would overcome the tendency to selfishness and jealousy and rejoice in the successes of all the children of my Heavenly Father" (*Teachings*, 138–39).

Because our Redeemer lives so shall we.
I bear you witness that He does live. I know it,
and I hope you know that divine truth.

DAVID O. McKAY
TEACHINGS OF PRESIDENTS OF THE CHURCH, 59

Jesus Christ lives. That truth can make all the difference in our lives. He is our Savior; he is there for us not just in the great adversities but in the struggles of daily life. When we're discouraged, he lifts us with his radiant life. When we feel alone and afraid, he beckons, "Come unto me, all ye that labour and are heavy laden, and I will give you rest" (Matthew 11:28–29). When we feel that we can't go on, he offers sweet assurance, "I am come that they might have life, and that they might have it more abundantly" (John 10:10). He is our Redeemer and counsels us to "fear not" (Luke 5:10). His undaunted courage and pure love for us saw him through the agonies of Gethsemane and Golgotha. He lives. President David O. McKay has said, "As Christ lived after death so shall all men. . . . The message of the resurrection, therefore, is the most comforting, the most glorious ever given to man" (*Teachings of Presidents of the Church,* 67).

APRIL 6

*The Standard of Truth has been
erected; no unhallowed hand can stop the
work from progressing.*

JOSEPH SMITH
HISTORY OF THE CHURCH, 4:540

On this day in 1830 the Church of Jesus Christ was organized in this dispensation by the Prophet Joseph Smith under the authority of the priesthood of God and subject to the laws of the land. Who could have imagined from its inauspicious beginning in a small farmhouse in upstate New York that the Church would eventually fill the earth and usher in the return of the Lord? In the 1842 Wentworth Letter, the Prophet Joseph proclaimed that the Standard of Truth had been erected and nothing would stop its progress: "Persecutions may rage, mobs may combine, armies may assemble, calumny may defame, but the truth of God will go forth boldly, nobly, and independently, till it has penetrated every continent, visited every clime, swept every country, and sounded in every ear, till the purposes of God shall be accomplished, and the Great Jehovah shall say the work is done" (*History of the Church,* 4:540).

We believe in the Lord Jesus and in his divine, saving mission into the world, and in the redemption, the marvelous, glorious redemption, that he wrought for the salvation of men.

JOSEPH F. SMITH
GOSPEL DOCTRINE, 138

The everlasting gospel is centered on Jesus Christ. We have confidence in him, rely upon his mercy, and trust in his redeeming grace. This is the Christ who calmed the raging wind and waters of Galilee and healed countless numbers with his matchless power and all-encompassing love. And though his miracles were many, the greatest miracle of all is his divine grace and bounteous mercy extended to each one of us. President Joseph F. Smith said, "We believe in [Christ], and this constitutes the foundation of our faith. . . .We are his by adoption, by being buried with Christ in baptism, by being born of the water and of the spirit anew into the world, through the ordinances of the gospel of Christ, and we are thereby God's children, heirs of God and joint heirs with Jesus Christ through our adoption and faith" (*Gospel Doctrine,* 138). May we look forward to that life which is in Christ, believe in him, and deny him not (2 Nephi 25:27–28).

*There is no being that has power to save the souls
of men and give them eternal life, except the Lord Jesus Christ,
under the command of His Father.*

WILFORD WOODRUFF
TEACHINGS OF PRESIDENTS OF THE CHURCH, 74

Even though we live in a time of uncertainty, we need not be troubled or afraid. Peace can dwell in our souls, even in the midst of turmoil. The Lord said, "Peace I leave with you, my peace I give unto you: not as the world giveth, give I unto you. Let not your heart be troubled, neither let it be afraid" (John 14:27). The peace that Christ won for us could not have been made available in any other way. Elder Wilford Woodruff said, "The object of Christ's mission to the earth was to offer himself as a sacrifice to redeem mankind from eternal death. . . . He acted strictly in obedience to his Father's will in all things from the beginning, and drank of the bitter cup given him. Herein is brought to light, glory, honour, immortality, and eternal life, with that charity which is greater than faith or hope, for the Lamb of God has thereby performed that for man which [man] could not accomplish for himself" (*Teachings of the Presidents of the Church*, 69–70).

In life we all have our Gethsemanes. A Gethsemane is a necessary experience, a growth experience. A Gethsemane is a time to draw near to God, a time of deep anguish and suffering.

JAMES E. FAUST
IN THE STRENGTH OF THE LORD, 250

Elder James E. Faust has said, "The Gethsemane of the Savior was without question the greatest suffering that has ever come to mankind, yet out of it came the greatest good in the promise of eternal life" (*In the Strength of the Lord,* 250). No other suffering can compare in its intensity to that of Jesus as he wrought the infinite Atonement. Incomprehensible to us, the Lord took upon him the sin and suffering of all people because of his pure love for us. We, too, will have our Gethsemanes—times of anguish, suffering, and intense pain. Although our trials are small in comparison, they are not small to us. Jesus perfectly understands and will help: "Come unto me, all ye that labour and are heavy laden, and I will give you rest. Take my yoke upon you, and learn of me; for I am meek and lowly in heart: and ye shall find rest unto your souls" (Matthew 11:28–29). If we endure our Gethsemanes in faith, not only will we find rest, we will be blessed with some of "the greatest good."

*When you are married,
be fiercely loyal one to another. Selfishness is the
great destroyer of happy family life.*

GORDON B. HINCKLEY
TEACHINGS, 328–29

The foundation upon which an eternal marriage and family grows is Jesus Christ. All other temporal foundations will ultimately fail. The sacred building blocks of happy and enduring marriages and families are tenets of the gospel of Jesus Christ: selflessness and sacrifice, charity and commitment, friendship and fairness, love and loyalty, forgiveness and forbearance—and a host of other principles (see, for example, Moroni 7:45–48; 1 Corinthians 13:1–13; D&C 121:41–46). President Hinckley has counseled husbands and wives to be more like Jesus, "If you will make your first concern the comfort, the well-being, and the happiness of your companion, sublimating any personal concern to that loftier goal, you will be happy, and your marriage will go on throughout eternity" (*Teachings*, 329). We will have the blessed opportunity to be together as spouses and families in eternity by being loyal and loving here in mortality, staying true to our covenants, and humbly following the Lord.

If I have injured any person,
I ought to confess to that person and make
right what I did wrong.

BRIGHAM YOUNG
TEACHINGS OF PRESIDENTS OF THE CHURCH, 61

True repentance is manifest in remorse that leads to an honest admission of wrongdoing—to ourselves, to the Lord, and to any person whom we may have injured. Unwillingness to confess our sins indicates that true repentance has not yet taken place, for our desire to be cleansed of sin and make things right must be far greater than our desire to protect our pride and hide our faults. The Lord has said, "Behold, he who has repented of his sins, the same is forgiven, and I, the Lord, remember them no more. By this ye may know if a man repenteth of his sins—behold, he will confess them and forsake them" (D&C 58:42–43). Those who are soft-hearted and truly remorseful are willing to confess and forsake, admit and abandon, in order to be cleansed and forgiven. The Lord's promise is reassuring: "I, the Lord, forgive sins, and am merciful unto those who confess their sins with humble hearts" (D&C 61:2).

*With one voice and one accord, we bear witness that the
gospel of Jesus Christ is the only way to satisfy ultimate spiritual
hunger and slake definitive spiritual thirst.*

JEFFREY R. HOLLAND
TRUSTING JESUS, 13

If we choose to partake of the bread of life and living
water offered by Jesus Christ, we shall never know spiritual hunger or thirst. Faith in Christ and complete surrender to him make us vessels of his righteousness,
inspired instruments through which his light and love
are conveyed to the children of God. The Lord has said,
"Unto him that keepeth my commandments I will give
. . . a well of living water, springing up unto everlasting
life" (D&C 63:23). Elder Jeffrey R. Holland taught:
"Only One who was with God, and was God (see John
1:1), can answer the deepest and most urgent questions
of our soul. Only His almighty arms could have thrown
open the prison gates of death that otherwise would
have held us in bondage forever. Only on His triumphant shoulders can we ride to celestial glory—if we
will but choose through our faithfulness to do so"
(*Trusting Jesus,* 13). The incomparable Christ is the only
way to satisfy spiritual hunger and thirst.

I would invite all members of the Church to live with ever-more attention to the life and example of the Lord Jesus Christ, especially the love and hope and compassion he displayed.

HOWARD W. HUNTER
TEACHINGS, 44

True spirituality is not manifest in how many scriptures we memorize or historical sites we visit. Real righteousness is manifest in how we *live* day in and day out: what we *become* because of the merits and mercy of the Lord. Too many look for "spiritual markers" as some kind of measuring rod for righteousness. But President Hunter exhorted real spirituality: "I pray that we might treat each other with more kindness, more courtesy, more humility and patience and forgiveness. . . . Christ's supreme sacrifice can find full fruition in our lives only as we accept the invitation to follow him. This call is not irrelevant, unrealistic, or impossible. To follow an individual means to watch him or listen to him closely; to accept his authority, to take him as a leader, and to obey him; to support and advocate his ideas; and to take him as a model. Each of us can accept this challenge" (*Teachings*, 44). The perfect model is the Savior with his largeness of heart, his kindness, and his compassion.

If there is any one thing that will bring peace and contentment into the human . . . family, it is to live within our means. And if there is any one thing that is grinding and discouraging and disheartening, it is to have debts . . . that one cannot meet.

HEBER J. GRANT
TEACHINGS OF PRESIDENTS OF THE CHURCH, 122

Life is filled with unplanned events. Tragedies occur, and inevitably, unexpected expenses seem to come our way. Even so, the Lord wants us to live full, happy lives. By living within our means we'll be free from financial bondage and crippling acquisitiveness. The home-spun advice of a wise grandfather who lived through the Great Depression has paid enormous dividends for his descendants: "Earn a little, spend a little less. Follow this advice and you'll always have enough." We don't need to have the most glamorous or highest-paying jobs. We simply need to know how to live within our means. In Proverbs we read, "The rich ruleth over the poor, and the borrower is servant to the lender" (22:7). In a time when credit is easily available and so many people struggle with the pressures of devastating debt, earning a little and spending a little less is more than just a good suggestion; it is a road map to happiness.

*Christ's agony in the garden is unfathomable
by the finite mind, both as to intensity and cause.*

JAMES E. TALMAGE
JESUS THE CHRIST, 568

Elder James E. Talmage wrote of Christ's agony in Gethsemane: "He struggled and groaned under a burden such as no other being who has lived on earth might even conceive as possible. It was not physical pain, nor mental anguish alone, that caused Him to suffer such torture as to produce an extrusion of blood from every pore; but a spiritual agony of soul such as only God was capable of experiencing. . . . In some manner, actual and terribly real though to man incomprehensible, the Savior took upon Himself the burden of the sins of mankind from Adam to the end of the world" (*Jesus the Christ*, 568). The glorified Lord himself also spoke of his suffering (D&C 19:16–19; 18:11–13). No mere mortal could atone for the sin of another (Alma 34:10–14), nor could any ordinary mortal have endured what Christ endured and remained alive. Now and forever, we must strive to understand the majesty and scope of the Lord's atoning sacrifice.

*The Lord expects us to do all we can to save ourselves, and . . .
after we have done all we can to save ourselves, then we can lean
upon the mercies of the grace of our Heavenly Father.*

HAROLD B. LEE
TEACHINGS OF PRESIDENTS OF THE CHURCH, 34

The words of Nephi echo down the centuries: "For we labor diligently to write, to persuade our children, and also our brethren, to believe in Christ, and to be reconciled to God; for we know that it is by grace that we are saved, after all we can do" (2 Nephi 25:23). The enabling power of the Lord's Atonement is what makes forgiveness and salvation possible. We are not saved by our works alone, but by what our works signify we are *becoming*. Righteousness is not a checklist, but a quality of heart, a way of living, manifest in our becoming true disciples of the Lord in our daily walk and talk. President Harold B. Lee said of the Father, "He gave his Son that through obedience to the laws and ordinances of the gospel we might gain our salvation, but not until we have done all we can do for ourselves" (*Teachings of Presidents of the Church,* 34). We are to be spiritually self-reliant and do our part, all while relying solely upon the grace of God.

Now there is a difference between immortality and eternal life.
Immortality is the gift to live forever. It comes to every creature.
Eternal life is to have the kind of life that God has.

JOSEPH FIELDING SMITH
DOCTRINES OF SALVATION, 2:8

Elder Joseph Fielding Smith helped us understand the difference between immortality and eternal life: "What is eternal life? It is to have 'a continuation of the seeds forever and ever' (D&C 132:19). No one receives eternal life except those who receive the exaltation. Eternal life is the greatest gift of God; immortality is not" (*Doctrines of Salvation,* 2:9). Immortality is a free gift for all mankind, to live everlastingly in a resurrected state with body and spirit inseparably connected. As the Fall brought death to the world, so the Atonement of Christ brought life. Eternal life is life in the presence of the Father and Son; it is the quality of life that God himself enjoys; it is to become a member of the Church of the Firstborn and become like God, being heirs as his sons and daughters; it is to receive a fulness of blessings and become a joint-heir with Jesus Christ (Romans 8:14–17; D&C 76:67, 94; 93:22).

*We are meeting the adversary every day. We must
be close to Christ, we must daily take His name upon us, always
remember Him, and keep His commandments.*

EZRA TAFT BENSON
A WITNESS AND A WARNING, 58

Perhaps we underestimate the battle for our souls, waged every day in the choices we make. Like Joshua of old, we must "choose . . . this day whom [we] will serve" (Joshua 24:15). To withstand the fiery darts of the adversary, we need the courage to stay well on the Lord's side of the line. That courage comes from daily devotion, scripture study, prayer, and Christlike service. Think how much better a day passes when we remember to ask ourselves: What would Jesus do? What better time to ask that question than during the weekly sacrament? When we sincerely think about Jesus and what it means to take his name upon us, we are better prepared for another week's worth of spiritual battles. When we sincerely commit to keep the commandments, our heightened resolve leads to a heightened awareness of what temptations we may face and how we can prepare to overcome them. Staying close to Christ is the only way to conquer the enemy of our souls.

Our Lord and Master came to the earth not to do His own will but that of His Father, and He successfully fulfilled His mission. He has triumphed over death, hell and the grave and has earned the reward of a throne at the right hand of His Father.

HEBER J. GRANT
TEACHINGS OF PRESIDENTS OF THE CHURCH, 224

For God so loved the world, that he gave his only begotten Son, that whosoever believeth in him should not perish, but have everlasting life" (John 3:16). In these twenty-five words uttered by Jesus we have the gospel plan summarized, affirming God's encompassing love for his children and tying together the Father, the Son, and his atoning sacrifice. The Savior, doing the will of his Father, "so loved the world that he gave his own life, that as many as would believe might become the sons of God" (D&C 34:3). As we follow his "more excellent way" (Ether 12:11) and receive his image in our countenances, we experience a mighty change of heart (Alma 5:14). Then, even though life is hard, we do not give up; even though we die, we do not perish. The Lord makes it possible for the faithful to have everlasting life, to receive exaltation in the kingdom of God.

We have nothing to fear if we are faithful.

JOSEPH SMITH
ENCYCLOPEDIA OF JOSEPH SMITH'S TEACHINGS, 246

Fear and doubt are among the chief weapons used by the adversary of righteousness. The father of lies whispers to us that faith in the Lord is folly, that true prophets are false, that those who sincerely strive to live the gospel are hypocrites and fools. The Lord, on the other hand, speaks clearly to our hearts: "Treasure up wisdom in your bosoms . . . ; but if ye are prepared ye shall not fear" (D&C 38:30). Certainly, life is not without trial and testing, without worry and sorrow. But this is the time to stand fast in righteousness, to move forward with faith, to look to God and live (Alma 37:47). If our lamps are trimmed and burning with faith, humility, and prayer, we carry with us the oil of spiritual preparedness. We will be ready for the coming of the Bridegroom and have no need to fear (D&C 33:17; Matthew 25:1–13).

*If you will not be loyal in the small things you
will not be loyal in the large things.*

BOYD K. PACKER
THAT ALL MAY BE EDIFIED, 238

Some mistakenly think they can sustain the prophet while refusing to sustain local ecclesiastical leaders. Elder Boyd K. Packer observed, "A man who says he will sustain the President of the Church or the General Authorities, but cannot sustain his own bishop, is deceiving himself. The man who will not sustain the bishop of his ward and the president of his stake will not sustain the President of the Church" (*That All May Be Edified,* 238). In some ways, it may be easier to sustain the prophet whom we see at a distance than to sustain our local leaders whom we see regularly and up close. Because we know our local leaders, we see some of their weaknesses and shortcomings—and we all have a few. Ego is more likely to crowd in on the local level. Nevertheless, our responsibility is to sustain our local leaders, and consequently, we will better sustain our prophet.

*We can best exemplify our love for our God by
living our religion. It is vain to profess a love for God while
speaking evil of or doing wrong to His children.*

WILFORD WOODRUFF
TEACHINGS OF PRESIDENTS OF THE CHURCH, 246

The essence of the gospel is love—not Church programs and procedures, but rather charity in our hearts
for all the sons and daughters of God. The surest indication of our love for God is how we treat the people
around us. The scriptures attest, "If a man say, I love
God, and hateth his brother, he is a liar: for he that
loveth not his brother whom he hath seen, how can he
love God whom he hath not seen? And this commandment have we from him, That he who loveth
God love his brother also" (1 John 4:20–21). Pure love
is its own reward; the more we give, the more we will
receive. It grows as we serve and sacrifice for one
another. Those who truly love God love his children,
all his children, even those who are difficult to love.
We live our religion best by loving those around us.

*No pain suffered by man or woman upon the
earth will be without its compensating effects if it be suffered
in resignation and if it be met with patience.*

SPENCER W. KIMBALL
TEACHINGS, 167

While wrongfully imprisoned in Liberty Jail, the Lord taught the Prophet Joseph that followers of Christ are not promised freedom from tribulation but strength to endure all things: "My son, peace be unto thy soul; thine adversity and thine afflictions shall be but a small moment; And then, if thou endure it well, God shall exalt thee on high. . . . All these things shall give thee experience, and shall be for thy good" (D&C 121:7–8; 122:7). Life is a school, and part of that education is hardship. Elder Spencer W. Kimball taught: "Being human, we would expel from our lives, sorrow, distress, physical pain, and mental anguish and assure ourselves of continual ease and comfort. But if we closed the doors upon such, we might be evicting our greatest friends and benefactors. Suffering can make saints of people as they learn patience, long-suffering, and self-mastery. The sufferings of our Savior were part of his education" (*Teachings,* 168).

We cannot repent for someone else.
But we can forgive someone else, refusing to hold hostage
those whom the Lord seeks to set free!

NEAL A. MAXWELL
QUOTE BOOK, 129

It has been said that lack of forgiveness toward another is akin to consuming poison and waiting for the other person to die. Vindictiveness and hardheartedness stifle spiritual growth and happiness. On the other hand, nothing enlarges the soul more than genuine forgiveness and compassion. The Lord's directive is clear: "Ye ought to forgive one another; for he that forgiveth not his brother his trespasses standeth condemned before the Lord; for there remaineth in him the greater sin. I, the Lord, will forgive whom I will forgive, but of you it is required to forgive all men" (D&C 64:9–10). The Lord, who is perfectly merciful, knows our hearts as well as the hearts of every offender. And since we all walk imperfectly before the Lord, we all need mercy. If we wish to be forgiven and draw upon the Atonement, we must forgive. Forgiveness is the greatest gift we can give others— and ourselves.

Be upright, just, and merciful, exercising a spirit of nobility and godliness in all your intentions and resolutions—in all your acts and dealings. Cultivate a spirit of charity.

LORENZO SNOW
TEACHINGS, 10

Lorenzo Snow, fifth President of the Church, was beloved for his kindliness and compassion. He had fully brought into his life the wisdom of Micah the prophet: "What doth the Lord require of thee, but to do justly, and to love mercy, and to walk humbly with thy God" (Micah 6:8). The Lord's standard of righteousness remains unchanged in every generation: do good works and treat people fairly, extend mercy and forgiveness, be meek and humble. If we want to have a place in Zion with the fellowship of the Saints, and in celestial glory with those who have their names written in heaven (D&C 76:68), we must live with integrity, be compassionate and kindhearted, and submissively seek to do the Lord's will. This is the gospel in action—*living* the gospel with full purpose of heart, a soft and sympathetic heart, a meek and merciful heart, a gracious and generous heart.

*I have never done anything with your
name of which you need be ashamed.*

GEORGE ALBERT SMITH
TEACHINGS, 132

George Albert Smith had an experience that
became a touchstone for the rest of his life. While
seriously ill, he lost consciousness. In a dream-vision,
he saw his beloved grandfather, who asked him, "I
would like to know what you have done with my
name." George Albert Smith said that his whole life
passed before him in retrospect. After this self-
examination, he was pleased to report that he had kept
his grandfather's name clean and honorable. When he
awoke from his dream-vision, his pillow was wet with
tears of gratitude that he could answer his grandfather
unashamed. President Smith later taught the youth of
the Church: "Honor the names that you bear, because
someday you will have the privilege and the obligation
of reporting to them (and to your Father in Heaven)
what you have done with their name" (*Teachings,*
132–33). Whatever your earthly name may be, honor
your eternal name as a son or daughter of God.

*Every man's religion should have practical issue,
not merely emotional responsiveness which delights in
hearing the gospel but lacks diligence in living it. We must
remember that religion is action, not diction.*

HUGH B. BROWN
VISION AND VALOR, 50

We have all heard the expression "talk is cheap"—especially when it comes to gospel living. How readily we lecture, speak, and speculate about gospel doctrines when the better part is to apply those principles in our lives. How much easier it can be to speak about love than to be kind to a person who is difficult to love. It requires much less of us to teach a class on service than to willingly give of our time and effort to help another. Elder Hugh B. Brown counseled: "Let us pray that God will deliver us from our dullness of conscience, from a feeble sense of duty, from thoughtless disregard of others, and from all halfheartedness in our work" (*Vision and Valor*, 50). If we put our "shoulder to the wheel" and do our best to love, serve, and follow the Lord, we will discover the true joy of gospel living.

An intelligent being, in the image of God, possesses every organ, attribute, sense, sympathy, affection of will, wisdom, love, power and gift, which is possessed by God himself. But . . . these attributes are in embryo, and are to be gradually developed.

PARLEY P. PRATT
KEY TO THE SCIENCE OF THEOLOGY, 100–101

Just as the Savior matured physically, mentally, socially, and spiritually, a full sense of his mission came in the process of time: "He received not of the fulness at first, but continued from grace to grace, until he received a fulness" (D&C 93:13; see Luke 2:52). As children of God, we grow line upon line, precept upon precept. We learn a little today, improve even more tomorrow, and, hopefully before we pass through the veil of death, we progress spiritually. We are here in this school of mortality, learning and proving ourselves. We are here to grow the seeds of godliness within us, to become more like our Father, to follow the more excellent way of the Master. One thing we know for certain: Our Heavenly Father never gives up on us, his children. He knows each of us and our inherent potential and divine worth. But we must come to know him and spend our best efforts in becoming like him.

Satan will be bound by the power of God;
but he will be bound also by the determination of the people of
God not to listen to him, not to be governed by him.

GEORGE Q. CANNON
GOSPEL TRUTH, 68

President George Q. Cannon taught an important truth with regard to the Millennium: "The Lord will not bind [Satan] and take his power from the earth while there are men and women willing to be governed by him. That is contrary to the plan of salvation. To deprive men of their agency is contrary to the purposes of our God. . . . Satan only gains power over man through man's exercise of his own agency; and when Satan shall be bound, as the Lord says he will be for a thousand years, one of the great powers that will help bring this to pass will be man's agency. The Lord has never forced men against their will to obey Him. He never will do so. If Satan, therefore, has power with man, it is because man yields to his influence" (*Gospel Truth,* 68). During the Millennium, Satan will be bound and have "no power over the hearts of the people" because righteousness and peace will prevail (1 Nephi 22:26; D&C 101:28–29).

In this Church there is a stream of living water that flows from the throne of God. . . . Oh, won't you drink of this living stream? For if you will your souls shall never thirst again.

CHARLES A. CALLIS
CONFERENCE REPORT, OCTOBER 1931, 67–68

A living church needs living water. Ancient words of holy writ, handed down from generation to generation, are not enough. We need *living water.* Living water is a symbol of the Savior and his teachings. Jesus Christ is the Fountain of Living Water from which eternal life springs. His stream of living water includes ancient and modern revelation, scriptures, words of apostles and prophets, and inspired teachings and writings of others as they are moved upon by the Holy Ghost (D&C 68:4). The stream of living water that leads to eternal life is manifest in the hearts of faithful Saints whose thoughts and deeds reflect the Fount of Every Blessing. Conversely, the world offers alluring temptations and transitory pleasures that lead to stagnant, stinking pools of disappointment and sorrow. Thankfully, living water slakes spiritual thirst and leads to "peace in this world, and eternal life in the world to come" (D&C 59:23).

MAY

~

*We need to remember that though
we make our friends, God has made our
neighbors—everywhere. Love should
have no boundary; we should
have no narrow loyalties.*

HOWARD W. HUNTER

*Heaven pity the man who is unconscious
of a fault! Pity him also who is ignorant of his ignorance!
Neither is on the road to salvation.*

DAVID O. MCKAY
GOSPEL IDEALS, 13

Blindness of mind and heart has often been condemned in scripture: "Wo unto the blind that will not
see; for they shall perish" (2 Nephi 9:32). Akin to
hardness of heart, blindness of mind is self-deception
of the worst kind (1 Nephi 7:8). Those who are puffed
up can't see their own weaknesses; their blindness
closes them to humility and meekness, charity and
integrity. Most often, the blind are arrogant, self-
righteous, and self-betrayed. Blindness can come from
looking beyond the mark for something grand and
glorious and thereby missing the sweet simplicity of
the gospel of Jesus Christ (Jacob 4:14). Blindness can
also come when we give ourselves so much to the
world that the Spirit of the Lord can no longer whisper its still, small voice of inspiration (Alma 10:25;
13:4). We must live truthfully and remember the
promise that the adversary cannot blind us if we hold
firmly to the iron rod (1 Nephi 15:24).

A choice to be good—even with the trials that come—
will allow the Atonement to change your heart. In time and after
persistence, your wants and even your needs will change.

HENRY B. EYRING
TO DRAW CLOSER TO GOD, 70

The people who believed King Benjamin's sermon found that a powerful change had come to them "because of the Spirit of the Lord Omnipotent, which has wrought a mighty change in us, or in our hearts, that we have no more disposition to do evil, but to do good continually" (Mosiah 5:2). The gospel is a message of change, of transformation and regeneration, as we strive to follow the Lord with full purpose of heart (Moroni 7:47–48). Elder Henry B. Eyring wisely counseled, "If we stay at it long enough, perhaps for a lifetime, we will have for so long felt what the Savior feels, wanted what he wants, and done what he would have us do that we will have, through the Atonement, a new heart filled with charity. And we will have become like him" (*To Draw Closer to God,* 71).

*Treat everybody well, and do
what is right to everybody, and cultivate the
spirit of kindness towards all.*

JOHN TAYLOR
TEACHINGS OF PRESIDENTS OF THE CHURCH, 25

One of the qualities of the heart most reflective of the Savior's life and teachings is goodwill toward all people. Largeness of soul is manifest in those who are considerate, gracious, and kindhearted toward people of varying ages and background, socioeconomic status and occupation, religious affiliation and ethnicity. So often we see the opposite: some treat the CEO different from the custodian, or the beautiful and powerful people different from the humble and unassuming people. But Christ treated all people the same—the sinner and saint, the publican and Pharisee, the believer and doubter—with gentleness, benevolence, fairness, and thoughtfulness. He taught and lived what has come to be known as the Golden Rule: "Therefore all things whatsoever ye would that men should do to you, do ye even so to them: for this is the law and the prophets" (Matthew 7:12). Treat all people the way you want to be treated.

Look to the President of the Church for
your instructions. If ever there is a conflict, you keep your
eyes on the President if you want to walk in the light.

HAROLD B. LEE
TEACHINGS, 532

President Harold B. Lee counseled the Saints to "keep in mind that the head of this church is not the President of the Church. The head of this church is the Lord and Master, Jesus Christ, who reigns and rules" (*Teachings,* 527). The Lord works through his authorized representative, his anointed prophet and seer, his spokesman and watchman on the tower. In this day of turmoil and trouble, we need the Lord's mouthpiece more than ever. "Let's not be foolish and suppose that because the sun is shining today there won't be clouds tomorrow. The Lord has told us by revelation some of the things that are ahead of us, and we are living in the day when the fulfillment of those prophecies is at hand. We are startled, and yet there is nothing happening today that the prophets didn't foresee. God help us to keep our own houses in order and to keep our eyes fixed upon those who preside . . . and to follow their direction, and we won't be led astray" (ibid., 315).

If you marry the proper "whom" and if you marry in the proper "where," then you will have an infinitely better chance of happiness throughout all eternity.

SPENCER W. KIMBALL
TEACHINGS, 301

Speaking to young men at a mission conference, President Spencer W. Kimball gave sound advice regarding the marriage decision: "The greatest single factor affecting what you are going to be tomorrow, your activity, your attitudes, your eventual destiny is the one decision you make that moonlit night when you ask that individual to be your companion for life. That's the most important decision of your entire life! It isn't where you are going to school . . . or how you are going to make your living. These, though important, are incidental and nothing compared with the important decision that you make when you ask someone to be your companion for eternity" (*Teachings*, 301). Truly, the decisions we make with regard to marrying the right person, in the right place, at the right time are eternally significant. Once married, the most important thing we can do to keep our marital love alive and growing is to honor our sacred covenants with complete fidelity.

Happiness in marriage is not so much a matter of romance as it is an anxious concern for the comfort and well-being of one's companion.

GORDON B. HINCKLEY
TEACHINGS, 325

Marriage and family life is not easy; it never was. It is filled with stress and anxiety, heartache and pain, financial and health concerns. But when a husband and wife come together in love and mutual respect, they can build a familial union that also brings the greatest of earthly joys and a partnership that can weather any storm. President Gordon B. Hinckley stated, "Marriage is a companionship. . . . We walk side by side with respect, appreciation, and love one for another. There can be nothing of inferiority or superiority between the husband and wife in the plan of the Lord. . . . If husbands and wives would only give greater emphasis to the virtues that are to be found in one another and less to the faults, there would be fewer broken hearts, fewer tears, fewer divorces, and much more happiness in the homes of our people" (*Teachings,* 322). Happiness in marriage and family life comes from charity, selflessness, and righteousness.

*If parents will continually set before their children
examples worthy of imitation and the approval of our Father in
Heaven, they will turn the . . . tide of feelings of their children,
and they eventually will desire righteousness more than evil.*

BRIGHAM YOUNG
DISCOURSES, 208

In a group discussion with several recently married
college students, some of the students commented
about how worried they were to bring children into
the world. One young wife said, "I've always wanted
children, but with all the wickedness today, I just don't
know." Another new husband said, "It terrifies me to
think of being a father. I wonder how I can support a
family and raise good children in such an immoral
world." These two comments are certainly not indica-
tive of all newly married couples, but they do reflect
some uncertainty about childrearing in this troubled
world. Parents today, as in times past, need to heed the
words of prophets: "God's commandment for His
children to multiply and replenish the earth remains
in force" (*Ensign,* November 1995, 102). The example
of parents—of courage, faithfulness, obedience, and
righteousness—will bless their children and grandchildren for generations to come.

We need to remember that though we make our friends,
God has made our neighbors—everywhere. Love should have no
boundary; we should have no narrow loyalties.

HOWARD W. HUNTER
TEACHINGS, 95

Those who feel the "pure love of Christ" in their hearts extend charity to all peoples (Moroni 7:47). The key is to love our neighbor—whether across the street or on the other side of the world—including our neighbor who is difficult to love. It is often easier to speak of our love for all of humanity than it is to love those in our family, neighborhood, ward, and stake who are so different from us or hard to get along with. But pure love requires an abundant, generous, forgiving heart—a heart that opens wide in kindness, understanding, and compassion for all people. Without this pure love that extends throughout the whole human race, we have little to commend us as followers of Jesus Christ. Let us, as Mormon counseled, "pray unto the Father with all the energy of heart, that ye may be filled with this love, which he hath bestowed upon all who are true followers of his Son, Jesus Christ" (Moroni 7:48).

Motherhood lies at the foundation of happiness in the home, and of prosperity in the nation. God has laid upon men and women very sacred obligations with respect to motherhood.

JOSEPH F. SMITH
GOSPEL DOCTRINE, 288

It has been said that a mother is the first and most important teacher in a child's life. No one can adequately take her place. She willingly walks into the valley of the shadow of death as she gives life, and then she walks alongside her children, sustaining them until they venture on their own. Even then, her heart follows close behind and skips a beat every time she hears their footsteps. Mothers are the heart of a home: they nurture and love; they create homes of harmony and warmth; they cultivate strengths and see potential. Motherhood is not merely a checklist of attributes. It's a description of a person who loves another more than life itself; a person who freely, lovingly gives her all for the happiness of another. No two mothers are just alike. And not a single one is expected to be perfect—or close to it. Mothers with eternal perspective know they do their best simply by doing a little better every day.

*We regard the mother as the one who gives shape to the
character of the child. I consider that the mother has a greater
influence over her posterity than any other person can have.*

WILFORD WOODRUFF
TEACHINGS OF PRESIDENTS OF THE CHURCH, 169

Poets and philosophers, scholars and sages, have long
believed that motherhood possesses the greatest
potential for good or ill in human life. Children
unconsciously model their parents' manner, speech,
and conduct. A mother's habits often become a child's
pattern for living. A mother's influence can be an
incomparably powerful force for good. Elder Wilford
Woodruff said it this way: "Show me a mother who
prays, who has passed through the trials of life by
prayer, who has trusted in the Lord God of Israel in
her trials and difficulties, and her children will follow
in the same path" (*Teachings of Presidents of the Church,*
169). Most mothers seem to have the God-given ability to nurture their children. They teach their children
to work hard, to persevere, and most of all, to love.
They model kindness and respect. They maintain a
positive attitude in the face of trials. Indeed, motherhood is the noblest responsibility in the world.

*Good mothers are truly Christ-like. Mother-love
in its real sense is an intimate application of God-love. It is
enduring, self-sacrificing, and pure, knowing no bounds.*

MARK E. PETERSEN
FAITH WORKS, 87

Sometimes it is only in retrospect that we fully cherish what mothers do. Good mothers have Christlike love. They sacrifice, love, forgive, love, hope, love, and love some more. While no earthly mother is perfect, many come close as they daily strive to cultivate greatness in a child, as they do their best to teach and nurture, as they realize that childrearing is not a competition but must be tailored to the temperaments and capacities of each child. Just as every child is different, so is every mother. Those unique attributes forge special bonds between mothers and children. And when mistakes are made, good mothers apologize and make amends—and teach their children to do the same. The desire to rear children in love and righteousness, the special ability to love and nurture, and the willingness to express that love in the selfless development of another human soul is surely the clearest application of Christlike living.

What you have to do is get on the straight and narrow path—thus charting a course leading to eternal life—and then, being on that path, pass out of this life in full fellowship. . . . There is no such thing as falling off the straight and narrow path in the life to come.

BRUCE R. McCONKIE
"PROBATIONARY TEST OF MORTALITY," 11

It has been wisely observed that the gospel of Jesus Christ is simply beautiful and beautifully simple; what we must do in this life is get on the gospel path and go forward with faithfulness to the end. We don't have to be perfect in this life or, because of shortcomings, spend our days feeling guilty and unworthy. We don't have to be truer than true and thereby become blinded by looking beyond the mark (Jacob 4:14). The gospel mark *is* Christ, and the mainstream of the Church is the course leading to eternal life. Those who have been born of the Spirit, those who with broken heart and contrite spirit receive the ordinances necessary to get on the path, stay on the path by looking to Christ and pressing forward with faith. If we humbly and steadfastly walk the path, we will not be lost or go astray, and ultimately, we'll taste the fruits of perfection.

Now, fathers and mothers, appreciate your children. Don't turn them over to somebody else to train and educate in regard to matters of eternal life. That is your privilege, and it is a privilege.

GEORGE ALBERT SMITH
CONFERENCE REPORT, OCTOBER 1948, 166

Children need parents who love and cherish them, who appreciate and enjoy them, who want to spend time with them. Indeed, children spell *love* T-I-M-E. Our opportunities to bless and teach our children may come in unexpected ways. For example, one night after basketball practice, a ten-year-old boy was more quiet than usual. Sensing something was wrong, the father created an opportunity to be alone with his son. After a few minutes, the son started to cry. Pouring out his feelings of rejection, the boy explained that some other boys had been mean to him. The father carefully listened with his arm around his son. He didn't try to solve the problem; he asked questions; he didn't hurry him. He listened and listened and then said, "Son, I wish I could take away the pain you're feeling." Then in a moment of intense bonding, the son hugged his father and said, "It feels like you already have."

This ability and willingness properly to rear children, the gift to love, and eagerness, yes, longing to express it in soul development, make motherhood the noblest office or calling in the world.

DAVID O. MCKAY
GOSPEL IDEALS, 453

Motherhood deserves to be honored not just one day a year but every day. In the way we think and talk, live and interact, we ought to demonstrate the highest regard for the highest of holy callings: motherhood. Elder David O. McKay eloquently gives perspective to motherhood: "She who can paint a masterpiece or write a book that will influence millions deserves the admiration and the plaudits of mankind; but she who rears successfully a family of healthy, beautiful sons and daughters, whose influence will be felt through generations to come, whose immortal souls will exert an influence throughout the ages long after paintings shall have faded, and books and statues shall have decayed or shall have been destroyed, deserves the highest honor that man can give, and the choicest blessings of God. In her high duty and service to humanity, endowing with immortality eternal spirits, she is co-partner with the Creator himself" (*Gospel Ideals*, 453–54).

*To do well those things which God
ordained to be the common lot of all man-kind,
is the truest greatness.*

JOSEPH F. SMITH
GOSPEL DOCTRINE, 285

True greatness is the composite of life's prosaic moments, when day after day, the small, usually unrecognized acts of service, integrity, and discipleship we render reveal our real character. The things that come from the heart, the things that strengthen ties between family and friends, are what give us the most joy here and hereafter. And they require our utmost attention and energy. Unfortunately, we often become preoccupied with things of little consequence: the size of our house or bank account, the power and prestige of the world. But these accomplishments fade with the passage of time. As President Joseph F. Smith said, "To be a successful father or a successful mother is greater than to be a successful general or a successful statesman. One is universal and eternal greatness, the other is ephemeral" (*Gospel Doctrine,* 285). The praise and honor of the world never lasts, but the love of family and the knowledge of God can endure forever.

*Keep your eye on the prophet—
for the Lord will never permit His prophet to
lead this Church astray.*

EZRA TAFT BENSON
TEACHINGS, 44

Of all mortal men we must keep our eyes firmly riveted on the Lord's anointed prophet, seer, and revelator. He is called of God and endowed with the power and authority of the keys of the priesthood— and empowered by the gifts of God—to act in the name of God in all things (D&C 107:91–92; 132:7). Although we realize he is mortal and imperfect, we also know that it is he who stands closest to the fountain of living waters and is the mouthpiece of the Lord; it is he who reveals to us the mind and will of the Lord to guide us in these latter-days. If we hearken to his counsel, we will be led out of the darkness and captivity of Babylon into the joy and salvation of Zion.

*The fall of man came as a blessing in disguise, and
was the means of furthering the purposes of the Lord in the
progress of man, rather than a means of hindering them.*

JOSEPH FIELDING SMITH
DOCTRINES OF SALVATION, 1:114

Elder Joseph Fielding Smith has enlightened us in
regards to the Fall: "When Adam was driven out of the
Garden of Eden, the Lord passed a sentence upon him.
Some people have looked upon that sentence as being a
dreadful thing. It was not; it was a blessing. I do not
know that it can truthfully be considered even as a
punishment in disguise" (*Doctrines of Salvation,* 1:113).
Adam and Eve praised God because of the blessing of
mortality: "Blessed be the name of God, for because of
my transgression my eyes are opened, and in this life I
shall have joy and again in the flesh I shall see God"
(Moses 5:10–12). Without mortality we would not be
given the promised blessing of immortality or the
potential of eternal life. Because of Adam and Eve, we
have been granted the privilege to pass through a mortal experience. Because of Adam and Eve, we can know
joy and sorrow, pleasure and pain, gain a body, and
prove ourselves worthy to receive an eternal reward.

The time has now come for every Latter-day
Saint, who calculates to be prepared for the future . . . to do
the will of the Lord and to pay his tithing in full.

LORENZO SNOW
TEACHINGS, 155

On this date in 1899, President Lorenzo Snow announced a renewed emphasis on the payment of tithing. The Church was drowning in debt, and the Saints in southern Utah were suffering under a devastating drought. President Snow had pleaded mightily with the Lord for the solution. While on a trip to St. George, Utah, to preside over a conference, it was revealed to him that the solution to both problems lay in the Saints paying an honest tithing on their income. Carrying this message to the Saints throughout the region, he stimulated a renewed commitment to tithing. As the Saints covenanted to obey this commandment, not only did the Church begin to move into financial solvency but the drought was also lifted. The Saints were saved from temporal disaster by heeding the words of the prophet.

Good parents . . . have lovingly, prayerfully, and earnestly
tried to teach their children . . . "to pray, and to walk uprightly
before the Lord" (D&C 68:28). . . . Successful parents are
those who have . . . struggled to do the best they can.

JAMES E. FAUST
ENSIGN, MAY 2003, 61

No greater joy in life can come to parents than to
see their children grow in truth and righteousness
(3 John 1:4), become responsible adults, and then
become loving parents themselves. Parenting is the
hardest work most of us will ever do, and things may
not turn out the way parents hope. Ultimately, the
person a child becomes is not entirely up to the parents. That's why parents cannot revel too much in
"successful" children or give in to despair with struggling children. President James E. Faust counseled,
"Let us not be arrogant but rather humbly grateful if
our children are obedient and respectful of our teachings of the ways of the Lord. To those brokenhearted
parents who have been righteous, diligent, and prayerful in the teaching of their disobedient children, we
say to you, the Good Shepherd is watching over them.
God knows and understands your deep sorrow. There
is hope" (*Ensign,* May 2003, 68).

*A testimony comes when the Holy Ghost gives the earnest
seeker a witness of the truth. . . . Conversion, on the other hand,
is the fruit of, or the reward for, repentance and obedience.*

MARION G. ROMNEY
LOOK TO GOD AND LIVE, 111

Elder Marion G. Romney explained the difference between conversion and testimony: "Conversion is effected by divine forgiveness which remits sins. The sequence is something like this: An honest seeker hears the message. He asks the Lord in prayer if it is true. The Holy Spirit gives him a witness. This is a testimony. If one's testimony is strong enough, he repents and obeys the commandments. By such obedience he receives divine forgiveness which remits sin. Thus, he is converted to a newness of life. His spirit is healed" (*Look to God and Live,* 111–12). While membership in the Church reflects association with the kingdom of God on earth, conversion reflects a change of heart that brings us to Christ. In other words, while Church membership and testimony are essential, a deep-down and abiding commitment to Christ is a newness of life manifest in who we are *becoming.* The conversion we seek is a lifelong process of putting off the natural man and becoming a saint (Mosiah 3:19).

MAY 21

The men and women of Christ are constant,
being the same in private as in public. We cannot keep
two sets of books while Heaven has but one.

NEAL A. MAXWELL
QUOTE BOOK, 142

A microbiology professor once told his class that he keeps his science in one pocket and his faith in another. He said they do not overlap and are kept apart from one another. But our lives cannot be so compartmentalized. We are to live with integrity: being the same at home as at the office, and letting our faith infuse our life and work (D&C 88:118). Would it not be appropriate for a physician to say a silent prayer before surgery, a farmer to pray over his flocks, a teacher to petition heaven's help for her students? Of course, that same physician, farmer, and teacher must use all the tools of reason and intelligence. Faith and reason, study and prayer, are the keys to being the same in private and in public—one person, not two. As James said, "A double minded man is unstable in all his ways" (James 1:8).

*In the service of the Lord, it is not where
you serve but how. In The Church of Jesus Christ of Latter-day
Saints, one takes the place to which one is duly called,
which place one neither seeks nor declines.*

J. REUBEN CLARK JR.
CONFERENCE REPORT, APRIL 1951, 154

J. Reuben Clark's twenty-eight-year tenure in the First Presidency was the longest in Church history, serving as counselor to three presidents. On April 9, 1951, people became concerned when new Church President David O. McKay named J. Reuben Clark as his second counselor, perceiving it as a demotion since he had most recently been serving for several years as first counselor to George Albert Smith. President McKay explained that he had done it only because Stephen L Richards (who had been named as first counselor) had seniority over President Clark as an apostle. In that April 1951 general conference President Clark delivered one of the greatest sermons on consecration to the Lord's cause, teaching that it is not in which calling we serve that matters but how we serve. Because callings change and the kingdom of God rolls forth, our aim and sole desire, like President Clark's, must be to seek the welfare of Zion (2 Nephi 26:29).

Always tell the truth. He is a coward who does
not tell the truth; she is a coward who does not tell the truth. . . .
You are cowardly when you do not tell the truth.

GEORGE Q. CANNON
GOSPEL TRUTH, 451

The father of lies is given that epithet because he has been a liar from the beginning (D&C 93:25). In him, the ultimate coward, there is no truth. His way is the way of deception. In today's world, some do not prize truthfulness as they once did. They rationalize deceit as a means to an end, just another way to get ahead. They deem it acceptable to: "lie a little, take the advantage of one because of his words, dig a pit for thy neighbor." They mistakenly reason that "there is no harm in this . . . for tomorrow we die" (2 Nephi 28:8; D&C 10:25). But when we lie or bear false witness, we cross the line into the adversary's territory. We cannot lie to the Lord (Alma 5:17). Quite simply, true Saints "believe in being honest," not in being mostly honest or sometimes honest (Article of Faith 13). President George Q. Cannon counseled: "Always remember that it is . . . brave to tell the truth" (*Gospel Truth,* 451). May we be courageous enough to be truthful.

Parents have a sacred duty to rear their children in love and righteousness. . . . Husbands and wives—mothers and fathers—will be held accountable before God for the discharge of these obligations.

THE FIRST PRESIDENCY AND QUORUM
OF THE TWELVE APOSTLES
ENSIGN, NOVEMBER 1995, 102

The scriptures instruct parents to teach the gospel to their children by precept and by example. "Teach them to walk in the ways of truth and soberness; ye will teach them to love one another, and to serve one another" (Mosiah 4:15). As parents we are admonished to "teach one another the doctrine of the kingdom" (D&C 88:77) and teach our children repentance and faith in Christ (D&C 68:25). The scriptures explain that parents should study the Savior's life and teachings and strive to teach as he taught (3 Nephi 27:27); they should prepare to teach (D&C 1:37; 11:21; John 5:39); they should not cease to pray (3 Nephi 20:1); they should strive to be a good example, as was Jesus (1 Peter 2:21, 2 Nephi 31:5–10); they should cultivate humility (John 8:50; 13:14–15; Proverbs 3:5–6; Ether 12:27; D&C 112:10) and be dedicated in love (John 15:12; 13:34–35; Moroni 7:48). The scriptures and teachings of the prophets are a parenting Liahona.

*May God help me, and give me strength to do what
is right. . . . This is my greatest desire, and that I may be true and
faithful, and useful in doing good, proclaiming the word of
God, and sustaining the authorities of the Church.*

ABRAHAM O. WOODRUFF
CONFERENCE REPORT, OCTOBER 1897, 45

Abraham Owen Woodruff, son of President
Wilford Woodruff, was called to the Quorum of the
Twelve Apostles in 1897 when he was only twenty-
four years old. In his first remarks as a new apostle, he
said, "I do covenant with you, as I have done with my
God . . . , that I will seek with all my power which He
will give me . . . to dedicate my life . . . to the building
up of His kingdom" (Conference Report, October
1897, 45). He served faithfully in various assignments,
including as chief colonizer of the Latter-day Saint
settlement in the Big Horn Basin of Wyoming. In
1904 Elder Woodruff traveled to Mexico with his wife
and four children to visit Mormon settlements. While
there his wife contracted smallpox and died. Two
weeks later, this faithful apostle died at age thirty-one,
having been stricken with the same disease while caring for his beloved wife.

*It has been and is a principle of my life never
to betray a friend, my religion, my country or my God.*

DANIEL H. WELLS
PROPHETS AND APOSTLES OF THE LAST DISPENSATION, 257

Daniel H. Wells served as an apostle and member of the First Presidency of the Church for twenty years, until the death of Brigham Young. He then served for fourteen years as a counselor to the Twelve Apostles until his death in 1891. He was held in prison by enemies of the Church for contempt of court because he refused to reveal the details of the temple ceremony. Loyal and true to the end, he would not break the sacred oath of his temple covenants. Those who knew him attested to his integrity and character, his honesty and trustworthiness. His example of loyalty is one to be emulated. Are we faithful to family, friends, and others—even during difficult times? Are we steadfast in our devotion to truth? Are we fair? Are we the same when a person is present as when he or she is absent? Far from the fickle crowd is One who watches over us with perfect love and unsurpassed fidelity. Let us be unwaveringly loyal to him, and with his help, be more loyal to others.

Take some time . . . each day to have a quiet hour, . . .
an hour of prayerful meditation where you can tune in with God
and discuss with Him problems that are too much for human
understanding, too great for human strength.

HAROLD B. LEE
TEACHINGS, 152

Revelation and understanding can come to those who combine sincere prayer with pondering the things of God. For example, as Nephi sat pondering in his heart the things his father had taught, he was caught away in the Spirit and saw the vision of the tree of life (1 Nephi 11:1). This kind of pondering is much more than casual thinking or occasional reflecting; it requires rigorous effort and a willing, consecrated heart. When the Lord visited the New World, he exhorted them to "ponder upon the things which I have said, and ask of the Father, in my name, that ye may understand" (3 Nephi 17:3). Elder Harold B. Lee said, "Take time to meditate. Many times you will be wrestling with problems, the solution of which can be spiritually discerned. Don't get so busy that you don't have time to meditate. Take the time" (*Teachings of Presidents of the Church*, 183).

No law in scripture has been more clearly defined than that of the Sabbath. From the time of Genesis to our own day, there has been no subject spoken of more directly or repeatedly than the Sabbath.

MARK E. PETERSEN
CONFERENCE REPORT, APRIL 1975, 70

Carelessness and apathy in keeping the Sabbath holy always lead to a decay in righteousness. Elder Mark E. Petersen observed, "[The Sabbath] is one of the laws most dear to the heart of God. Yet it is noted far more in its desecration than in its acceptance and proper observance" (Conference Report, April 1975, 70). We follow the Creator's example and the teachings of the prophets as we observe a weekly day of rest (Genesis 2:2–3; Exodus 20:8–11). The Sabbath is a sacred day set apart for spiritual sustenance, a day to more fully separate ourselves from the world, a holy day "to rest from your labors, and to pay thy devotions unto the Most High" (D&C 59:10). We grow spiritually as we take a break from our temporal concerns, as we more sincerely contemplate the everlasting things, as we assemble in love and fellowship to worship together, and do our duty before God.

Our enemies have never done anything that has
injured this work of God, and they never will.

HEBER J. GRANT
GOSPEL STANDARDS, 85

The latter-day kingdom of God, like a stone that will grow to fill the whole earth (Daniel 2:34–35), will flourish unimpeded until the Lord returns in glory. There will be temporary setbacks and disappointments, but as a whole, the work will move ever forward. Elder Heber J. Grant said, "Where are the men who have assailed this work? Where is their influence? They have faded away like the dew before the sun. We need have no fears, we Latter-day Saints. God will continue to sustain this work; He will sustain the right. If we are loyal, if we are true, if we are worthy of this gospel, of which God has given us a testimony, there is no danger that the world can ever injure us. We can never be injured, my brethren and sisters, by any mortals, except ourselves. If we fail to serve God, if we fail to do right, then we rob ourselves of the ability and power to grow, to increase in faith and knowledge, to have power with God, and with the righteous" (*Gospel Standards,* 85).

*There is no labor in which the
Latter-day Saints feel more deeply interested than in
the building and completing of temples.*

WILFORD WOODRUFF
TEACHINGS OF PRESIDENTS OF THE CHURCH, 175

Today, as in times past, temples are places where heaven and earth come together. Temples allow for communion between God and man. Temples are places of learning, of sweet assurance, and of unity for the Saints. Prophets have long been concerned with and responsible for the construction of temples. In this dispensation, just one year after the organization of the Church, the Lord directed Joseph Smith and other elders to build a temple in the "center place" of Zion (D&C 57:1–3). Over the next fifteen years and despite great persecution, temples were constructed at Kirtland and Nauvoo. In our day, temples are beginning to dot the earth in fulfillment of prophecy. With the expansion in temple building worldwide has come a corresponding advance in family history work as the hearts of fathers and children are turned to one another (Malachi 4:6; D&C 138:47).

*Those who have done wrong always
have that wrong gnawing them. . . . You cannot go
anywhere but where God can find you out.*

JOSEPH SMITH
HISTORY OF THE CHURCH, 6:366

On April 7, 1844, in Nauvoo, just two months before his martyrdom, Joseph Smith opened his authentic heart as he spoke to the Saints: "You don't know me; you never knew my heart. No man knows my history. I cannot tell it: I shall never undertake it. I don't blame any one for not believing my history. If I had not experienced what I have, I would not have believed it myself. I never did harm any man since I was born in the world. My voice is always for peace" (*History of the Church,* 6:317). The Prophet understood that we mortals do not see the whole picture. After all, what can we ever really know of another's authentic heart? But God knows. He knows us at our best and our less-than-best. He knows what we are capable of and what we have the potential to become. That is why you can never feel right doing wrong. If you want to be happy, be good. Those with a clear conscience go to sleep in peace.

JUNE

*Man can transform himself
and he must. Man has in himself the seeds
of godhood, which can germinate
and grow and develop.*

SPENCER W. KIMBALL

Let us not love the things of this world above the things of God. . . . How contracted in mind and short-sighted we must be to permit the perishable things of this world to swerve us in the least degree from our fidelity to the truth.

BRIGHAM YOUNG
DISCOURSES, 231

Brigham Young, known as the Lion of the Lord, was born on this date in Whitingham, Vermont, in 1801. Some have called him the "American Moses" because he led an exodus of Latter-day Saints through the wilderness to settle in the West. He was a great colonizer, dynamic apostle, tireless missionary, temple builder, dedicated family man, and president of the Church for nearly thirty years. His was always a voice of forthrightness and common sense as he exhorted the Saints to love the things of God more than the things of the world. Brother Brigham admonished the Saints to more fully follow the pattern of Christ as the means to combat spiritual apathy. He firmly believed that becoming distracted by worldly pursuits and thereby becoming disaffected from the fellowship of the Saints and the influence of the Spirit of God would be to suffer everlasting disappointment.

JUNE 2

*The great criterion of success in the
world is that men can make money. But I want to say to you
Latter-day Saints that to do this is not true success.*

HEBER J. GRANT
TEACHINGS OF PRESIDENTS OF THE CHURCH, 125

This life is the time for us to pursue *true, lasting* success, even as the world stands at the door preaching only monetary success. Elder Heber J. Grant said, "As a man grows and increases in the things of this world, if he is not careful, he will lose the Spirit of the Lord, and he will set his heart upon the things of this world. And if he loses the Spirit of the Lord, and fails to be honest with God in the payment of his tithes as strictly and honestly as he would account to a partner if he were engaged in business, that man will lessen his strength, will lessen his power, will lessen the testimony of the Spirit of God within his soul. . . . Therefore, that which is counted by the world as success is failure" (*Teachings of Presidents of the Church,* 125). We are here to keep faithfully our second estate, to recognize our eternal potential and priorities, and to be found worthy to return where God and Christ dwell.

Integrity is that golden key which
will unlock the door to almost any success.

HOWARD W. HUNTER
TEACHINGS, 92

Recently, a man was given an opportunity that could have made him large sums of money. The business proposition was not a complete rip-off, but he felt in his heart that it was less than honest and would compromise his integrity. He asked himself, "How would I feel if a family member was involved in this company?" Even more important, he asked: "What would Jesus do?" In good conscience, he knew he could not be involved. Integrity means that we avoid anything that has even the appearance of evil, anything that takes advantage of another, anything that tries to circumvent honesty. Integrity means that we are the same person whether alone or in a public place. "One of the greatest accomplishments of our lives is to promote an honest, earnest integrity within ourselves," said President Hunter. "This means that we become spiritually sound, intellectually sincere, morally honest, and always personally responsible to God" (*Teachings,* 92).

JUNE 4

*Try, keep trying daily and hourly in all your
avocations, in all your walks of life, in all your associations,
to be perfect, even as our Father in Heaven is perfect.*

LORENZO SNOW
TEACHINGS, 38

The great Christian apologist C. S. Lewis said: "The real problem of the Christian life comes where people do not usually look for it. It comes the very moment you wake up each morning. All your wishes and hopes for the day rush at you like wild animals. And the first job each morning consists simply in shoving them all back; in listening to that other voice, taking that other point of view, letting that other larger, stronger, quieter life come flowing in. And so on, all day. . . . We can only do it for moments at first. But from those moments the new sort of life will be spreading through our system: because now we are letting Him work at the right part of us. It is the difference between paint, which is merely laid on the surface, and a dye or stain which soaks right through. He never talked vague, idealistic gas. When he said, 'Be perfect,' He meant it. He meant that we must go in for the full treatment" (*Mere Christianity*, 154).

170

*Happiness is the object and design of our existence;
and will be the end thereof, if we pursue the path that leads to it;
and this path is virtue, uprightness, faithfulness, holiness,
and keeping all the commandments of God.*

JOSEPH SMITH
TEACHINGS, 255

Each life has purpose. Our loving Heavenly Father did not send us to earth without providing a plan for our happiness. If we will pursue the path that leads to it, we can find the joy and peace that God intended for us. All too often, however, we are like the child who cannot find the next number on a dot-to-dot puzzle. Maybe we lack knowledge or need assistance to proceed. Perhaps we're looking for a shortcut or we have a different picture in mind. We may want to start over, or even stay in place—refusing to move forward. But finding happiness in life requires both humble submission to God's plan and steady progression. As we willingly follow the plan of happiness, the big picture will unfold for our view, and we can see how customized challenges can shape us into the kind of person God knows we can become. We will see his hand in all things and give thanks (Alma 26:37).

The very foundation of the kingdom of God, of righteousness, of progress, of development, of eternal life and eternal increase in the kingdom of God, is laid in the divinely ordained home.

JOSEPH F. SMITH
GOSPEL DOCTRINE, 304

The home is a divinely ordained sanctuary. A sanctuary is a holy place where sacred feelings and experiences happen. A sanctuary is also a defense, a refuge, a haven from the storms and fiery darts that descend upon all of us, whether in the form of adversity or temptation or evil. We are commanded to "stand . . . in holy places, and be not moved, until the day of the Lord come; for behold, it cometh quickly, saith the Lord" (D&C 87:8; see also 45:32). The hallmark of a holy place is not its size or location, but what goes on *inside* its walls. No matter the size of the home, it can be filled to overflowing with joy and contentment and grounded in goodness and decency. The path to home as a holy place is always paved with Christlike virtues of love and kindness, charity and selflessness. And no matter how far we travel, we always come back—even if only in our memories—to such holy places. These holy places are the foundation of the kingdom of God.

*While few human challenges are greater
than that of being good parents, few opportunities
offer greater potential for joy.*

JAMES E. FAUST
IN THE STRENGTH OF THE LORD, 378

It has been said that biologically, adults produce children; but spiritually, children produce adults. Nothing tests our patience, expands our hearts, and deepens our joys and sorrows more than parenting. Elder James E. Faust said, "Surely no more important work is to be done in this world than preparing our children to be God-fearing, happy, honorable, and productive. Parents will find no more fulfilling happiness than to have their children honor them and their teachings. It is the glory of parenthood. . . . In my opinion, the teaching, rearing, and training of children requires more intelligence, intuitive understanding, humility, strength, wisdom, spirituality, perseverance, and hard work than any other challenge we might have in life. . . . To have successful homes, values must be taught, and there must be . . . standards" (*In the Strength of the Lord,* 378–79). Good parents live forever in the hearts of those who cherish, honor, and love them.

*[The Lord] has heard our prayers, and by revelation has con-
firmed that the long-promised day has come when every faithful,
worthy man in the Church may receive the holy priesthood.*

THE FIRST PRESIDENCY
DOCTRINE AND COVENANTS, OFFICIAL DECLARATION 2

On this day in 1978, the First Presidency issued a letter announcing that "all worthy male members of the
Church may be ordained to the priesthood without
regard for race or color" (D&C Official Declaration 2).
President Spencer W. Kimball said of that glorious
experience, "I want you to know, as a special witness of
the Savior, how close I have felt to him and to our
Heavenly Father as I have made numerous visits to the
upper rooms in the temple. . . . The Lord made it very
clear to me what was to be done" (*Teachings,* 452). What
a glorious blessing that the heavens are still open, that
God continues to reveal his will to his anointed prophet.
We are the beneficiaries of this open revelatory canon
because of the living head, the Lord's prophet. Joseph
Smith said it succinctly: "We believe all that God has
revealed, all that He does now reveal, and we believe
that He will yet reveal many great and important things
pertaining to the Kingdom of God" (Article of Faith 9).

I promise you that daily family prayer and scripture study will build within the walls of your home a security and bonding that will enrich your lives and prepare your families to meet the challenges of today and the eternities to come.

L. TOM PERRY
LIVING WITH ENTHUSIASM, 32

Daily family prayer and scripture study are spiritual patterns that we have been counseled to weave into the fabric of family life in order to fortify family members during times of trial, give them strength against temptation, and help them withstand "the fiery darts of the adversary" (1 Nephi 15:24). We influence our families not so much by sparks of spirituality during journal-worthy events, but more often by the day-to-day spiritual habits for which we make time. No matter the outcome of our efforts, the Lord will bless us for trying. He is aware of our sincere efforts in behalf of our families. When we are intentional about establishing spiritual patterns in the home, we move toward making our homes places of peace and joy, sanctuaries from the world. Armed with spiritual power, we will benefit from the protection of the "whole armour of God" (Ephesians 6:11).

Your obligation is as serious in your sphere of
responsibility as is my obligation in my sphere. No calling
in this Church is small or of little consequence.

GORDON B. HINCKLEY
DISCOURSES, 1:18

A faithful stake president was released not long ago and within a week was called to serve in his ward's Primary organization. One day he was the spiritual leader of a flock numbering in the thousands; the next day, he became the shepherd for a small class of seven-year-olds. He is happy to serve there. In a sense, one area of responsibility is as important as another. One of the great blessings in the Church is that we have opportunities to serve in various callings throughout our lives. President Gordon B. Hinckley said, "You have as great an opportunity for satisfaction in the performance of your duty as I do in mine. The progress of this work will be determined by our joint efforts. Whatever your calling, it is as fraught with the same kind of opportunity to accomplish good as is mine. What is really important is that this is the work of the Master. Our work is to go about doing good, as did He" (*Discourses*, 1:18). Each calling is important because every individual matters.

JUNE 11

*We come here to this Holy House to learn,
to know God as He really is, and just how each of us, for
ourselves, might obtain an exaltation in his presence.*

HAROLD B. LEE
TEACHINGS OF PRESIDENTS OF THE CHURCH, 100

The temple is our Heavenly Father's university, a place where we are spiritually strengthened as we learn the things of eternity. In these holy places we learn more of the great plan of happiness and we get a sense of our divine nature and destiny. The temple is the place to learn more about God and more about godliness; it is the place to learn the things of greatest worth. Elder Harold B. Lee said, "Down here on the earth outside of His sacred presence there are the things that money can buy, there are things that we call the honors of men and the things that we strive for and seem to think are most important. But [the temple] is where we climb high above the smoke and the fog of these earthly things and we learn to read by God's eternal stars a course that will lead us safely back home" (*Teachings,* 99). In the temple, the Spirit is the teacher. Consistent temple attendance helps us continue to learn and stay prepared to receive knowledge from on high.

I feel it is only a question of time, if we do our part, until most of our Father's children who are in the world and do not now understand, will learn of the truth and will be glad to be identified with the Church of Jesus Christ of Latter-day Saints.

GEORGE ALBERT SMITH
CONFERENCE REPORT, OCTOBER 1933, 25

The work of preaching the gospel of Jesus Christ to all persons—both here on this earth and in the post-mortal spirit world—continues to accelerate and expand in preparation of the Lord's triumphant return. Faithful believers on both sides of the veil talk of Christ, rejoice in Christ, preach of Christ, and prophesy of Christ, so that all may know that redemption comes only through the blood of the Lamb (2 Nephi 25:26). In time, all people will hear the message of Christ and the story of the Restoration—along with its saving ordinances—and all will have opportunity to accept or reject the good news of the gospel. If we do our part to live and teach truth, to emulate Christ in our daily walk and talk, we will be instruments in the hands of God to bring others into the fold. As always, there will be the lazy and hard-hearted who will choose to walk in darkness at noonday, but those whose hearts are honest will gratefully learn and accept the truth of the gospel of Jesus Christ.

*It is not sufficient to have a vague understanding
of truth or the reality of the Father and His Son, our Savior.
Each of us must come to know who They really are.*

RICHARD G. SCOTT
ENSIGN, NOVEMBER 2005, 80–81

Among the important things we do in this life, drawing closer to the Father and the Son is paramount. In the process of time, through prayer and study, through service and sacrifice, we come to know our Father and our Savior in a more intimate way. We each have something of divinity within us and therefore we do not really comprehend who we are if we do not understand and appreciate the character of the Father and the Son. Elder Richard G. Scott has said, "You must feel how very much They love you. You must trust that as you consistently live the truth the best you can, They will help you realize the purpose of your earth life and strengthen you to qualify for the blessings promised" (*Ensign,* November 2005, 81). Our lives will change for the better, our joys will deepen, and our understanding will expand as we truly come to know the Father and Son.

*The work of reactivation is no task for the
idler or daydreamer. Children grow, parents age, and time
waits for no man. Do not postpone a prompting; rather,
act on it, and the Lord will open the way.*

THOMAS S. MONSON
ENSIGN, MAY 2005, 55

Among the painful struggles of life is disappointment over loved ones who have wandered from the path of full activity in the Church. Our hearts ache as we see them make choices that distance themselves from family and spiritual traditions. At these difficult crossroads, we must simply love, wholeheartedly, with the "pure love of Christ" (Moroni 7:47). Christ is the great healer; he can heal our hearts and the hearts of those we love. We can choose to dwell on the good in the person, wait patiently, love constantly, and respect their agency all while offering a spiritual safety net to which they can return (see, for example, Luke 15:11–32). If our efforts to influence a family member seem to have made little difference, we can continue to seek guidance from the Spirit and the strength to remain steadfast. As we partner with Christ in the great work of loving and blessing the children of God, he will inspire us, prompt us, and open a way.

JUNE 15

Let us strive for peace and harmony in the home. If we cannot keep quarreling, bickering, and selfishness out of our home, how can we ever hope to banish these evils from our society?

DAVID O. MCKAY
GOSPEL IDEALS, 169

Parents would be wise to carefully consider King Benjamin's directive: "And ye will not suffer your children that they . . . fight and quarrel one with another, and serve the devil, who is the master of sin. . . . But ye will teach them to walk in the ways of truth and soberness, ye will teach them to love one another, and to serve one another" (Mosiah 4:14–15). Through the ages, prophets have counseled us not only to object to contention in the home but also to teach our children a better way. The adversary would have us believe that contention is an unavoidable, natural part of family living. But contention is harmful. It diminishes the influence of the Spirit in our homes and hearts, and it plants seeds of discord and divisiveness. The Spirit of the Lord invites peace: "There was no contention in the land, because of the love of God which did dwell in the hearts of the people" (4 Nephi 1:15). Peace and harmony is the answer; love is the means: "A soft answer turneth away wrath" (Proverbs 15:1).

If you endure to the end, and if you are valiant
in the testimony of Jesus, you will achieve true greatness
and will live in the presence of our Father in Heaven.

HOWARD W. HUNTER
TEACHINGS, 72

To be a successful Primary president or den mother or Spiritual Living teacher or loving neighbor or listening friend is much of what true greatness is all about," said Elder Howard W. Hunter. "To do one's best in the face of the commonplace struggles of life, and possibly in the face of failures, and to continue to endure and persevere with the ongoing difficulties of life—when those struggles and tasks contribute to the progress and happiness of others and the eternal salvation of one's self—that is true greatness. . . . To those who are doing the commonplace work of the world but are wondering about the value of their accomplishments; to those who are the workhorses of this Church, who are furthering the work of the Lord in so many quiet but significant ways; to those who are the salt of the earth and the strength of the world and the backbone of each nation—to you we would simply express our admiration" (*Teachings*, 72). God has placed us here to achieve true greatness.

I thank God that none of us are dependent
upon others for the testimony of the gospel. I thank Him that
each and all can obtain a testimony for themselves.

HEBER J. GRANT
TEACHINGS OF PRESIDENTS OF THE CHURCH, 64

An unshakeable testimony of Jesus Christ, his Church, and his anointed apostles and prophets is among our most precious endowments in mortality. This sacred gift is given to all who sincerely desire it. A testimony can be acquired by humbly seeking for truth and righteousness; a testimony can be kept vital by staying on the path of virtue and remaining valiant. But a testimony can also be lost if we aren't vigilant. A testimony is never static; it's either getting stronger or weaker. To keep a testimony alive, we nourish our spirits. We study, pray, and ponder. We attend church, serve others, and remain obedient. As we continue to grow our testimonies by humbly striving to keep the commandments, we are entitled to the whisperings of the Holy Spirit to lead us along. To gain and then continue to strengthen our testimony is the quest of a lifetime.

*The enlarging of the soul requires not
only some remodeling, but some excavating.*

NEAL A. MAXWELL
QUOTE BOOK, 149

Some things in our soul need to be refined; while other things need to be completely removed. For example, we all can increase in love, patience, and compassion (among other virtues); whereas enmity, animosity, and smallness of heart need to be taken right out of our souls. Mortality is the time for us to enlarge and purify our souls, to stretch and strengthen our inner selves, and to be tutored in the things of lasting value. Elder Neal A. Maxwell observed, "I don't think God [is] too interested in real estate. He owns it all anyway. He does seem to be incredibly interested in what happens to us individually and will place us in those circumstances where we have the most opportune chances to grow and to carry out our purposes" (*Quote Book,* 149). In the Lord's loving and omnipotent micromanaging of our lives, we each have been given customized challenges and opportunities that can prepare our souls for eternity.

A father should . . . magnify his priesthood and be an
example of righteousness. . . . He should be the source of stability
and strength for the whole family. By his uncompromising
example he should instill character into his children.

JAMES E. FAUST
ENSIGN, MAY 2001, 46

The story is told of a father who overheard his son praying, "Dear God, make me the kind of man my daddy is." Later that night, the father prayed, "Dear God, make me the kind of man my son needs me to be." Good fathering is the most important, and sometimes the most difficult, kind of work men do. It stretches, molds, and refines men as nothing else. No matter who the child is or what his circumstance, every child needs a father's consistent influence and good example. Children need fathers with inner strength and humility, fathers who are strong enough to apologize and gentle enough to discipline with love. Over the course of countless one-on-one moments, accumulated over many years, fathers and their children form deep bonds of love and loyalty. Most fathers are sincerely trying to do their best. And with Heavenly Father's help, their best is good enough when their hearts are right and their intentions pure.

This mortal probation was to be a brief period,
just a short span linking the eternity past with the eternity future.
Yet it was to be a period of tremendous importance.

JOSEPH FIELDING SMITH
DOCTRINES OF SALVATION, 1:69

We are in the second act of a three-act play—an act with eternal consequences. Elder Joseph Fielding Smith said of mortality: "It would either give to those who received it the blessing of eternal life, which is the greatest gift of God, and thus qualify them for godhood as sons and daughters of our Eternal Father, or, if they rebelled and refused to comply with the laws and ordinances which were provided for their salvation, it would deny them the great gift and they would be assigned, after the resurrection, to some inferior sphere according to their works. *This life is the most vital period in our eternal existence.* . . . We have to pass through pain and sorrow and are constantly in need of protection against sin and error. This is given us through the Spirit of God if we will but heed it. All of this was made known to us in the pre-existence, and yet we were glad to take the risk" (*Doctrines of Salvation,* 1:69).

*We have been sent into the world to do good to others;
and in doing good to others we do good to ourselves.*

LORENZO SNOW
TEACHINGS, 61

It is so much easier to do good to those who do good to us. But the Savior taught a higher law: "Love your enemies, bless them that curse you, do good to them that hate you, and pray for them which despitefully use you, and persecute you" (Matthew 5:44). A true test of Christian living is to do good to *all* people. "There is always opportunity to do good to one another," taught President Lorenzo Snow. "When you find yourselves a little gloomy, look around you and find somebody that is in a worse plight than yourself; go to him and find out what the trouble is, then try to remove it with the wisdom which the Lord bestows upon you; and the first thing you know, your gloom is gone, you feel light, the Spirit of the Lord is upon you, and everything seems illuminated" (*Teachings,* 61). Forget yourself and find someone who needs your love, your interest, your service, and you will discover the great secret to a happy, fulfilled life.

*Keep an account of the dealings of God
with you daily. I have written all the blessings I have
received, and I would not take gold for them.*

WILFORD WOODRUFF
TEACHINGS OF PRESIDENTS OF THE CHURCH, 129

Wilford Woodruff's well-known record keeping was an enduring gift to his descendants and to all members of the Church. We are the beneficiaries of more than six decades' worth of detailed journal entries of his life and travels, meetings attended, doctrines taught, lessons learned, and glimpses into the early people and history of the Church. He said, "Some may say [journal keeping] is a great deal of trouble. But we should not call anything trouble which brings to pass good. I consider that portion of my life which has been spent in keeping journals and writing history to have been very profitably spent" (*Teachings of Presidents of the Church,* 128). President Woodruff encouraged Church members to keep a journal: "Let every man who can, keep a journal and record events as they pass before our eyes day by day. This will make a valuable legacy to our children and a great benefit to future generations" (ibid., 130).

JUNE 23

No cause under the heavens can stop the work of God.
Adversity may raise its ugly head. The world may be troubled
with wars and rumors of wars, but this cause will go forward.

GORDON B. HINCKLEY
ENSIGN, NOVEMBER 2001, 6

Gordon B. Hinckley, fifteenth President of the Church, was born on this day in 1910. Known for his keen intelligence and quick wit, his deep spirituality and unfailing sanguinity, President Hinckley has worked to move the work of the Lord forward in visionary, remarkable ways during his nearly fifty years as a General Authority. Of valiant pioneer ancestry, President Hinckley frequently acknowledges those brave men and women of the past who labored tirelessly to establish Zion. At the same time he is known for his undaunted optimism for the future. He said: "It is a wonderful time to be a member of the Church. I envy these young people who are here today. Their lives are ahead of them. They will see marvelous things in the years that lie ahead. I have no doubt of it whatever. The Church will grow and grow and grow, and no force under the heavens can stop it" (*Ensign,* August 2000, 5).

*If you need a transfusion of spiritual
strength, then just ask for it. We call that prayer.
Prayer is powerful spiritual medicine.*

BOYD K. PACKER
ENSIGN, NOVEMBER 1987, 18

Life can change in an instant. No matter what comes our way, we can always turn to God in prayer—and not just in petitions, but in praise and thanks. Prayer can see us through to the other side of sorrow; it can buoy up our spirits when we feel like giving up; it can prompt us with inspiration and guidance about what to do and how to do it. To learn how to pray and how to receive answers to prayers is one of our most important opportunities in life. The apostle Paul said we should "pray without ceasing" (1 Thessalonians 5:17) and "by prayer and supplication with thanksgiving let your requests be made known unto God" (Philippians 4:6). Some answers come soon, some come later, but they come to those who sincerely pray. It matters not how simple the words may be. If we come before the Lord with a humble heart, the Lord will draw near unto us (D&C 88:63).

JUNE 25

*Learn to like your work. . . . God has blessed us
with the privilege of working. When he said, "Earn thy bread by
the sweat of thy brow," he gave us a blessing. . . . Too much
leisure is dangerous. Work is a divine gift.*

DAVID O. MCKAY
GOSPEL IDEALS, 497

Work is a divine principle. It brings happiness and joy, feelings of self-worth and self-reliance, as well as contentment. Work engenders humility as we realize our dependence upon God and recognize the law of the harvest in our lives. It is the means by which dreams become reality and hopes are realized. Those who work will be blessed, and those who are indolent and lazy "shall be had in remembrance before the Lord" (D&C 68:30). Indeed, neither temporal nor spiritual salvation can be had without work. Idleness breeds idolatry (Alma 1:32); slothfulness engenders discouragement; laziness leads to hopelessness. Work, on the other hand, is purposeful and invigorating. Few things are as satisfying and inspiring as experiencing a job well done or a tedious task accomplished. The work of salvation stretches our souls and expands our hearts. Let us roll up our sleeves and get to work.

Today we are being tested and tried by
another kind of test that I might call the "test of gold"—
the test of plenty, affluence, ease—more than perhaps the
youth of any generation have passed through.

HAROLD B. LEE
TEACHINGS, 328–29

Our greatest tests in life may come from the easiness of the way. When we've never really had to sacrifice or extend ourselves in any meaningful way, never really become acquainted with God in our extremities, our faith can be thin and our resolve weak. Elder Harold B. Lee noted, "May the Latter-day Saint youth, youth of the noble birthright, whose parents have passed through the rigors of trials and testing, consider now the trials through which they are passing today—ease and luxury and perhaps too easy ways to learning and education. Theirs may be the most severe test of any age. God grant that they will not fail, that they will develop the faith that can keep them true when they are in the darkness and humble when they are in the spotlight" (*Teachings*, 329). These latter days require men and women, boys and girls, who are steadfast and immovable, faithful and strong, in their dedication to the principles of truth and righteousness.

*Joseph Smith, the Prophet and Seer of the Lord,
has done more, save Jesus only, for the salvation of men in this
world, than any other man that ever lived in it.*

JOHN TAYLOR
DOCTRINE AND COVENANTS 135:3

John Taylor remained loyal to the Prophet Joseph Smith from the day he met him in Kirtland, Ohio, in 1837 until his own death fifty years later. While incarcerated at Carthage Jail on June 27, 1844, the Prophet asked John Taylor to sing "A Poor, Wayfaring Man of Grief" to help lift their spirits. A short while after he sang, the mobs with blackened faces stormed the jail, killing Joseph and Hyrum. John Taylor, though shot multiple times, was an eyewitness to the martyrdom and—for many more decades—was an unwavering testator to the prophetic calling of Joseph Smith. Nearly twenty years after the Prophet's death, Elder Taylor proclaimed, "If there is no other man under the heavens that knows that Joseph Smith is a prophet of God I do" (*Teachings of Presidents of the Church,* 79). Like Joseph and Hyrum, John Taylor was ever steadfast and true to the end.

*Man can transform himself and
he must. Man has in himself the seeds of godhood,
which can germinate and grow and develop.*

SPENCER W. KIMBALL
TEACHINGS, 28

We are each created in the image of God; we are his beloved sons and daughters. The essence of the great plan of happiness is that we can truly become like our Father. President Spencer W. Kimball said, "As the acorn becomes the oak, the mortal man becomes a god. It is within his power to lift himself by his very bootstraps from the plane on which he finds himself to the plane on which he should be. It may be a long, hard lift with many obstacles, but it is a real possibility" (*Teachings,* 28). On another occasion he said, "Perfection is a long, hard journey with many pitfalls. It's not attainable overnight. . . . It cannot be accomplished in little spurts and disconnected efforts. There must be constant and valiant, purposeful living—righteous living" (ibid., 29). Because of our divine nature and because of the enabling power of the Atonement, we can overcome every weakness, combat every temptation, and become like God, our Father.

We must know Christ better than we know him;
we must remember him more often than we remember him;
we must serve him more valiantly than we serve him.

HOWARD W. HUNTER
TEACHINGS, 43

Three steps, all with the same upward pull, make the biggest difference in our lives: knowing, remembering, and serving Christ. Nothing else has the power to transform us and make of us new creatures (Mosiah 27:25–26). President Howard W. Hunter asked, "How often do we think of the Savior? How deeply and how gratefully and how adoringly do we reflect on his life? How central to our lives do we know him to be? For example, how much of a normal day, a working week, or a fleeting month is devoted to 'Jesus, the very thought of thee'? Perhaps for some of us, not enough. Surely life would be more peaceful, surely marriages and families would be stronger, certainly neighborhoods and nations would be safer and kinder and more constructive if more of the gospel of Jesus Christ 'with sweetness' could fill our breasts" (*Teachings,* 43–44). Indeed, we must come to *know* Christ better, *remember* him more sincerely, and *serve* him with all our might, mind, and strength.

*I am grateful that I belong to a church that
does not compel obedience. The Church of Jesus Christ
of Latter-day Saints does not coerce.*

GEORGE ALBERT SMITH
TEACHINGS, 97

Our greatest endowment in life is our moral agency. We have been given the freedom to choose whether or not we will obey. A well-known hymn teaches an everlasting principle:

> *Know this, that ev'ry soul is free*
> *To choose his life and what he'll be;*
> *For this eternal truth is giv'n:*
> *That God will force no man to heav'n.*
> *He'll call, persuade, direct aright,*
> *And bless with wisdom, love, and light,*
> *In nameless ways be good and kind,*
> *But never force the human mind.* (Hymns, no. 240)

Just as God will not force us to heaven, the devil cannot coerce us to hell. We are free to choose life or death, liberty or captivity, good or evil. Agency is an essential component of God's kingdom. All that is right and good could not be so if righteousness were compelled or goodness forced.

JULY

To live in a land in which each
individual has the right to life and
liberty is a glorious privilege.

DAVID O. MCKAY

When the Lord makes promises, and the conditions of those promises are observed, one need not entertain the slightest doubt that the Lord will do His part and fulfill those promises.

LORENZO SNOW
TEACHINGS, 12

In a world of conditional promises and provisional agreements, it is reassuring to know that there is a steady source we can count on without fear or doubt: the Lord, "the way, the truth, and the life" (John 14:6). He will not let us down or break a promise. He cannot lie or deceive, or he would cease to be God (Alma 42:22–25). We can have perfect confidence that what he says is true and that his promises will be fulfilled: "I, the Lord, am bound when ye do what I say; but when ye do not what I say, ye have no promise" (D&C 82:10). When we do what the Lord says, when we faithfully honor our covenants and remain true to the truth, the Lord promises us peace here and eternal life hereafter. If we choose not to keep covenants, the Lord is not bound (D&C 130:20–21). Oaths and covenants with the Lord that are kept seal us to him with a bond that cannot—that will not—be broken.

*I would rather have God for my friend
than all other influences and powers outside.*

JOHN TAYLOR
GOSPEL KINGDOM, 343

What aspiration could be greater than to have God for a friend? Not a distant connection or casual acquaintance, but a true and loyal friend, a steadfast companion and confidant through all the ups and downs of life. To be a friend to God is to strive to become like him, to wish to enjoy his presence and eternal association, to follow his pathway to happiness. Developing a friendship with God means that we commune with him through sincere prayer. We listen to the whisperings of the Holy Ghost. We learn of God through earnest scripture study and by pondering the words of the prophets. We serve God by reaching out in charity and compassion to all his children. We obey God by honoring our covenants and keeping the commandments. All of these nurture a relationship of trust and caring, a heavenly rapport that stands the test of time.

*To live in a land in which each individual has
the right to life and liberty is a glorious privilege.*

DAVID O. MCKAY
GOSPEL IDEALS, 316

We are blessed to live in a land that affords us the freedom to think and believe as we wish, to act and interact as we choose, and to come and go as we please. But with this sacred privilege comes accountability. Truly, where much is given much is expected. We have a responsibility as free citizens to support those measures that strengthen the family and ensure freedom, that promote civility and conscientious citizenship, that extend to each individual the right to life, liberty, and the pursuit of happiness. President David O. McKay said, "Next to being one in worshiping God, there is nothing in this world upon which this Church should be more united than in upholding and defending the Constitution of the United States" (*Gospel Ideals,* 319). In the wisdom of the Lord, the Church was organized in a free land. Today we do our part by upholding these priceless freedoms.

This nation was established by the God of heaven as a citadel of liberty. A Constitution guaranteeing those liberties was designed under the superintending influence of heaven.

EZRA TAFT BENSON
TEACHINGS, 569

On this day in 1776, revolutionaries claimed their independence from Great Britain, a day Americans still celebrate as their nation's birthday. Every year, thousands leave their homelands to come to the "land of the free and the home of the brave" to begin their own American Dream. The Fourth of July is a day to rejoice in our blessings and remember the sacrifices of those who vouchsafed our freedom; it is a day to thank God for our liberty. A devoted patriot, President Ezra Taft Benson, said: "Consider how very fortunate we are to be living in this land of America. The destiny of this country was forged long before the earth was even created. This choice land was set apart by God to become a cradle of freedom. Men of unflinching courage established this nation and under God's guiding hand provided a Constitution, guaranteeing freedom to every one of its citizens" (*Teachings*, 587).

An effort must be put forth to learn the gospel, to understand it, to comprehend the relationship of its principles. The gospel must be studied, otherwise no test of its truth may sanely be applied to it.

JOHN A. WIDTSOE
EVIDENCES AND RECONCILIATIONS, 16

John A. Widtsoe was known for his intellectual brilliance and absolute devotion to the Church. Born in Norway, he graduated from Harvard and then with his master's and Ph.D. from Goettingen in Germany, he went on to a distinguished career in science and education (he served as president of both Utah State University and the University of Utah). He became an apostle at age forty-nine and served until his death thirty-one years later. His was a uniquely qualified voice on issues of science and religion: "It is a paradox that men will gladly devote time every day for many years to learn a science or an art; yet will expect to win a knowledge of the gospel, which comprehends all sciences and arts, through perfunctory glances at books or occasional listening to sermons. The gospel should be studied more intensively than any school or college subject" (*Evidences and Reconciliations*, 16–17).

The Kingdom of God is a Kingdom of freedom;
the gospel of the Son of God is the gospel of liberty.

JOSEPH F. SMITH
TEACHINGS OF PRESIDENTS OF THE CHURCH, 288

T he law of Moses was given as a preparatory law to bring men and women to Jesus Christ. It was a law of ordinances and sacrifices, rules and restrictions, proscriptions and prohibitions. Today the law of Christ, which fulfilled the law of Moses, is the fulness of the eternal gospel, the new and everlasting covenant, "the perfect law of liberty" (James 1:25). Ultimately, we are judged by this law of liberty: "So speak ye, and so do, as they that shall be judged by the law of liberty" (James 2:12). All the commands of God are volitional; we are permitted to act for ourselves. We are free to choose virtue or vice, freedom or captivity, good or evil, light or darkness (Helaman 14:30–31). The gospel of liberty gives us "soul freedom"—for that is the only way we can learn to make righteous choices and thus develop the attributes of godliness. Above all things, the Lord wants us to offer the sacrifice of a broken heart and a contrite spirit (3 Nephi 9:20).

Heaven help us to be our best, and make for all a hallowed and a happy home—for home is "the healing place of the soul."

RICHARD L. EVANS
MESSAGES FROM MUSIC AND THE SPOKEN WORD, 181

M any decades ago, Edgar A. Guest, known as the people's poet, explained in "The Path to Home" why a happy home is the very essence and purpose of life.

> There's the mother at the doorway, and the children at the
>   gate,
> And the little parlor windows with the curtains white and
>   straight.
> There are shaggy asters blooming in the bed that lines the
>   fence,
> And the simplest of the blossoms seems of mighty consequence.
> Oh, there isn't any mansion underneath God's starry dome
> That can rest a weary pilgrim like the little place called home.
> Men have sought for gold and silver; men have dreamed at
>   night of fame;
> In the heat of youth they've struggled for achievement's
>   honored name;
> But the selfish crowns are tinsel, and their shining jewels paste,
> And the wine of pomp and glory soon grows bitter to the taste.
> For there's never any laughter howsoever far you roam,
> Like the laughter of the loved ones in the happiness of home.

*I have an abiding and perfect faith in
the Latter-day Saints, and a perfect and abiding faith
in the triumph of this great country of ours.*

HEBER J. GRANT
GOSPEL STANDARDS, 94

This great country was founded so freedom would flourish and bless God's children everywhere. This nation was established so the restored gospel would have a seedbed on which to be nourished and strengthened. In preparation for the Lord's return, this country cannot fail but must triumph in faith and freedom. President Heber J. Grant proclaimed: "It is a land choice above all other lands, so the Lord has declared. I am thoroughly converted to the fact that in no other part of the world except America could the Church of Jesus Christ have been again established on the earth" (*Gospel Standards,* 94). To carry the work of the Lord forward and prosper the cause of freedom, we must do our part as conscientious, liberty-loving people.

*Those who turn against the Church do so to play
to their own private gallery, but when, one day, the applause has
died down and the cheering has stopped, they will face
a smaller audience, the judgment bar of God.*

NEAL A. MAXWELL
QUOTE BOOK, 16

Those who trade eternal salvation for thirty pieces of silver or fifteen minutes of supposed fame will one day find themselves face-to-face with the God who made them. At that moment, clarity will come with the sharpness of a knife, and heartache at missed opportunities or wasted chances will cut the deepest. Those whose lives are centered on transitory things will find that they have marginalized the things of the Spirit. When we think back on our lives, none of us will wish we had watched more television or held more grudges or given in to more temptation. In the same way, possessions, power, and prestige are all but forgotten when life comes to an end. But things of the heart endure and grow sweeter with time's passage. Opportunities to help, to love, to learn, and to nurture relationships are among life's greatest gifts. Are we spending our time on that which stands the test of time?

We should cultivate a meek,
quiet and peaceable spirit.

JOSEPH SMITH
HISTORY OF THE CHURCH, 5:517

In a Psalm of David we read: "But the meek shall inherit the earth; and shall delight themselves in the abundance of peace" (Psalm 37:11). Jesus quoted the first part of this Psalm as one of his beatitudes in the Sermon on the Mount (Matthew 5:5). The meek person is one who controls his or her emotions, one who demonstrates poise under pressure and provocation, and one who is also strong and valiant. Joseph Smith and all the prophets are worthy examples of the virtue of meekness. They are people most fearless, yet most humble; courageous, yet peaceable; assertive, yet quiet. Because they have tamed their own souls, they are able to preach peace and live meekly. Only the meek, those who have dispelled the noise within themselves, will know peace forevermore. The Lord's promise is sure: "Learn of me, and listen to my words; walk in the meekness of my Spirit, and you shall have peace in me" (D&C 19:23).

If you take each challenge one step at a time, with faith in every footstep, your strength and understanding will increase. You cannot foresee all of the turns and twists ahead.

JAMES E. FAUST
IN THE STRENGTH OF THE LORD, 307

Character is built and manifest as we bravely face the ups and downs, the twists and turns of life. Although we do not know what tomorrow will bring, we can trust that God is in his heaven, that we are his beloved children, "that all things work together for good to them that love God" (Romans 8:28). If we have faith in the future and hope in the present, we can face every challenge with courage and every difficulty with determination. That doesn't mean our knees won't shake from time to time, but with faith in the Lord and his purposes we can weather any storm, surmount any trouble, overcome any obstacle. Things will work out for those who are humble, faithful, and patient—either here or hereafter. The best advice is to follow the direction of the Savior of the world: "Be not afraid, only believe" (Mark 5:36).

*Simple truth, simplicity, honesty, uprightness,
justice, mercy, love, kindness, do good to all and evil to
none, how easy it is to live by such principles! A thousand
times easier than to practice deception!*

BRIGHAM YOUNG
DISCOURSES, 232

President Brigham Young said: "It is much better to be honest; to live here uprightly, and forsake and shun evil, than it is to be dishonest. It is the easiest path in the world to be honest,—to be upright before God" (*Discourses*, 232). They that deal truly are the Lord's delight (Proverbs 12:22). The fact is, to be deceitful is hard work: one has to remember the fabrications, the lies and falsehoods of the past; one has to practice lying eyes and cover tracks so as to not be discovered; one has to rationalize within oneself (and with others and God) and hope that it will come out all right in the end. Deceivers are forever wondering what is real, what is truth. It is so much easier to come clean, to be truthful in thought and deed, to shun evil and live uprightly, to manifest integrity of heart. The psalmist's plea resounds down the centuries: "Deliver my soul, O Lord, from lying lips, and from a deceitful tongue" (Psalm 120:2).

I do not think it requires a great deal of argument
to prove to us that union is strength, and that a united
people have power which a divided people do not possess.

WILFORD WOODRUFF
TEACHINGS OF PRESIDENTS OF THE CHURCH, 243

The opposition mounting to thwart the purposes of the Lord is increasing in intensity and subtlety in these latter days. No longer is a casual, occasional commitment to the truth enough. We need to be intentional in our devotion to Christ and his kingdom in order to withstand the fiery darts of the adversary. One of our greatest sources of strength is to join together with fellow believers, having "hearts knit together in unity and in love one towards another" (Mosiah 18:21). A righteous union of hearts and minds is a powerful force for good—whether a family, a ward or branch, a neighborhood, or a group of friends. If we fortify and serve one another in the midst of difficulty and opposition, we gain power over the adversary of righteousness; we win the battle for the souls of men and women. The wicked will have little power to bring to pass evil if we are united as fellow citizens in the household of faith.

The payment of a generous fast offering,
which will bless the lives of the poor and needy, will also make
our prayers more meaningful and bring additional
spiritual and temporal blessings into our lives.

HOWARD W. HUNTER
TEACHINGS, 109

Fast offerings are the Lord's financial law given for the blessing of the poor. Prophets have encouraged us to contribute generously each month in conjunction with our monthly fasting. On this day we abstain from food and drink and pay fast offerings to the needy. The monthly fast benefits the body and the spirit, turning our thoughts and desires more fully to the Lord. We recognize our dependence upon him. Additionally, as we charitably open our pocketbooks and think of others, our hearts enlarge with compassion and love for those who are in need. And we never know when we ourselves might be needy. The amount of our offering is not what matters. Unlike tithing, the amount is left to our individual discretion. When we offer liberally and willingly, in an attitude of rejoicing and prayer, our offering is pleasing to the Lord (D&C 59:14).

The price of leadership is loneliness. . . .
The price of adherence to conscience is loneliness. The
price of adherence to principle is loneliness.

GORDON B. HINCKLEY
GO FORWARD WITH FAITH, 447

Sometimes walking the path of righteousness means walking alone. President Gordon B. Hinckley spoke of the loneliness of leadership and discipleship: "A man has to live with his principles. A man has to live with his convictions. A man has to live with his testimony. Unless he does so, he is miserable—dreadfully miserable. And while there may be thorns, while there may be disappointment, while there may be trouble and travail, heartache and heartbreak, and desperate loneliness, there will be peace and comfort and strength" (*Go Forward with Faith*, 447). Disciples of Christ are never fully alone. The Lord will walk with those who turn to him. The Lord will strengthen those who seek after righteousness. As we live worthy of the guidance of the Holy Ghost, the Lord will tread the sometimes thorny path of life with us. His promise is sure: "I will not leave you comfortless: I will come to you" (John 14:18).

God knows all things, the end from the beginning, and no man becomes President of the Church of Jesus Christ by accident, nor remains there by chance, nor is called home by happenstance.

EZRA TAFT BENSON
TEACHINGS, 140

All things are in the Lord's omnipotent hands. He knows the end from the beginning—and everything in between. Our omniscient Lord is not surprised or caught off guard with regard to his earthly kingdom; there are no accidents or happenstances with regard to the term of service of his mortal representatives. Some Presidents of the Church serve a long time, others don't; some prophets in modern Israel live a long time, others don't. It is all in the Lord's hands. He who governs the universe surely knows the longevity of his anointed prophet. And just as assuredly, the Lord knows who will become President of his Church. A prophet's call to be President begins when he is called to the Quorum of the Twelve Apostles. It is not an issue of who simply lives the longest; it is a matter of whom the Lord has appointed to preside in Israel for a season. We can have total confidence in the Lord's plan and timetable and purposes.

Happiness in family life is most likely to be achieved when founded upon the teachings of the Lord Jesus Christ.

THE FIRST PRESIDENCY AND QUORUM
OF THE TWELVE APOSTLES
ENSIGN, NOVEMBER 1995, 102

The Family: A Proclamation to the World" is an inspired blueprint for happy marriages and family life. Issued to the world by prophets, seers, and revelators, the Proclamation expounds the foundational truths of the great plan of salvation: "The family is ordained of God. Marriage between man and woman is essential to His eternal plan. Children are entitled to birth within the bonds of matrimony, and to be reared by a father and a mother who honor marital vows with complete fidelity. . . . Successful marriages and families are established and maintained on principles of faith, prayer, repentance, forgiveness, respect, love, compassion, work, and wholesome recreational activities" (*Ensign,* November 1995, 102). The Proclamation testifies that gender is an eternal attribute of each individual, that men and women are to fulfill their sacred responsibilities as parents, and that the disintegration of the family undermines all of society.

*The Prophet Joseph Smith declared . . . that the
eternal sealings of faithful parents and the divine promises made
to them for valiant service in the Cause of Truth, would
save not only themselves, but . . . their posterity.*

ORSON F. WHITNEY
CONFERENCE REPORT, APRIL 1929, 110

Elder Orson F. Whitney illuminated a most comforting doctrine: "Though some of the sheep may wander, the eye of the Shepherd is upon them, and sooner or later they will feel . . . Divine Providence reaching out after them and drawing them back to the fold. Either in this life or the life to come, they will return. They will have to pay their debt to justice; they will suffer for their sins; and may tread a thorny path; but if it leads them at last, like the penitent Prodigal, to a loving and forgiving father's heart and home, the painful experience will not have been in vain. Pray for your careless and disobedient children; hold on to them with your faith. Hope on, trust on, till you see the salvation of God" (Conference Report, April 1929, 110). The divine sealing power makes possible eventual redemption (D&C 138:58–59). Through sacred covenants made in holy temples, God has provided a way that families can be together forever.

*May I say for the consolation of those who
mourn, and for the comfort and guidance of all of us,
that no righteous man is ever taken before his time.*

JOSEPH FIELDING SMITH
ENSIGN, DECEMBER 1971, 10

Joseph Fielding Smith, tenth President of the Church, was born on this date in Salt Lake City in 1876. He would die ninety-five years later after serving more than sixty-two years as a General Authority. He lived as he taught: with no fear of death. The righteous are not afraid of dying. Of course they desire to live as long as the Lord will permit them. But they are not terrified of death. When the time comes, they go in peace knowing that a loving Lord is in charge. "Those that die in me shall not taste of death, for it shall be sweet unto them; and they that die not in me, wo unto them, for their death is bitter," the Lord reassured (D&C 42:46–47; see also Alma 40:23–26). While imprisoned in Liberty Jail, the Prophet Joseph was promised by the Lord: "Thy days are known, and thy years shall not be numbered less; therefore, fear not what man can do, for God shall be with you forever and ever" (D&C 122:9; see also Mosiah 13:3).

I bear you my witness that the Savior is closer to us than you have any idea. He will be close to you and powers divine will be at your side when you have nowhere else to turn.

HAROLD B. LEE
TEACHINGS, 10

The Lord has said, "Verily, I say unto you that mine eyes are upon you. I am in your midst and ye cannot see me" (D&C 38:7). Truly, the Lord is watching over us. President Harold B. Lee said: "The Lord is in His heavens; He is closer to us than you have any idea. You ask when the Lord gave the last revelation to this church. The Lord is giving revelations day by day, and you will witness and look back on this period and see some of the mighty revelations the Lord has given in your day and time" (*Teachings,* 427). We are blessed as a Church to know that the heavens are open, that God watches over his kingdom, that apostles and prophets are watchmen upon the towers. But we are also blessed personally and individually as we know that God slumbers not as he watches over us, that we are his beloved sons and daughters, and that his merciful and loving hand is stretched out still.

*The Sabbath is ordained as a day of rest and a day
on which the Saints should specially devote their attention
and turn their thoughts to spiritual matters.*

GEORGE Q. CANNON
GOSPEL TRUTH, 394

The Sabbath is a day set apart, a sanctified day of rest and renewal. It is a day to help us keep more fully unspotted from the world: a day of thanksgiving and cheerfulness, of fasting and prayer, of reverence and rejoicing (D&C 59:9–15). Rather than thinking of all that we cannot do on Sunday, think of all that we *can* do: visit the sick or lonely, write in our personal histories or journals, spend time with family, study the scriptures. President George Q. Cannon said, "The Saints should not . . . be more anxious on the Sabbath to serve God than they are upon any other day. But there is an appropriateness of conduct and of action which all Latter-day Saints should adopt on Sunday which will cause them to refrain from light-mindedness and folly and prompt them to make it indeed a day of worship and of rest" (*Gospel Truth,* 394).

*We like enjoyment here. . . . God designs that we
should enjoy ourselves. I do not believe in a religion that makes
people gloomy, melancholy, miserable, and ascetic.*

JOHN TAYLOR
GOSPEL KINGDOM, 61

A wise bishop counseled a husband and wife who were struggling to find happiness in their relationship and joy in life to find some interest or activity they could enjoy together. He also advised them to smile and laugh more, to go on a weekly date, to look for the good. The bishop's counsel, so simple and clear, was sincerely followed by the couple and they began to find more joy in life. Whether in a relationship or for us personally, we would do well to remember that this is not a gospel of doom and gloom. It is the good news of Jesus Christ and the joyful, abundant life found in him. True Saints of God love life; they enjoy themselves, they are lighthearted and upbeat despite the realities of life. They have a larger perspective that keeps them going and helps them focus on everlasting things. Because of Christ and the great plan of happiness, we can have joy in this life—even in the midst of trial and heartache (2 Nephi 2:25).

Our heritage will not save us; the deeds of the pioneers were their deeds. We, as their descendants, must stand on our own feet.

EZRA TAFT BENSON
TEACHINGS, 421

We remember with gratitude the courage and dedication of faithful pioneers who gave so much, including their very lives, that the Church of Jesus Christ could be established and prosper in these latter days. While we honor the pioneers of the past, we also acknowledge that the burden of our own salvation rests squarely on us. Elder Spencer W. Kimball said, "Could the thousands of our pioneers have voice this morning, I am sure that they would ask for no shrine, no monuments to their name, no words of praise, but . . . that we, their posterity, should consecrate our lives, our fortunes, our energies, and ourselves to the work of the Lord, the cause for which they gave so much" (*Teachings,* 156). The blessings that we enjoy today are the direct result of valiant men and women and their posterities, who have given their all to build Zion and move the work of the Lord forward. Our responsibility today is just as sacred as theirs.

*Whether you are among the posterity of the
pioneers or whether you were baptized only yesterday,
each is the beneficiary of their great undertaking.*

GORDON B. HINCKLEY
ENSIGN, MAY 1997, 65

The noble pioneers who gathered to Zion left us a
wonderful heritage. But the days of pioneering are not
over. As we hold on to the iron rod of truth, repent and
overcome bad habits, expand our talents and serve others, and live worthy of the guidance of the Holy Ghost,
we not only enrich our lives, we also prepare a better way
for those who come after us. Anyone who is preparing
the way for others is a pioneer. Anyone who is a transitional character, who changes for good the entire course
of a lineage, is a pioneer. Even though the frontiers we
explore are usually not geographical, they are just as real
and can be as purposeful and important. Today, all of us
enjoy the benefits of the efforts and sacrifices of the pioneers, and all of us have sacred responsibilities which go
along with that heritage. Although our challenges are different, we too face perils and difficulties. We honor the
past and future by doing our best to build Zion with personal righteousness and familial solidarity.

Through the great atonement, the expiatory
[or atoning] sacrifice of the Son of God, it is made possible that
man can be redeemed, restored, resurrected and exalted to
the elevated position designed for him in the creation.

JOHN TAYLOR
TEACHINGS OF PRESIDENTS OF THE CHURCH, 49

On this day in 1887, President John Taylor died at age seventy-eight after serving for more than forty-eight years as a General Authority. Shortly before his death, President Taylor expressed the hope he had through the Atonement: "I pray God the Eternal Father that when we have all finished our probation here, we may be presented to the Lord without spot or blemish, as pure and honorable representatives of the Church and kingdom of God on the earth, and then inherit a celestial glory in the kingdom of our God, and enjoy everlasting felicity with the pure and just in the realms of eternal day, through the merits and atonement of the Lord Jesus Christ" (*Teachings of Presidents of the Church,* 49). Through his divine grace, Jesus' Atonement overcomes mortal death for all mankind. The enabling power of the Atonement makes of us new creatures in Christ and true Saints of God.

A great person is reverent. He will be deferential in a house of worship even though he be the only soul therein.

SPENCER W. KIMBALL
TEACHINGS, 222

Reverence has been described as profound respect mingled with love. Reverence is an attitude of awe, honor, appreciation, respect, and deference to the holy. It is reflected in the way we talk and think, the way we treat others, the way we regard sacred things. Reverence is an integral part of good character. "We must remember that reverence is not a somber, temporary behavior that we adopt on Sunday," observed President Spencer W. Kimball. "True reverence involves happiness, as well as love, respect, gratitude, and godly fear. It is a virtue that should be part of our way of life. In fact, Latter-day Saints should be the most reverent people in all the earth. . . . The home is the key to reverence, as it is to every other godlike virtue" (*Teachings,* 223–24). The home is where we instill a respect and love for God, for the inherent worth of all God's children, for sacred places and holy things.

*The Lord has revealed in this dispensation that our
rewards in the eternities are predicated on our level of obedience.
If we are fully obedient to celestial law, fulfilling the laws of
Christ, we will be worthy of a celestial glory.*

DELBERT L. STAPLEY
ENSIGN, NOVEMBER 1977, 20

Delbert L. Stapley encouraged us to "reassess our-selves to determine where we presently stand in rela-tion to the fundamental law of the celestial kingdom—the law of obedience. The results should reveal to us which kingdom we have chosen as our goal." We should seriously consider the answers to such questions as:

Do I study and ponder the scriptures?

Do I follow the counsel of God's living prophet?

Do I seek the advice and counsel of my bishop on matters of concern to me and my family?

Am I earnestly striving to discipline myself?

Am I making every effort to repent of wrongdo-ings and correct them by doing right?

Do I have faith in God even though I experience trials, adversity, and affliction?

Do I bear my burden without a complaining spirit? (*Ensign,* November 1977, 20–21).

JULY 28

*May the Lord bless our government and lead
those that hold the power in their hands to do that which
is righteous, pleasing and acceptable unto God.*

JOSEPH F. SMITH
TEACHINGS OF PRESIDENTS OF THE CHURCH, 125

Those who serve in public office need our prayers. Whether or not we agree with all their political positions, the public servants of the nation surely need heaven's help. A grandmother can well remember her staunch Republican father praying for Democratic Presidents Roosevelt and Truman during World War II. We, too, should teach by example and precept the importance of praying for our government leaders and being good citizens ourselves. President Joseph F. Smith exhorted parents: "Teach your children to honor the law of God and the law of our country. Teach them to respect and hold in honor those who are chosen by the people to stand at their head and execute justice and administer the law. Teach them to be loyal to their country, loyal to righteousness and uprightness and honor, and thereby they will grow up to be men and women choice above all the men and women of the world" (*Teachings of Presidents of the Church,* 123).

*Your happiness will be in proportion
to your charity and to your kindness and to your love
of those with whom you associate here on earth.*

GEORGE ALBERT SMITH
TEACHINGS, 146

President George Albert Smith was known for his love and charity toward all people. His life is worthy of emulation as we remember that when the final curtain is drawn and we are left to be judged, our loving deeds and kind actions, our charitable thoughts and good desires, will be our greatest legacy. Suppose you were allowed to call back a day or even an hour and relive that small portion of your life. What would you do differently? Would you spend more time with children? With family and friends? Would you take the opportunity to show more love? To apologize? To forgive? Or simply to listen? Opportunities to extend love and forgiveness, to reach out in kindness and charity, are all about us. Charity, kindness, and love endure forever and even grow sweeter as the years pass—for both the giver and the receiver.

*My father used to tell me that the difference
between a man when he has a testimony and when he does not
have one is the difference between a living, growing tree
and a dry stump. I am sure he was right.*

MARION G. ROMNEY
LOOK TO GOD AND LIVE, 43

Marion G. Romney served for forty-seven years as a General Authority, including as counselor to two Presidents of the Church. When he was a young man in Colonia Juarez, Mexico, the Mormon settlers there were forced to leave their homes. The Romney family was robbed at gunpoint of their last pesos by members of a rebel army. Fifty years later he would return to Mexico as an apostle. His was an unwavering, fearless testimony: "I know that God lives and that Jesus Christ lives. I shall not be more certain when I stand before them to be judged of my deeds in the flesh. The Holy Ghost has revealed these truths to me. I know that God can hear prayers; he has heard mine on many occasions. I have received direct revelation from him. . . . I have heard the voice of God in my mind and I know his words" (*Look to God and Live,* 44–45).

*Let each of us every day live an exemplary life,
that our influence may be felt for good and that others,
seeing our good works, may be led to glorify God.*

N. ELDON TANNER
ENSIGN, FEBRUARY 1980, 5

N. Eldon Tanner served as counselor to four Presidents of the Church and was admired by people worldwide. Known for his great integrity, he exhorted the Saints to be true to the gospel at all times, in all places. He said: "The people with whom you associate respect you if you live according to the teachings of the church of Jesus Christ. People expect a great deal from the members of this Church because we profess much. I have never at any time found that my membership in the Church and living according to the teachings of the gospel were deterrents. . . . Parents, be an example every day to your children—and you children and young people, live to show the world that you are 'not ashamed of the gospel of Christ: for it is the power of God unto salvation to every one that believeth' (Rom. 1:16)" (*Ensign*, February 1980, 5).

AUGUST

*The gift of the Holy Ghost . . . is,
as it were, marrow to the bone, joy to the
heart, light to the eyes, music to the
ears, and life to the whole being.*

PARLEY P. PRATT

*Do we realize that in our daily walk
and work we are not alone, but that angels attend us
wherever our duty causes us to go?*

JAMES E. TALMAGE
COLLECTED DISCOURSES, 3:291

What a comfort to know that angels will attend us as we choose the right and do our duty. "It is only when we stray into unholy places, only when we tread upon forbidden ground, that they leave us to ourselves; and then they watch us from the distance with sorrow and tears," said Elder James E. Talmage (*Collected Discourses*, 3:291). This is not some strange, mysterious or mythological concept. Angels with an assigned stewardship to watch over us, angels who love us, will attend us as we walk in righteousness. "Who are [these] guardian angels?" asked Elder Harold B. Lee. "Well, it would appear that someone who is quickened by some influence, not yet celestialized, is permitted to come back as a messenger for the purpose of working with and trying to aid those who are left behind" (*Teachings*, 59). As we daily strive to do our best, as we walk humbly before God, we can have the sweet assurance that we are not alone and that angels from the other side will watch over us.

To accomplish this work there will have to be not only one temple but thousands of them, and thousands and tens of thousands of men and women will go into those temples and officiate for people who have lived as far back as the Lord shall reveal.

BRIGHAM YOUNG
DISCOURSES, 394

Considering the forty years it took to build the Salt Lake Temple, President Brigham Young truly was visionary when he spoke of thousands of temples. From Joseph Smith to our living prophet, we are a Church devoted to temple building. Everywhere the early Saints traveled, whether to Ohio, Missouri, Illinois, or Utah, one of the first things they did was dedicate a spot for the Lord's holy house, a place where the highest priesthood ordinances could be performed and families could be sealed together forever. Today is the greatest temple-building season in the history of the world, and while we have more temples than ever before, we have barely scratched the surface. More temples will be built, hundreds more—both in the next generations and during the Millennium, which will usher in a season of even more accelerated temple work.

No man is safe unless he is master of himself;
and there is no tyrant more merciless or more to be dreaded
than an uncontrollable appetite or passion.

JOSEPH F. SMITH
GOSPEL DOCTRINE, 247

The natural man has given his will to his appetites instead of to God; hence, he is an enemy to God (Mosiah 3:19). The natural man abdicates to the enemy within. "For my part I do not fear the influence of our enemies from without, as I fear that of those from within," observed President Joseph F. Smith. "An open and avowed enemy, whom we may see and meet in an open field, is far less to be feared than a lurking, deceitful, treacherous enemy hidden within us, such as are many of the weaknesses of our fallen human nature, which are too often allowed to go unchecked, beclouding our minds, leading away our affections from God and his truth, until they sap the very foundations of our faith and debase us beyond the possibility or hope of redemption, either in this world or that to come. These are the enemies that we all have to battle with" (*Gospel Doctrine,* 341). We must put off the natural man and become saints.

*I promise you that the Book of Mormon
will change the lives of your family.*

EZRA TAFT BENSON
TEACHINGS, 517

Ezra Taft Benson, thirteenth President of the Church, was born on this day in Whitney, Idaho, in 1899. He spent much of his ministry testifying of the power of the Book of Mormon: "Reading the Book of Mormon together as a family will especially bring increased spirituality into your home and will give both parents and children the power to resist temptation and to have the Holy Ghost as their constant companion. Individual scripture reading is important, but family scripture reading is vital" (*Teachings,* 517); "I promise you that from this moment forward, if we will daily sup from [the Book of Mormon] and abide by its precepts, God will pour out upon each child of Zion and the Church a blessing hitherto unknown" (*Ensign,* May 1986, 77). The Book of Mormon is the keystone of our religion because of how it establishes the truthfulness of the restored gospel and the prophetic mission of Joseph Smith and how it leads one and all to Jesus Christ.

*We as a people have one supreme
thing to do, and that is to call upon the world to
repent of sin, to come to God.*

HEBER J. GRANT
GOSPEL STANDARDS, 104

We are on the Lord's errand to stand as witnesses of Christ, to share the gospel in word and deed, and to be examples of the believers in charity and faith (1 Timothy 4:12). We are all missionaries to the extent that we do our best to live the gospel and share it with others. A missionary mindset is not one of standing on soapboxes and preaching in a loud voice; it is a way of seeing the world through the lens of brotherhood for all of God's children. Most often the gospel is shared intimately, even quietly, as we go about our lives with integrity and honor, with love and compassion, looking for opportunities to share the good news of the gospel. President Heber J. Grant said, "It is our duty above all others to go forth and proclaim the gospel of the Lord Jesus Christ, the restoration again to the earth of the plan of life and salvation" (*Gospel Standards,* 104). We best call people to repent and come unto God as we ourselves repent and come unto God.

Love is the highest attribute of the human soul,
and fidelity is love's noblest offspring.

DAVID O. McKAY
GOSPEL IDEALS, 489

Love is manifest in devotion and affection. Love for God includes adoration, reverence, service, gratitude, kindness. The greatest example of God's love for his children is found in the infinite atonement of Jesus Christ. The scriptures are filled with this highest attribute of the human soul: "Thou shalt love the Lord thy God with all thine heart" (Deuteronomy 6:5); "A friend loveth at all times" (Proverbs 17:17); "God so loved the world, that he gave his only begotten Son" (John 3:16); "Love one another; as I have loved you" (John 13:34); "If ye love me, keep my commandments" (John 14:15); "Greater love hath no man than this, that a man lay down his life for his friends" (John 15:13); "God is love" (1 John 4:8); "Press forward with . . . a love of God and of all men" (2 Nephi 31:20); "Teach [your children] to love . . . and to serve one another" (Mosiah 4:15); "Charity is the pure love of Christ" (Moroni 7:47).

I . . . invite the members of the Church to establish
the temple of the Lord as the great symbol of their membership
and the supernal setting for their most sacred covenants.

HOWARD W. HUNTER
TEACHINGS, 238

So that we can withstand the slow stain of the world, we must keep our eyes firmly riveted on the Lord and his holy house. The temple is the connecting link between heaven and earth, the hallowed place where covenants are made, and the sacred symbol of our Church membership and eternal aspirations. The temple is a place of peace and holiness, of love and learning, of beauty and blessings. Truly, it is a focal point of our sincere longing for godliness and selfless service. President Howard W. Hunter exhorted the Saints: "It is the deepest desire of my heart to have every member of the Church worthy to enter the temple. It would please the Lord if every adult member would be worthy of—and carry—a current temple recommend. The things that we must do and not do to be worthy of a temple recommend are the very things that ensure we will be happy as individuals and as families" (*Teachings,* 238).

*Adulation is poison. It is so very important
that you do not let praise and adulation go to your head.*

GORDON B. HINCKLEY
STAND A LITTLE TALLER, 5

Alma taught the people of his day that in order to
be saved all people must repent and be born again, be
humble, and keep the commandments. He asks a
series of penetrating questions that provoke introspec-
tion for us today. One of them gets to the heart of a
mighty change: "Behold, are ye stripped of pride? I say
unto you, if ye are not ye are not prepared to meet
God" (Alma 5:28). The pride and praise of the world
are so fickle, so fleeting. And those who let temporal
trappings go to their head and heart are in for ultimate
disappointment. President Gordon B. Hinckley said,
"Never lose sight of the fact that the Lord put you
where you are according to His design, which you
don't fully understand. Acknowledge the Lord for
whatever good you can accomplish and give Him the
credit and the glory" (*Stand a Little Taller*, 5). Everything
we do, everything we are, is because of the Lord and
his gifts of life and grace.

*The time will come when no man nor
woman will be able to endure on borrowed light. Each
will have to be guided by the light within himself.*

HEBER C. KIMBALL
LIFE OF HEBER C. KIMBALL, 450

Those who do not have a testimony by the power of the Holy Ghost that Jesus is the Christ will falter as the world sinks deeper into darkness. The most powerful weapon we have against the evils of the day is an unshakeable testimony of our Savior. We cannot borrow someone's testimony or live on another's faith. When our faith is weak and we are young in the gospel, we may temporarily lean on the believing arm of another—but that will not suffice for the future. We must know for ourselves. We must seek the confirming witness of the Spirit (Moroni 10:4–5). We each have too many moments alone, too many tests and temptations ahead, to not have a firm testimony of Christ and his Church. A steadfast and immovable testimony comes to those who humbly seek the Lord: "Draw near unto me and I will draw near unto you; seek me diligently and ye shall find me; ask, and ye shall receive; knock, and it shall be opened unto you" (D&C 88:63).

Let us lengthen our stride.

SPENCER W. KIMBALL
TEACHINGS, 174

Spencer W. Kimball was beloved far and wide for his deep spirituality and love and tireless devotion to truth. During his presidency (1973–1985), his personal slogan became an exhortation to the Saints: "Lengthen your stride." Battling health problems and the effects of age for several years, President Kimball was indefatigable in his efforts to build the kingdom. He said, "So much depends upon our willingness to make up our minds . . . that present levels of performance are not acceptable, either to ourselves or to the Lord. . . . The 'lengthening of our stride' suggests urgency instead of hesitancy . . . ; it suggests not only an acceleration, but efficiency. It suggests, too, that the whole body of the Church move forward in unison with a quickened pace and pulse, doing our duty with all our heart, instead of halfheartedly" (*Teachings,* 174). President Kimball's example continues to inspire all who strive to move the work of the Lord forward.

There is safety for us only on the Lord's side of the line.

GEORGE ALBERT SMITH
TEACHINGS, 19

President George Albert Smith said, "My grandfather used to say to his family, 'There is a line of demarcation well defined between the Lord's territory and the devil's territory. If you will stay on the Lord's side of the line you will be under his influence and will have no desire to do wrong; but if you cross to the devil's side of that line one inch, you are in the tempter's power, and if he is successful, you will not be able to think or even reason properly, because you will have lost the Spirit of the Lord.' When I have been tempted sometimes to do a certain thing, I have asked myself, 'Which side of the line am I on?' If I determined to be on the safe side, the Lord's side, I would do the right thing every time. So when temptation comes, think prayerfully about your problem, and the influence of the Lord will aid you to decide wisely" (*Teachings,* 19). The only safe course for us is to stay on the Lord's side of the line.

*Evil is going to be dressed up until it
will be more difficult, as the years come, to distinguish between
the good and the bad, the false and the true.*

HAROLD B. LEE
TEACHINGS, 40

The adversary's deceptions and temptations are more subtle and beguiling than ever. The great deceiver and his minions would have us "Eat, drink, and be merry . . . for tomorrow we die" (2 Nephi 28:8). The devil wishes to confuse the distinction between good and evil: "Woe unto them that call evil good, and good evil; that put darkness for light, and light for darkness; that put bitter for sweet, and sweet for bitter!" (Isaiah 5:20). Satan tries to mislead us with a bit of truth and a lie about our divine nature, about sin, about the plan of happiness. Elder Harold B. Lee said, "There is never going to be a truth that isn't going to have a counterfeit by Satan's forces. And the counterfeit is going to be made to look as much like the truth as the devil knows how to make it" (*Teachings,* 40). Our best defense is to hold on to the iron rod and follow Christ.

We should, of all people upon the face of the earth, be the best tempered, the kindest, the most forbearing, the most loving, the least disposed to quarrel.

GEORGE Q. CANNON
GOSPEL TRUTH, 439

True Saints of God desire to develop within themselves the attributes of godliness; they seek to emulate the Savior in word, thought, and deed as they strive to be "example[s] of the believers, in word, in conversation, in charity, in spirit, in faith, in purity" (1 Timothy 4:12). The surest manifestation of our commitment to Christ and his kingdom is how we treat others. What doth it profit us if we go to church every Sunday but fail to become more like Jesus by partaking of the divine nature (2 Peter 1:4)? How we interact and act toward others reveals, in large measure, who we really are. President George Q. Cannon said, "The Spirit of God produces peace and quiet and good-temper. Men and women who have the Spirit are amiable, are kind and loving one towards another. They control their tempers, because the Spirit of God will not dwell where the spirit of anger and hatred and violence exist" (*Gospel Truth*, 439).

*The gift of the Holy Ghost . . . is, as it were,
marrow to the bone, joy to the heart, light to the eyes,
music to the ears, and life to the whole being.*

PARLEY P. PRATT
KEY TO THE SCIENCE OF THEOLOGY, 61

The gift of the Holy Ghost enlivens and enhances our every capacity. Indeed, Paul's description of charity could well define what feeling the Holy Ghost is like: "Charity suffereth long, and is kind; charity envieth not; charity vaunteth not itself, is not puffed up, . . . is not easily provoked, thinketh no evil; rejoiceth not in iniquity, but rejoiceth in the truth; beareth all things, believeth all things, hopeth all things, endureth all things. Charity never faileth" (1 Corinthians 13:4–8). And neither does the Holy Ghost fail. But we can withdraw ourselves from its influence when we make unrighteous choices. When we make righteous choices, we feel spiritual strength, guidance, and power. Our hearts are filled with love, and our capacities for good are enlarged. Elder Parley P. Pratt taught that the gift of the Holy Ghost "inspires virtue, kindness, goodness, tenderness, gentleness and charity" (*Key to the Science of Theology*, 61).

*I never told you I was perfect; but there is
no error in the revelations which I have taught.*

JOSEPH SMITH
HISTORY OF THE CHURCH, 6:366

A year before his martyrdom, the Prophet Joseph spoke about the good that can come of adversity: "I am like a huge, rough stone rolling down from a high mountain; and the only polishing I get is when some corner gets rubbed off by coming in contact with something else, striking with accelerated force against religious bigotry . . . and the authority of perjured executives, backed by . . . corrupt men and women—all hell knocking off a corner here and a corner there. Thus I will become a smooth and polished shaft in the quiver of the Almighty, who will give me dominion over all and every one of them, when their refuge of lies shall fail, and their hiding place shall be destroyed, while these smooth-polished stones with which I come in contact become marred" (*History of the Church,* 5:401). By enduring well the trials of life, we can become smooth and polished shafts in the quiver of the Almighty.

The Lord never has, nor will He
require things of His children which it is
impossible for them to perform.

LORENZO SNOW
TEACHINGS, 37

From the realm of glory an angel proclaimed the coming birth of Jesus: "For with God nothing shall be impossible" (Luke 1:37). The Savior, now grown, taught the same truth concerning who shall be saved: "With men this is impossible; but with God all things are possible" (Matthew 19:26). Faith, a principle of power, makes all things possible. After Christ cast out a devil, his disciples wondered why they could not perform the same miracle. Jesus taught them the principle of faith: "If ye have faith as a grain of mustard seed, ye shall say unto this mountain, Remove hence to yonder place; and it shall remove; and nothing shall be impossible unto you" (Matthew 17:20). Our faith is not mere positive thinking. Our faith is centered in Jesus Christ and his atoning sacrifice. Our faith is activated by sincere efforts to keep the commandments. If we rest our hope in him and seek to do his will, we will have the faith to do what may seem impossible.

*This is our labor, our business,
and our calling—to grow in grace and in knowledge
from day to day and from year to year.*

BRIGHAM YOUNG
DISCOURSES, 248

Among the instruction given by the Prophet Joseph at Ramus, Illinois, April 2, 1843, was this doctrine: "Whatever principle of intelligence we attain unto in this life, it will rise with us in the resurrection. And if a person gains more knowledge and intelligence in this life through his diligence and obedience than another, he will have so much the advantage in the world to come" (D&C 130:18–19). We must continue learning and growing in knowledge and truthfulness, for that is among the very few things we will retain as we cross to the other side of the veil. President Brigham Young taught: "I shall not cease learning while I live, nor when I arrive in the spirit-world; but shall there learn with greater facility; and when I again receive my body, I shall learn a thousand times more in a thousand times less time; and then I do not mean to cease learning, but shall still continue my researches" (*Discourses,* 248). This is a gospel of continuing education.

Worldly pleasures do not match up to heavenly joy.

JAMES E. FAUST
IN THE STRENGTH OF THE LORD, 354

The temporal trappings of this fallen world will never have the power to satisfy us here or exalt us on high. We may experience the transitory pleasures that come and go with mortality, but real joy, the kind that is felt deep in the soul and that transcends time and space, comes from drawing closer to the Infinite. Elder James E. Faust said: "The odyssey to happiness seems to depend almost entirely upon the degree of righteousness to which we attain in terms of the degree of selflessness we acquire, the amount of service we render, and the inner peace which we enjoy. . . . Instant and unrestrained gratification is the shortest and most direct route to unhappiness" (*In the Strength of the Lord,* 354–55). The joys awaiting those who have fought a good fight, have finished their course, and have kept the faith far exceed any of the fleeting pleasures of this world (2 Timothy 4:7).

A true community of Saints will . . .
have a high ratio of those who are meek, being low
demanders and high performers.

NEAL A. MAXWELL
QUOTE BOOK, 209

No virtue is more needed, both in the Church and in the world, than the virtue of meekness. Meekness is not a passive attribute or a kind of lackadaisical humbleness. Instead, meekness is spiritual and intellectual strength. The meek are courageous enough to recognize their dependence upon God, to express their gratitude for the bounties of life, to open their hearts with love and kindness to all peoples. "Meekness also protects us from the fatigue of being easily offended," said Elder Neal A. Maxwell. "There are so many just waiting to be offended. They are so alerted to the possibility that they will not be treated fairly, they almost invite the verification of their expectations! The meek, not posted on such a fatiguing alert, find rest from this form of fatigue" (*Quote Book,* 207–8). The meek experience an authentic inner peacefulness and a deepening spirituality as they humbly look to God and live.

*If our religion does not lead us to love our
God and our fellowman and to deal justly and uprightly
with all men, then our profession of it is vain.*

WILFORD WOODRUFF
TEACHINGS OF PRESIDENTS OF THE CHURCH, 246

The gospel of Jesus Christ is a message of love that is manifest in our daily life. What commends our profession of faith more than to love God and all peoples, live with integrity, and grow in goodness and righteousness? The Lord's requirements of his covenant people remain unchanged in every generation: "O man, what is good; and what doth the Lord require of thee, but to do justly, and to love mercy, and to walk humbly with thy God?" (Micah 6:8). The power of the everlasting gospel to change lives is not found in theorizing, conjecturing, or debating. The essence of what the Lord requires is doing our best to live the gospel with fairness and equity, with integrity and honesty, with love and compassion. This is the gospel of the Son of God in action.

*Even with such a solemn mission given to Him, the
Savior found delight in living; He enjoyed people and told His
disciples to be of good cheer. He said we should be as thrilled with
the gospel as one who had found a great treasure.*

JEFFREY R. HOLLAND
TRUSTING JESUS, 22

The gospel weaves hope and joy into the fabric of
our lives. We should laugh and have fun, look on the
bright side, and enjoy the amusements of life. The
Savior enjoyed life. All was not serious and somber for
him—and it doesn't have to be for us either. Light-
mindedness is condemned in scripture; lighthearted-
ness is not. Of course, there is an appropriate level of
fun and laughter to be enjoyed by the Saints (D&C
88:69). The Lord said, "Therefore, cease from all your
light speeches . . . from all your pride and light-
mindedness, and from all your wicked doings" (D&C
88:121). Sacred things should be treated with dignity
and respect, and solemnity appropriately accompanies
holiness. We never trivialize or make light of sacred
things (D&C 6:12; 8:10). We who have found the
great treasure of the gospel, should be of good cheer.

No man, however strong he may be in the faith,
however high in the Priesthood, can speak evil of the Lord's
anointed and find fault with God's authority on the
earth without incurring His displeasure.

GEORGE Q. CANNON
GOSPEL TRUTH, 217

George Q. Cannon, who served for many years as a member of the First Presidency, spoke of sustaining our leaders: "God has chosen His servants. He claims it as His prerogative to condemn them, if they need condemnation. He has not given it to us individually to censure and condemn them. . . . However difficult it may be for us to understand the reason for any action of the authorities of the Church, we should not too hastily call their acts in question and pronounce them wrong" (*Gospel Truth,* 217). We understand our leaders are human and imperfect; nonetheless, we sustain them as the Lord's anointed servants, as those called to preside, as those who are authorized to represent the Lord. The Holy Ghost will not abide with murmurers and faultfinders. All through the course of life, we need to cultivate meekness and humility that we might faithfully follow the counsel of the Lord's anointed.

The sacrament meeting is the most sacred,
the most holy, of all the meetings of the Church.

JOSEPH FIELDING SMITH
DOCTRINES OF SALVATION, 2:340

We gather as Saints in sacrament meetings all over the world to renew covenants and rejuvenate our minds and spirits with gospel teachings. In the spirit of repentance, we remember the Lord's sufferings and meekly examine ourselves. Elder Joseph Fielding Smith taught: "For this purpose we are called together once each week to partake of these emblems, witnessing that we do remember our Lord, that we are willing to take upon us his name, and that we will keep his commandments. This covenant we are called upon to renew each week, and we cannot retain the Spirit of the Lord if we do not consistently comply with this commandment. . . . This is an occasion when the gospel should be presented, when we should be called upon to exercise faith, and to reflect on the mission of our Redeemer" (*Doctrines of Salvation,* 2:341–42). Sacrament meeting is a sacred, holy hour.

*There is no room in the true Christian life
for an attitude of "holier than thou." Each one who claims to
be a Christian could with better grace pray as did the
publican, "God be merciful to me, a sinner."*

HUGH B. BROWN
VISION AND VALOR, 170

The apostle Paul speaks to each of us today: "For all have sinned, and come short of the glory of God" (Romans 3:23; see also 5:8). No one is without sin or blemish; therefore we humbly acknowledge that we need divine help from a Savior. Jesus Christ is the mediator between God and man. His atonement makes possible a way for us to repent of our sins and become reconciled to God. To be perfect is to be complete, whole, and fully developed. Perfect can also mean without sin or evil. Only Christ was totally perfect. True followers of Christ may become perfect in process of time, but only through his grace and atonement. We all need help and love and compassion from our fellow "sinners." No true Christian would ever look upon others with a condescending or condemning, "holier than thou" attitude. Christ, who truly was holier than all, humbly said, "Love one another, as I have loved you" (John 15:12).

We are engaged in a great eternal struggle that concerns the very souls of the sons and daughters of God. We are not losing. We are winning. We will continue to win if we will be faithful and true.

GORDON B. HINCKLEY
ENSIGN, NOVEMBER 1986, 44

We know the outcome of the aggregate battle for the souls of the sons and daughters of God: Christ and his people will win, truth will prevail, righteousness will triumph. The ultimate conclusion of this struggle has been clearly set forth. What is in question is how each individual will stand at that great and last day. In the macro, we know the cause of Christ will succeed; in the micro, it is up to each one of us personally to stand for truth and hold fast to the iron rod. God's amassed army is only as great as the individual righteousness of each person. Let us do as Joshua of old exhorted, "Choose you this day whom ye will serve; whether the gods which your fathers served that were on the other side of the flood, or the gods of the Amorites, in whose land ye dwell: but as for me and my house, we will serve the Lord" (Joshua 24:15). In this grand battle for souls, the Lord needs every one of us to be faithful and true disciples.

*Enduring to the end means that we have
planted our lives firmly on gospel soil, staying in the
mainstream of the Church, humbly serving our fellow
men, living Christlike lives, and keeping our covenants.*

JOSEPH B. WIRTHLIN
ENSIGN, NOVEMBER 2004, 101

In living the gospel we do not have to be truer than
true. Danger lies in overzealousness and looking
beyond the mark (Jacob 4:14). Safety, on the other
hand, lies in staying with the mainstream of the
Church, following the prophets, listening to the
promptings of the Spirit, doing our part to serve others and build the kingdom. To be zealous is good if
kept within the bounds the Lord has set. To the extent
that we are zealous in keeping the commandments
and our covenants, living humbly and obediently, we
will stay on the gospel path that leads to happiness and
salvation. Overzealousness, however, leads to pride
and fanaticism, to attitudes that alienate us from the
Spirit of the Lord and diminish our influence for good
with others. Elder Joseph B. Wirthlin said, "Those
who endure are balanced, consistent, humble, constantly improving, and without guile" (*Ensign,*
November 2004, 101).

*We learn to pray by praying. One can devote
countless hours to examining the experiences of others,
but nothing penetrates the human heart as does a personal,
fervent prayer and its heaven-sent response.*

THOMAS S. MONSON
ENSIGN, OCTOBER 2004, 4

Prayer is the soul's sincere desire,
Uttered or unexpressed,
The motion of a hidden fire
That trembles in the breast. . . .
Prayer is the simplest form of speech
That infant lips can try;
Prayer, the sublimest strains that reach
The Majesty on high. (*Hymns*, no. 145)

We build a relationship of love and trust with Heavenly
Father through sincere and frequent prayer. Heartfelt
communion with the Infinite can soften souls and
draw our thoughts and desires heavenward. In humble
prayer, we realize our dependence upon God, the Giver
of life and everything in it. As we express sincere gratitude and meekly supplicate, we remember that we are
his children and that he loves us with a pure and constant love. May we ever seek to pray.

*Obedience to God can be the very highest expression
of independence. Just think of giving to Him the one thing, the
one gift, that He would never take. Think of giving Him
that one thing that He would never wrest from you.*

BOYD K. PACKER
THAT ALL MAY BE EDIFIED, 256

Obedience has been called the "first law of heaven."
It is the means by which humble consecration is
manifest, the way by which blessings are vouchsafed:
"When we obtain any blessing from God, it is by obedience to that law upon which it is predicated" (D&C
130:21). There is no compulsion in all the commands
of God. We each have been given the freedom to
choose to be obedient, and we increase our freedom
by using our agency to obey. Elder Boyd K. Packer
observed, "Obedience—that which God will never
take by force—He will accept when freely given. And
He will then return to you freedom that you can
hardly dream of—the freedom to feel and to know, the
freedom to do, and the freedom to *be,* at least a thou-
sandfold more than we offer Him. Strangely enough,
the key to freedom is obedience" (*That All May Be
Edified,* 256).

It is not the amount of money an individual earns that brings
peace of mind as much as it is having control of his money.
Money can be an obedient servant but a harsh taskmaster.

N. ELDON TANNER
ENSIGN, NOVEMBER 1979, 81

Human wants are insatiable. We are seldom satisfied, and restraining the impulse that would lead us deeper into debt requires both self-control and self-respect. Too many of us are troubled by keeping up with neighbors or family members, by giving in to desires of immediate gratification, by living beyond our capacity to pay the debt. It has been said that he who owes another does not altogether own himself. Debt is a sort of slavery, as the debtor is in perpetual servitude to the creditor. President N. Eldon Tanner spoke often about staying out of debt: "Those who structure their standard of living to allow a little surplus, control their circumstances. Those who spend a little more than they earn are controlled by their circumstances. They are in bondage" (*Ensign,* November 1979, 81). In all honor and integrity, we must pay our debts, live within our means, and keep our financial promises. We are not truly free if we are not solvent.

Never do an act that you would be ashamed
of man knowing, for God sees us always, both day and night, and
if we expect to live and reign with him in eternity, we
ought to do nothing that will disgrace us in time.

JOHN TAYLOR
GOSPEL KINGDOM, 343

When missionary companions Alma and Amulek caught Zeezrom in his lying and deceiving, he began to tremble under an awareness of his guilt. Alma contended with him: "Now Zeezrom, seeing that thou hast been taken in thy lying and craftiness, for thou hast not lied unto men only but thou hast lied unto God; for behold, he knows all thy thoughts, and thou seest that thy thoughts are made known unto us by his Spirit" (Alma 12:3). We may be able to deceive some people some of the time, but God cannot be deceived. He knows the beginning and the end and everything in between. He knows what we are capable of as well as the thoughts and intents of our heart—every hour of every day. He is also perfectly merciful and forgiving. Developing integrity of heart is not simply a matter of personal determination and willpower. It is accomplished only through the enabling power of the atonement of Jesus Christ.

*Forsake the philosophy of self-sufficiency,
which is the philosophy of the world, and adopt the philosophy
of faith, which is the philosophy of Christ.*

STEPHEN L RICHARDS
WHERE IS WISDOM? 419

Korihor's fallacy was that of self-interest and self-sufficiency: "There could be no atonement made for the sins of men, but every man fared in this life according to the management of the creature; therefore every man prospered according to his genius, and that every man conquered according to his strength; and whatsoever a man did was no crime" (Alma 30:17). No Savior is needed in that philosophy, no atonement, no repentance. The false reasoning of the world leads away from God and his prophets, away from humility and consecration. Elder Stephen L Richards stated: "In direct contrast to the philosophy of self-sufficiency, faith brings to a man humility—not servility, but a modest, unpretentious, submissive attitude which makes him conscious of and amenable to powers and forces higher and more potential than himself" (*Where Is Wisdom?* 401). Apostles and prophets teach the philosophy of faith.

SEPTEMBER

*Let wisdom be sown in your hearts,
and let it bring forth a bountiful harvest. It
is more profitable to you than all the gold
and silver and other riches of earth.*

BRIGHAM YOUNG

*The saints are peculiar. This is true of them
both regarding their habits and their religious belief. If they are
true to their faith, they cannot help being different from
other peoples. Their religion requires it of them.*

JOSEPH FIELDING SMITH
DOCTRINES OF SALVATION, 1:234

Peter describes true Saints in all dispensations: "But ye are a chosen generation, . . . that ye should shew forth the praises of him who hath called you out of darkness into his marvellous light" (1 Peter 2:9). The Saints of God are different from others around them. Elder Joseph Fielding Smith said, "The Latter-day Saints should be all that their name implies. . . . However, in accepting the title of Saints they are not arrogant, pretentious or self-righteous. *They did not choose the name, it was given them by divine commandment*" (*Doctrines of Salvation,* 1:235). The Church's name, including the designation *Saints,* was revealed by the Lord: "For thus shall my church be called in the last days, even The Church of Jesus Christ of Latter-day Saints. . . . Arise and shine forth, that thy light may be a standard for the nations" (D&C 115:4–5).

*In my office at home . . . I have a little sign
and it says, "Do it!"*

SPENCER W. KIMBALL
TEACHINGS, 173

The Lord taught Abraham: "There is nothing that the Lord thy God shall take in his heart to do but what he will do it" (Abraham 3:17). The Lord's latter-day prophets spend their lives doing the Lord's will. President Spencer W. Kimball was tireless in his efforts to advance the Church's three-fold mission: proclaim the gospel, redeem the dead, and perfect the Saints. He said, "We are not here for the fun of it. We are here for the joy of it, and we want to go forward and do our work as we should do it. . . . I suppose if I have learned anything in life, it is that we are to keep moving, keep trying—as long as we breathe! If we do, we will be surprised at how much more can still be done" (*Teachings*, 173).

*An important part of the gospel message is that we
not be too rigid, that we open up our minds, that we develop some
tolerance and not be too quick to render judgment.*

JAMES E. FAUST
IN THE STRENGTH OF THE LORD, 340

The gospel of Jesus Christ overflows with love, compassion, and forgiveness. A narrow-minded, fanatical, or self-righteous approach is antithetical to all that the gospel is. Those imbued with the love of Christ and a knowledge of his gospel delay judgments, develop more tolerance, and live a balanced life. That doesn't mean they think it's all right to rationalize adherence to principle. True disciples are secure enough in the truth that they are charitable, kind, and generous with all the sons and daughters of God. Elder James E. Faust said, "As I have blessed newborn children . . . I have blessed them with a sense of humor . . . with the hope that it will help guard them against being too rigid, in the hope that they will have balance in their lives" (*In the Strength of the Lord,* 340).

We have no occasion for fear or cause for
trembling: . . . If we will do right and keep His commandments,
He will surely deliver us from every difficulty.

LORENZO SNOW
TEACHINGS, 172

A recurrent theme in holy writ is the plea for deliverance from evil (Psalm 79:9; Matthew 6:13; Galatians 1:4; 1 Nephi 7:11). As in days of old, we also need deliverance from the fiery furnaces of sin (Daniel 3:17); we need relief from the enemies of righteousness (Mosiah 9:17); we need rescue from the bondage of iniquity (Mosiah 7:17). The Good Shepherd is also the Great Rescuer to those who put their confidence in him: "O Lord my God, in thee do I put my trust: save me from all them that persecute me, and deliver me" (Psalm 7:1). In the strength of the Lord, we have no fear of failure, no worry about ultimate triumph. As Pahoran exhorted, "We should put our trust in [the Lord], and he will deliver us" (Alma 61:13).

Real hope is much more than wishful musing. It stiffens, not slackens, the spiritual spine. It is composed, not giddy, eager, without being naïve, and pleasantly steady without being smug.

NEAL A. MAXWELL
QUOTE BOOK, 162

Alma taught that faith, hope, and charity are connected: "Be led by the Holy Spirit, . . . having faith on the Lord; having a hope that ye shall receive eternal life; having the love of God always in your hearts, that ye may be lifted up at the last day and enter into his rest" (Alma 13:28–29). When we have faith in the Lord, we hope for eternal life, and the love of God dwells in our hearts. *Faith* is the principle of power that moves us to trust the Lord and his purposes. *Hope* is sweet and realistic anticipation, taking the form of determination—not merely to survive but to "endure . . . well" to the end (D&C 121:8). *Love* is the pure love of Christ which endures forever and is manifest as charity for all people (Moroni 7:47).

*Are we living so that if the summons should come to us,
that we are worthy to go back to our Heavenly Father, when
we leave this earth, and be welcomed there?*

HEBER J. GRANT
GOSPEL STANDARDS, 172

Although we want to live as long as possible, do we feel that if we were to die, all would be well? Though we are far less than perfect, do we feel that we are doing our best to live true to the truth? These are not questions for the fainthearted. Life's realities demonstrate that the heavenly summons could come to us at any time. If we do our best, if we are obedient, if we strive to endure well the trials and sorrows of life, we can have confidence that our Heavenly Father will welcome us home with open arms, saying: "Well done, thou good and faithful servant: thou hast been faithful over a few things, I will make thee ruler over many things: enter thou into the joy of thy lord" (Matthew 25:21).

Don't start the day without family prayer;
don't get so careless that you forget to kneel together.

HAROLD B. LEE
TEACHINGS, 280

Through the ages, prophets have been concerned with personal and familial righteousness. One of their principal exhortations has always been that we cultivate a spirit of devotion and trust in God through prayer. Truly, prayer can "change the night to day" in our homes and hearts. President Harold B. Lee said: "There may have been some rough edges through the day and a good way to smooth them out is by kneeling together in prayer. Don't neglect to have your little ones taught early to have family prayer. Family prayer is a safeguard to the individual members of the family as they leave from the home each day and go out into the uncertainties of the world" (*Teachings*, 280). Let us join in the sacred circle of family prayer.

*In no marriage circle can true peace, love,
purity, chastity, and happiness be found, in which is not present
the spirit of Christ, and the daily, hourly striving after
loving obedience to his divine commands.*

DAVID O. MCKAY
TEACHINGS OF PRESIDENTS OF THE CHURCH, 150

David O. McKay was born in Huntsville, Utah, on this day in 1873. He married his beloved sweetheart Emma Ray in the Salt Lake Temple twenty-seven years later. President McKay was admired throughout the world for his love for his wife, and for his example and teachings on marriage and family. He said: "We may have that sweet companionship between husband and wife which grows dearer and dearer as the troubles of life come on. We can have homes in which children will never hear father and mother wrangle or quarrel. God help us . . . to build such homes, and to teach our young men and young women who are anticipating home life, to cherish such an ideal" (*Teachings of Presidents of the Church*, 150).

*If we go forward with our family home
evenings, our homes will be enriched, our wards and branches
will grow and prosper, our lives will be purified, and the
gates of hell will not prevail against us.*

JAMES E. FAUST
ENSIGN, JUNE 2003, 6

Regular family home evening helps families combat the world's evil influences and stay on the Lord's side. President James E. Faust said, "I wonder if having unplanned and infrequent family home evenings will be enough to fortify ourselves and our children with sufficient moral strength to meet the complexities of our day. . . . Where in the world will we learn chastity, integrity, honesty, and basic human decency if not at home? These values will, of course, be reinforced at church, but teaching them in family home evening can be particularly consistent and effective. To combat the world's evil influences, we need the strength that comes from family home evening" (*Ensign,* June 2003, 6). Family home evenings can become a vital spiritual pattern in the home that strengthens the family for the battles ahead.

Each of us is unique. Each child is unique. . . .
We must not assume that the Lord will judge the success of
one [child] in precisely the same way as another.

HOWARD W. HUNTER
TEACHINGS, 148

Any parent will attest, each child is a unique son or daughter of God. We know our children come from the premortal realm where they were learning, growing, and making decisions—just as they do here. And we know that they come as distinctive individuals. Elder Howard W. Hunter said, "Just as each of us starts at a different point in the race of life, and just as each of us has different strengths and weaknesses and talents, so each child is blessed with his own special set of characteristics" (*Teachings,* 148). Our challenge and opportunity as parents is to help our children grow in light and truth and assist them in reaching their potential. So we strive for Christian goodness and teach them gospel principles. As we do, we will see that each child is a unique gift from God.

I wish to say to the Latter-day Saints, all that we have to do is to be faithful, to keep His commandments, to be humble, to seek Him in mighty prayer, and all will be well with us.

WILFORD WOODRUFF
TEACHINGS OF PRESIDENTS OF THE CHURCH, 106

We live in troubled, worrisome times. It is a time that calls for resolute faith, stalwart commitment, and immovable dedication to the principles of righteousness. What we must do in these latter days of fear and worry is to be faithful and humble, keep the commandments, and seek the Lord in sincerity and truth. The words of the Master have resounded in hearts through the centuries: "Be not afraid, only believe" (Mark 5:36). If we are true and faithful to our covenants, we have the Lord's promise: "If thou wilt do good, yea, and hold out faithful to the end, thou shalt be saved in the kingdom of God, which is the greatest of all the gifts of God; for there is no gift greater than the gift of salvation" (D&C 6:13).

*You had better take seriously that which should
be taken seriously but, at the same time, we can bring in a touch
of humor now and again. If the time ever comes when
we can't smile at ourselves, it will be a sad time.*

GORDON B. HINCKLEY
TEACHINGS, 432

The gospel blesses us to be more buoyant, to rise above our trials, and to cultivate a lightness of heart and a vibrancy of mind. Although we know that life has its sorrow and suffering, the eternal perspective of the gospel reassures us that God is in his heaven and that joy and peace will come to those who are faithful. A little humor goes a long way in helping us survive the hard times and enjoy the other times. Those who are true and faithful to the Lord are not characterized by woeful countenances and solemn demeanors. Certainly there are reasons for seriousness and solemnity, but we should also enjoy the lighter side of life. Humor and laughter help brighten the difficult pathways of life.

*Prayer is the means by which men
communicate with God. Revelation . . . is the means
by which God communicates with men.*

MARION G. ROMNEY
LOOK TO GOD AND LIVE, 64

We don't come to everlasting truth by speculating and sermonizing, by hypothesizing and imagining. Our intellect alone is insufficient to discover the ultimate truth contained in the gospel. As the apostle Paul said, "For what man knoweth the things of a man, save the spirit of man which is in him? even so the things of God knoweth no man, but the Spirit of God" (1 Corinthians 2:11). Elder Marion G. Romney explained: "The spirit of revelation turns the key which opens the mind and spirit of man to an understanding of the gospel. There is no other approach to such knowledge. Thinkers have philosophized, poets have dreamed, and scientists have experimented; but only God speaks with a sure knowledge of all truth" (*Look to God and Live,* 65). We gain a witness of truth by the power of personal revelation.

SEPTEMBER 14

*We should stamp out profanity, and
vulgarity, and everything of that character that exists among
us; for all such things are incompatible with the gospel
and inconsistent with the people of God.*

JOSEPH F. SMITH
GOSPEL DOCTRINE, 241

The Lord and his servants have always exhorted people to avoid profanity, vulgarity, and cursing of any kind. "But above all things . . . swear not," said James (James 5:12; see also Matthew 5:33–37). One of the Lord's Ten Commandments was to not take the name of deity in vain (Exodus 20:7). We know that every idle word we speak we shall account for in the day of judgment (Matthew 12:34–37); and we know that our words will condemn us (Alma 12:14; Mosiah 4:30). Strength of character is needed to shun the ungodliness that comes of profane and vain babblings (2 Timothy 2:16). Controlling the tongue exhibits both self-discipline and richness of expression not found in those who are profane, blasphemous, or irreverent. Abstaining from profanity and vulgarity refines our expression, bringing us closer to the divine.

*One truth revealed from heaven is
worth all the sectarian notions in existence.*

JOSEPH SMITH
HISTORY OF THE CHURCH, 6:252

During the spring of 1842, the Prophet Joseph taught the Saints eternal truths regarding the principles of adversity, obedience, and faith: "All difficulties which might and would cross our way must be surmounted. Though the soul be tried, the heart faint, and the hands hang down, we must not retrace our steps; there must be decision of character. . . . When instructed, we must obey that voice, observe the laws of the kingdom of God, that the blessing of heaven may rest down upon us" (*History of the Church,* 4:570). Come what may, the faithful Saints in all dispensations obey the voice of God as delivered through his earthly representative, his anointed prophet (Amos 3:7). How reassuring to know that there is a living prophet who will lead us in the paths of righteousness toward the promised blessings of heaven.

I know that Joseph Smith was a prophet of God;
I know that he was an honorable man, a moral man, and that he
had the respect of those who were acquainted with him.

LORENZO SNOW
TEACHINGS, 55

Although the Prophet Joseph Smith was not a perfect man, he was a remarkable servant, a prophet called of God to usher in the dispensation of the fulness of times. Those filled with the Spirit of the Lord saw his flaws and foibles, but they also saw his inspired leadership and prophetic mantle. President Lorenzo Snow, who knew the Prophet well, said: "There are very few men now living who were so well acquainted with Joseph Smith the Prophet as I was. I was with him oftentimes. I visited with him in his family, sat at his table, associated with him under various circumstances, and had private interviews with him for counsel. The Lord has shown me most clearly and completely that he was a prophet of God, and that he held the holy priesthood" (*Teachings,* 55).

*We have been very fortunate to hear all
the General Authorities who have borne testimony. . . . These
good men have testimonies of the gospel. They wouldn't
lie to you. They are telling you the truth.*

N. ELDON TANNER
ENSIGN, MAY 1982, 75

Nathan Eldon Tanner passed away on November 27, 1982, after suffering from Parkinson's disease for several years. Even so, at age eighty-four he had continued to fulfill his responsibilities as First Counselor in the First Presidency. Twenty-two years in the leading councils of the Church (nineteen of them as a counselor in the First Presidency) made President Tanner a familiar figure to all Church members. In April 1982, he said: "I have had the great privilege of being a counselor and working very closely with four of our Presidents. These prophets had entirely different personalities, but to see how the Lord works through them is a great privilege, and one can realize why they were chosen. Follow their teachings. . . . May the Lord give us a clear understanding of where we should improve to serve him" (*Ensign*, May 1982, 76).

The discouraging idea that a mistake . . . makes it everlastingly too late does not come from the Lord. He has said that if we will repent, not only will He forgive us our transgressions, but He will forget them and remember our sins no more.

BOYD K. PACKER
ENSIGN, MAY 1989, 59

Elder Boyd K. Packer spoke of the miraculous power of repentance and forgiveness: "Repentance is like soap; it can wash sin away. Ground-in dirt may take the strong detergent of discipline to get the stains out, but out they will come" (*Ensign,* May 1989, 59). Another apostle, Elder Mark E. Petersen, said of the redeeming power of Jesus Christ: "There is no place for weakness in the Kingdom, there is no place for sin. . . . There must be a complete cleansing. But the cleansing must be more than a washing off, as we might wash a car. The cleansing must be of the inner soul—with a reformation. . . . It must be the building of a true and Christ-like character" (*Faith Works,* 143–44). We experience a cleansing, mighty change of heart as we draw upon the enabling power of the atonement of Jesus Christ.

Christ must be our daily and
complete pattern. We must hew close to the line which
he has laid down, no matter what the cost.

MARK E. PETERSEN
FAITH WORKS, 145

The prophet Alma testified: "There is no other way or means whereby man can be saved, only in and through Christ. Behold, he is the life and the light of the world. Behold, he is the word of truth and righteousness" (Alma 38:9). The mortal Messiah said of himself: "I am the way, the truth, and the life: no man cometh unto the Father, but by me" (John 14:6). Christ is the *way:* "Follow thou me," he commands (2 Nephi 31:10). He is the *truth,* and his truth sets us free from sin (John 8:32). He is the *life;* he is our Redeemer who saves us from temporal and spiritual death: "In him was life; and the life was the light of men" (John 1:4). Truly, in the gift of his Son hath God prepared a more excellent way (Ether 12:11).

When you are finished with your earth life, you will be the sum of your thoughts. Don't spend time with unworthy thoughts. Be satisfied with the good you see around you—then increase it.

GEORGE ALBERT SMITH
TEACHINGS, 28

Examine me, O Lord, and prove me; try my reins and my heart" (Psalm 26:2). This life is a time of testing, of examination and refining to see if we will do all that the Lord commands. He will test our hearts, our resolve, our willingness to serve him and submit to his will. We must continually examine our hearts to discover areas of weakness, areas that need improvement and strengthening. If we are humble and teachable, we will see the blind spots and self-deceptions that keep us from living truthfully and developing a close relationship with the Lord. We would all do well to take inventory of our thoughts, what fills our mind and shapes our heart. "For as he thinketh in his heart, so is he" (Proverbs 23:7).

What then is the power of the Book of Mormon?
It will proclaim the everlasting gospel; it will gather Israel; it will
build the New Jerusalem; it will prepare a people for the
Second Coming; it will usher in the Millennium.

BRUCE R. McCONKIE
MILLENNIAL MESSIAH, 171

On this date in 1823, the angel Moroni delivered a message to Joseph Smith: "Behold, I will reveal unto you the Priesthood, by the hand of Elijah the prophet. . . . And he shall plant in the hearts of the children the promises made to the fathers, and the hearts of the children shall turn to their fathers. If it were not so, the whole earth would be utterly wasted at his coming" (D&C 2:1–3). Because Elijah came to the Kirtland Temple in April 1836 (D&C 110), there comes into our hearts a desire to enjoy the promises made to Abraham (Abraham 2:8–11). Through the spirit of Elijah we sense the need to make those blessings available to those who died without knowledge of the gospel's fulness. These blessings come only through the ordinances of the temple.

The Book of Mormon is the keystone of our religion—
the keystone of our testimony, the keystone of our doctrine, and
the keystone in the witness of our Lord and Savior.

EZRA TAFT BENSON
SERMONS AND WRITINGS, 86

September 22 is a date closely associated with the Book of Mormon. On this date in 1823, Moroni appeared to Joseph Smith at the Hill Cumorah and showed him the gold plates for the first time. He visited the Prophet on the same date for the next four years until, in 1827, Joseph received the plates, the Urim and Thummim, and the breastplate. The primary purpose of the Book of Mormon is to testify of Jesus Christ. The Book of Mormon changes lives as we learn of and draw closer to the Savior. The Prophet Joseph testified that "the Book of Mormon was the most correct of any book on earth, and the keystone of our religion, and a man would get nearer to God by abiding by its precepts, than by any other book" (*History of the Church,* 4:461).

*Let wisdom be sown in your hearts, and let it bring
forth a bountiful harvest. It is more profitable to you than all
the gold and silver and other riches of earth.*

BRIGHAM YOUNG
DISCOURSES, 261

Wisdom is the principal thing; therefore get wisdom: and with all thy getting get understanding" (Proverbs 4:7). Of all things vital to sow in our hearts, wisdom is most precious: "For wisdom is better than rubies" (Proverbs 8:11). Wisdom is far more than acquiring knowledge or the accumulation of facts. Wisdom is deeper, more insightful and perceptive, and is formed as we live truthfully and apply virtues to daily living. Wisdom comes from experience, from mistakes and defeats as well as from victories and successes. It comes of reading and pondering, from conversing with others who are wise, from observing and learning over time, and from being taught by the Spirit. Wisdom comes from hearkening to the words of righteous men and women who, guided by the Holy Ghost, can counsel and teach us. Humility is at the root of wisdom, and compassion and understanding are its offspring.

SEPTEMBER 24

Those who keep a book of remembrance are more
likely to keep the Lord in remembrance in their daily lives.
Journals are a way of counting our blessings and of leaving an
inventory of these blessings for our posterity.

SPENCER W. KIMBALL
TEACHINGS, 349

A journal is a place to remember the goodness of God; it is a place to record our spiritual development as we mature over the years; it is a place to document the events that have shaped our life. President Spencer W. Kimball said: "We renew our appeal for the keeping of individual histories and accounts of sacred experiences in our lives—answered prayers, inspiration from the Lord, administrations in our behalf, a record of the special times and events of our lives. . . . Stories of inspiration from our own lives and those of our forebears as well as stories from our scriptures and our history are powerful teaching tools. I promise you that if you will keep your journals and records they will indeed be a source of great inspiration to you, each other, your children, your grandchildren, and others throughout the generations" (*Teachings,* 349).

*The truths of the gospel of Jesus Christ
are plain, precious, and powerful. The lives of the
worthy are plain, precious, and powerful.*

MARVIN J. ASHTON
ENSIGN, MAY 1977, 67

Nephi declared, "For my soul delighteth in plainness" (2 Nephi 31:3). We are taught and touched by
the Spirit more powerfully when done in plainness.
"Glamour and mystery do not lead to eternal life," said
Elder Marvin J. Ashton. "Some overlook the great
rewards and the joys of the gospel because they feel
that the gift of eternal life and the knowledge of the
Savior can only be attained by ornamentation and
mystery. The Lord has told us that we must learn line
upon line and precept upon precept. May we learn the
plain and simple truths of the gospel by following the
plain and simple steps outlined by our leaders. . . .
Look not for glamour, but for humility in everyday
service. Learn obedience and understanding from the
plain truths of the gospel and then share them in can-
did, clear, and frank language and actions" (*Ensign,* May
1977, 68).

I have witnessed many, apparently good men and good women, turn away from the Church through indulging in this spirit of fault-finding and criticising the actions of the Priesthood.

MARRINER W. MERRILL
CONFERENCE REPORT, OCTOBER 1897, 4

Strength comes from sustaining the leaders of the Lord's Church. To sustain is to support, uphold, and defend in word and deed those duly called to preside over us. "Now, we must remember that there is not a single officer in the Church who has selected himself," said Elder Marriner W. Merrill. "There is not one of the Presidency, nor one of the Apostles, that has sought the position he occupies today. These men have not desired the position, and have not asked for it. But the Lord, in the dispensations of His providence, has placed them in office in the Church. And when we complain, and find fault, and criticise, we must surely know that we are criticising the actions of the Lord, because He is the one that has brought these things to pass and placed these men in their positions" (Conference Report, October 1897, 4).

*It is the first principle of the Gospel
to know for a certainty the Character of God.*

JOSEPH SMITH
TEACHINGS, 345

The character and attributes of God are known by the power of personal revelation when we humbly seek to know God and Jesus Christ. They are known through prayer and scripture study, through hearkening to the counsels of the Lord's anointed. Jeremiah said, "And ye shall seek me, and find me, when ye shall search for me with all your heart" (Jeremiah 29:13). We cannot understand our destiny if we don't understand our origin. The Prophet Joseph Smith explained, "Having a knowledge of God, we begin to know how to approach him, and how to ask so as to receive an answer. When we understand the character of God, and know how to come to him, he begins to unfold the heavens to us, and to tell us all about it. When we are ready to come to him, he is ready to come to us" (*Teachings,* 349).

*I just can't imagine living . . . after I pass out of this life
without the companionship of my sweet wife and my children.
How I thank God for . . . the knowledge that marriage and the
family unit are intended by Him . . . to endure forever.*

LeGrand Richards
Ensign, May 1982, 30

The new and everlasting covenant of marriage seals
us to our spouse and our posterity in unending familial bonds of love. This sacred and eternal association
will rise with the righteous in the resurrection; there
could be no greater joy and knowledge in time and
eternity. Elder LeGrand Richards observed: "I think
of my children one by one . . . , and I see what they are
accomplishing and the nobility of their lives. . . . I feel
that [fatherhood] is nearer to becoming a god than
anything else I can do here in mortality. . . . I have
tried to live before those children and descendants of
mine so that if they walked in my footsteps they would
be honoring their second estate and preparing themselves to have glory added upon their heads forever
and forever" (*Ensign,* May 1982, 30).

*There is no power given to the adversary
of men's souls to destroy us if we are doing our duty.*

HEBER J. GRANT
TEACHINGS OF PRESIDENTS OF THE CHURCH, 27

The devil is waging a battle he will not win. Paul has given us this reassuring promise: "God . . . will not suffer you to be tempted above that ye are able; but will with the temptation also make a way to escape" (1 Corinthians 10:13). And Elder Heber J. Grant said: "The devil . . . would gladly rob us of eternal life, the greatest of all gifts. But it is not given to the devil, and no power will ever be given to him to overthrow any Latter-day Saint that is keeping the commandments of God. . . . No man has ever lost the testimony of the Gospel, no man has ever turned to the right or to the left, who had the knowledge of the truth, who was attending to his duties" (*Teachings of Presidents of the Church,* 27).

Prayer is the pulsation of a yearning,
loving heart in tune with the Infinite. It is a message
of the soul sent directly to a loving Father.

DAVID O. MCKAY
TEACHINGS OF PRESIDENTS OF THE CHURCH, 73

The most repeated exhortation in holy writ is to pray, to give thanks, to acknowledge the Giver of all that is good. Prayer flows from an abundant heart, a grateful heart, a heart that is submissive and meek. Two things offend God: disobedience and ingratitude (D&C 59:21). We are to manifest our thankfulness and willingness to obey by sending our sincere and frequent messages of the soul to a loving Heavenly Father. President Heber J. Grant said, "In the quiet hours, in the heat of battle, and through the hazards of the day; in times of temptation, of sorrow, of peace and of blessing, let us pray always, both alone, and with our families gathered around us, with gratitude for the blessings of life, for understanding of its problems, and for strength to endure to the end" (*Teachings of Presidents of the Church,* 174).

OCTOBER

*Each of us has agency; each is free
to choose. Nothing can free us spiritually
more than obedience—obedience
to the laws, to the Lord.*

BOYD K. PACKER

OCTOBER 1

When you are prepared to see our Father,
you will see a being with whom you have long been acquainted,
and He will receive you into His arms, and you will be
ready to fall into His embrace and kiss Him.

BRIGHAM YOUNG
JOURNAL OF DISCOURSES, 4:55

Our Heavenly Father is not some disembodied essence. He is our Father, and he wants for us his joy and eternal life. His work and glory is to see us enjoy everlasting associations with our heavenly parents, our Savior, and our loved ones long departed: "That same sociality which exists among us here will exist among us there, only it will be coupled with eternal glory" (D&C 130:2). President Brigham Young said: "When you are qualified and purified, so that you can endure the glory of eternity, so that you can see your Father, and your friends who have gone behind the [veil], you will fall upon their necks and kiss them, as we do an earthly friend that . . . we have been anxiously desiring to see" (*Journal of Discourses*, 4:55). We will rejoice in that blessed day.

All of us stand on the shoulders of others. . . . All of us inherit so much from the past that we have an obligation to serve the present, and to pass on an improved world to the future.

RICHARD L. EVANS
MESSAGES FROM MUSIC AND THE SPOKEN WORD, 148

When all is well and life is good, we tend to forget those who have sacrificed on our behalf to make our present comforts possible. We all enjoy benefits and blessings that come from the work of others. How often do we pause to acknowledge them? We appreciate our blessings more deeply when we choose to remember those who have made them possible, when we reciprocate by doing our part to make the world a better place. Because we have all been given so much, we have a sacred responsibility to improve the world, build the kingdom, and lift and bless others around us. If the Giver is always close to our hearts, our lives will be enriched by the reverent acknowledgment of our every blessing and by our sincere efforts to leave behind a better world.

*I have not lived alone these five months. I have
dwelt in the spirit of prayer, of supplication, of faith and of
determination; and I have had my communication
with the Spirit of the Lord continuously.*
JOSEPH F. SMITH
TEACHINGS OF PRESIDENTS OF THE CHURCH, 362

On this date in 1918, President Joseph F. Smith sat pondering the scriptures when he received a remarkable vision now known to Latter-day Saints as the vision of the redemption of the dead (D&C 138). The vision was added to the canon of scripture at general conference in April 1976. President Smith died a few weeks later at the age of eighty, having served seventeen years as president. This marvelous vision came while pondering and meditating upon the things of God. How blessed we are to know that continuing revelation comes from God to his church through his prophets. These mighty men of God are the watchmen on the towers, the preachers of righteousness, who, guided by the inspiration of the Holy Spirit, reveal to us the mind and will of God.

Success is many things to many people,
but to every child of God it ultimately will be to inherit
His presence and there be comfortable with Him.

HAROLD B. LEE
TEACHINGS, 69

No one likes feeling uncomfortable in any given situation. We wish to associate with those with whom we are most alike, those with whom we are at ease and feel contented and relaxed. In the hereafter, we will find ourselves in our place of inheritance with those with whom we are most comfortable: a telestial person would certainly not be very comfortable in the presence of persons celestial, and vice versa. Our ultimate aim in life is to receive eternal life in the kingdom of God, which is Heavenly Father's greatest gift to his children (D&C 14:7). But to win that prize we must become more like our Father, develop his attributes, and follow his plan of happiness. Those who inherit that greatest of eternal gifts will feel at home and comfortable in the presence of God.

Each of us has agency; each is free to choose.
Nothing can free us spiritually more than obedience—
obedience to the laws, to the Lord.

BOYD K. PACKER
THINGS OF THE SOUL, 58

Joseph Smith taught us the first law of heaven: "There is a law, irrevocably decreed in heaven before the foundations of this world, upon which all blessings are predicated—And when we obtain any blessing from God, it is by obedience to that law upon which it is predicated" (D&C 130:20–21). We came to earth to prove our willingness to obey (Abraham 3:24–26). Commandments are given because God loves us and wants us to become like him. But obedience is always voluntary (Helaman 14:30–31). At times we may need to obey even when we don't fully understand (1 Nephi 3:7; Moses 5:5–6). Other times, it is by suffering that we learn to obey (D&C 105:6). Always, we show our love for the Father and Son by choosing to obey (John 14:15, 21, 23).

*Heavenly Father wants to save every
one of his children. . . . In his justice and mercy he
will give us . . . all that he can give, and in the reverse, . . . he
will impose upon us the minimum penalty . . . possible.*

J. REUBEN CLARK JR.
CONFERENCE REPORT, OCTOBER 1953, 84

The premortal Lord instructed and comforted his prophet Alma with these words: "Whosoever transgresseth against me, him shall ye judge according to the sins which he has committed; and if he confess his sins before thee and me, and repenteth in the sincerity of his heart, him shall ye forgive, and I will forgive him also. Yea, and as often as my people repent will I forgive them their trespasses against me" (Mosiah 26:29–30). The Lord is the perfect judge, the perfect advocate and mediator. He is perfectly loving and merciful and perfectly just and fair. We can have complete confidence and sweet assurance that in the coming day of our accounting before him, his judgment and his love will be perfect. We too are to strive to be merciful and just.

Let us treat one another with kindness and one another's
reputation with respect, and feel after one another's welfare,
treating everybody as we would like God to treat us.

JOHN TAYLOR
TEACHINGS OF PRESIDENTS OF THE CHURCH, 25

Treat others the way you want to be treated. If we all took the Golden Rule to heart, our homes and hearts, our communities and nations, would transform. This old world, which has seen sorrow and suffering, tribulation and difficulty, needs love and kindness more than ever. Although it's simple, essential common sense, it's often not common practice. President John Taylor said, "Treat one another aright. Have you sinned one against another? Then go and make restitution. Have you defrauded one another? Go and make it right. Have you spoken unkindly to your brother or sister? Then go and acknowledge your wrong and ask to be forgiven, promising to do better in the future" (*Teachings of Presidents of the Church,* 25). We can each do our part by filling our corner of the world with love and kindness.

*Mormonism . . . must stand or fall on the story of Joseph Smith.
He was either a prophet of God, divinely called, properly
appointed and commissioned, or he was one of the biggest frauds
this world has ever seen. There is no middle ground.*

JOSEPH FIELDING SMITH
DOCTRINES OF SALVATION, 1:188

The truthfulness of The Church of Jesus Christ of
Latter-day Saints rests on the story of Joseph Smith.
The life story of the Prophet Joseph reads like an
adventure epic—but it is true. His story is unique in
all the world—and authentic. One cannot say that the
organizational structure of the Church is impressive,
the Book of Mormon remarkable, the doctrines and
teachings inspiring—and disavow the contributions of
Joseph Smith. He, working in an inspired way under
the direction of the Lord, is the prophet of prophets,
the one who "has done more, save Jesus only, for the
salvation of men in this world, than any other man
that ever lived in it" (D&C 135:3). We thank thee, O
God, for the Prophet Joseph Smith.

If we are going to do our duty, we are going to need the powers of heaven. And if we are going to be given access to the powers of heaven, we are going to have to learn to wait upon the Lord.

HENRY B. EYRING
TO DRAW CLOSER TO GOD, 96

When storms rage, an eagle will set its wings so that the wind will pick it up and lift it high above the storm. Each of us can similarly respond to life's difficulties and sorrows. When the storms of sickness, failure, disappointment, and even tragedy strike, we can make it through them—even rise above them—by being spiritually prepared. God can carry us through adversities that would otherwise crush us. Just as the eagle is able to feel the calm above the storm, we too can feel God's peace even in the midst of tribulation. We can rise above the storms of life by setting our hearts on everlasting things, by drawing upon the powers of heaven, by allowing God's power to comfort our souls.

*The proud do not change to improve,
but defend their position by rationalizing. Repentance means
change, and it takes a humble person to change.*

EZRA TAFT BENSON
SERMONS AND WRITINGS, 287

Repentance is a lifelong process of "soul change."
We're all in need of it, and we all need to be humble
enough to draw upon the power of the Atonement to
change and improve. President Ezra Taft Benson said,
"As we cleanse the inner vessel, there will have to be
changes made in our own personal lives, in our families, and in the Church. . . . We must first cleanse the
inner vessel by awakening and arising, being morally
clean, . . . and finally conquering pride by humbling
ourselves. We can do it. I know we can" (*Sermons and
Writings,* 287–88). Repentance is not something to
dread or do casually; it is the process by which we
ascend ever upward to greater heights of spirituality.
Sincere repentance is hard work, but it can become
the greatest blessing, the greatest gift, we experience.

*The happiest people in this world are those
who love their neighbors as themselves and manifest their
appreciation of God's blessings by their conduct in life.*

GEORGE ALBERT SMITH
TEACHINGS, 147

Fulfilling the law and all righteousness, the Lawgiver spoke of a new command for true disciples: "That ye love one another; as I have loved you, that ye also love one another. By this shall all men know that ye are my disciples, if ye have love one to another" (John 13:34–35). This is the surest manifestation of our devotion to the Lord's ideals of living. Love is the essence of the gospel, the measure of our faith, and the substance of our discipleship. Our love for God is demonstrated in our actions and interactions with others. Our loving thoughts and deeds are an indication of what we are *becoming* because we have turned our hearts over to Christ. Those filled with this pure love also enjoy its accompanying virtues: happiness, kindness, and thankfulness.

*I make you a promise . . . that if you will
go to the House of the Lord, you will be blessed;
life will be better for you.*

GORDON B. HINCKLEY
TEACHINGS, 624

The temple is the place to become strengthened for the battles of the day. It is a powerful motivator and guide to keep the enticements of the world out of our lives. It protects us from getting too caught up in the temporal trappings and earthly events that consume so much of our time. Consistent temple attendance helps us stay prepared to receive knowledge and guidance through the Spirit. With such a strengthening influence available, why is it we don't go there more often? President Gordon B. Hinckley implored, "I know that your lives are busy, that you have much to do, but . . . avail yourselves of the great opportunity to go to the Lord's House" (*Teachings,* 624). The promise of prophets is powerful: go to the house of the Lord and you will be blessed.

*I have frequently said that the greatest
endowment God ever gave to man is good, sound,
solid sense to know how to govern ourselves.*

BRIGHAM YOUNG
DISCOURSES, 265

God has given to each of us a mind—and he expects
that we will use it. We are to observe and ponder, reason and reflect, continuing to learn and study over the
course of our life. In our Church callings, we are to
pray and seek the inspiration of the Lord to guide our
decisions. But we are also to study it out in our minds,
review options, and make a reasoned decision (D&C
9:7–9). The same is true in our families and personal
decisions—reason is a vital adjunct to revelation. Of
course, given the primacy of the Spirit, revelation
trumps reason. But reason and common sense can be
an accompanying safeguard and enhancement in the
process of inspiration and as an aid in governing
ourselves.

Let the motto be to every elder in Israel,
and to every person worthy to be called a Saint:
"Fear not, and never stand still, but move on."

LORENZO SNOW
TEACHINGS, 46

We know that if we are prepared we need not fear (D&C 38:30). Come what may, those who combat the adversary's siren call of doubt and fearfulness with the Lord's message of faith and hope will move forward with their lives and find peace in this world and eternal life in the world to come (D&C 59:23). It takes great conviction and strong testimony to trust the gospel plan of happiness when we cannot fully see the future. By obeying, by believing, by praying, and by pondering and feasting upon the words of eternal life, we will come to know the sweet assurance of the Lord: "Fear thou not; for I am with thee: be not dismayed; for I am thy God: I will strengthen thee; yea, I will help thee; yea, I will uphold thee with the right hand of my righteousness" (Isaiah 41:10).

*Unless you have the Holy Ghost
with you when you go out to preach the Gospel,
you cannot do your duty.*

WILFORD WOODRUFF
TEACHINGS OF PRESIDENTS OF THE CHURCH, 98

As a missionary, Wilford Woodruff helped thousands embrace the restored gospel. Of him, Heber J. Grant said, "I believe that no other man who ever walked the face of the earth was a greater converter of souls to the gospel of Jesus Christ" (*Gospel Standards,* 20). President Woodruff knew that successful missionaries seek the guidance of the Holy Ghost as they share the gospel. He said, "It does not make any difference what age a man is in preaching the gospel, . . . if he is only inspired by the Spirit and power of God" (*Teachings of Presidents of the Church,* 98). Like Wilford Woodruff, we cannot truly teach and testify of Christ unless we have received the Spirit (D&C 42:6, 14; 50:13–22). And when we have the Spirit, we shall know in the very hour what to say (D&C 84:85; 100:5–8).

*No man comes to the demanding position of the Presidency
of the Church except his heart and mind are constantly open to
the impressions, insights, and revelations of God.*

SPENCER W. KIMBALL
TEACHINGS, 466

Prophets have a way of jarring the carnal mind," said
President Spencer W. Kimball. "Too often the holy
prophets are wrongly perceived as harsh. . . . It is
because of their love and integrity that they cannot
modify the Lord's message merely to make people feel
comfortable. They are too kind to be cruel" (*Teachings*,
466). Prophets are preachers of righteousness and
teachers of truth—even if some take the truth to be
hard. Many would rather hear flattering words than a
call to repentance (Helaman 13:25–29). Prophets
know they will not be popular with the world or the
worldly; they say the hard things because they understand the doctrine and must speak the truth with love.
We thank God for inspired prophets in these latter
days who are loving but unyielding, meek but resolute.

*In the eyes of the Church and in the followers of Christ
there are no differences. Color makes no difference. Language
makes no difference. Nationality makes no difference. We
are all children of God, and we are brothers and sisters.*

HOWARD W. HUNTER
TEACHINGS, 97

Because the Lord knows fully the hearts and desires of all peoples, he loves them with perfect compassion and understanding. The Lord "denieth none that come unto him, black and white, bond and free, male and female . . . ; and all are alike unto God" (2 Nephi 26:33). We are all beloved spirit children of heavenly parents, created in the image of God with a divine nature and destiny (see *Ensign,* November 1995, 102). Elder Howard W. Hunter said: "Our Father loves all of his children. He desires all of them to embrace the gospel and come unto him. Only those are favored who obey him and keep his commandments. As members of the Lord's church, we need to lift our vision beyond personal prejudices. We need to discover the supreme truth that indeed our Father is no respecter of persons" (*Teachings,* 97).

Those who are on the other side
[of the veil] are just as anxious about us. They
are praying for us and for our success.

GEORGE ALBERT SMITH
TEACHINGS, 27

It is a comfort to know that our loved ones in the spirit world are praying for us. Those on the other side of the veil have not lost interest in those of us who now sojourn in mortality—they have great concern for our welfare, for our faithfulness, for our holding ever true to the iron rod. With their enlightened and expanded perspective, generations of long ago know of the challenges we face and what we must do to remain worthy of heaven's blessings and the gift of eternal life. Elder George Albert Smith said, "They are pleading, in their own way, for their descendants, for their posterity who live upon the earth" (*Teachings,* 27). The prayers of the faithful—on both sides of the veil—can join together to lift and strengthen, bless and comfort, our loved ones.

*Whom shall we teach? We shall teach every person whose life
we touch. It is real teaching when one's presence is an inspiration;
sometimes words are not necessary to teach effectively.*

HUGH B. BROWN
VISION AND VALOR, 26

We teach most clearly and effectively when our
lives exemplify the teachings we profess, the values
and principles we espouse. A teacher is not defined by
eloquence or head count, but by how he or she strives
to live the gospel, by how he or she strives to touch the
hearts of others for good. An effective teacher is one
who makes every effort to live as he or she teaches,
who is a lifelong learner, who is focused on helping
and blessing other people and not on how he or she
looks or sounds or impresses. To teach is not to put on
a show, not to astound others with obscure knowledge
or trivia. Good teachers are humble, not self-
aggrandizing; they are interesting, because they are
prepared and passionate about the gospel.

*Don't be limited in your views with regard to your
neighbor's virtue, but beware of self-righteousness, and be
limited in the estimate of your own virtues, and not
think yourselves more righteous than others.*

JOSEPH SMITH
HISTORY OF THE CHURCH, 4:606

A holier-than-thou attitude is not befitting the man
or woman of Christ. True disciples are meek and lowly
of heart, they are humble and teachable, they realize
that "of him unto whom much is given much is
required" (D&C 82:3). While it is true that we have
the fulness of the gospel, the fulness of truth, that
ought to fill us with gratitude and humility toward
God and reverence and love for all his creations.
Those filled with love for the Lord and his gospel
want to lift and bless, help and heal, share the gospel
and live so that others want to know more of the message of salvation. As we enlarge our souls with charity
and humility, we will see all people as brothers and sisters, fellow sons and daughters of God.

God does notice us, and he watches over us.
But it is usually through another mortal that he meets our
needs. Therefore, it is vital that we serve each other.

SPENCER W. KIMBALL
TEACHINGS, 252

Jesus was a man without property, wealth, or standing yet he influenced many. Peter said of him that he "went about doing good" (Acts 10:38). Jesus healed the sick, the lepers, the lame. He gave sight to the blind, hearing to the deaf, and hope to those whose lives were bound in sin and despair. Even in his final hours, hanging on the cross, Jesus pleaded, "Father, forgive them; for they know not what they do" (Luke 23:34). Jesus Christ's example encourages us to be more merciful and kind, to lift one another, to reach out with tender hearts to the downtrodden and the forgotten. His life reminds us that we can live kindly and generously. His was an inspiring message of love and compassion. Let it be said of each one of us that we too "went about doing good."

*One of Satan's methods is to distract and entice us so that we
will take our eyes off the dangerous crevasses. He has succeeded to
such an extent that many no longer recognize sin as sin.*

DAVID B. HAIGHT
ENSIGN, NOVEMBER 1986, 37

We live in a time when men "call evil good, and
good evil" (Isaiah 5:20). All around us the world is
darkening with sin and depravity. Much of the iniquity
is obvious, but there is wickedness that is subtle
and insidious. If we're not vigilant about holding
firmly to the iron rod, we may fall into these spiritual
crevasses. The light of the Lord will illuminate our
path so that we can see evil—and all its shades. We can
then shun evil influences that hinder the Spirit in our
lives. Elder David. B. Haight said: "Put your trust in
Him to avoid the crevasses of sin and evil. Hold on to
the lifeline of the gospel. You can make correct
choices—the ones you know in your heart will be for
your best good" (*Ensign*, November 1986, 38).

*To change . . . means to give up some behavior or habits
that have been very important to us in the past. . . . Every worthy
change means risk—the risk of losing an old and damaging
habit for a new and improved way of life.*

MARVIN J. ASHTON
ENSIGN, NOVEMBER 1986, 15

The prophet Lehi counseled his family: "Put on the armor of righteousness. Shake off the chains with which ye are bound" (2 Nephi 1:23). Many people are enslaved by the chains of addiction or of sin that restrict growth and happiness. We may be blind to these bad habits or they may seem too overwhelming to eliminate from our lives. Such chains limit our potential for good and make us captives to the adversary. "Chains weigh heavily on troubled hearts and souls," said Elder Marvin J. Ashton. "They relegate us to lives of no purpose or light. They cause us to become confused and lose the spirit. We need to arise from the dust and enjoy the fresh air of righteousness. . . . God help us to shake off and break the chains with which we are bound" (*Ensign,* November 1986, 14).

Think about your life and set your priorities.
Find some quiet time regularly to think deeply about where you
are going and what you will need to do to get there.

M. RUSSELL BALLARD
ENSIGN, MAY 1987, 14

To set priorities that focus on the things of greatest worth, we must develop an eternal perspective. Endlessly chasing things of little consequence will never give us the peace "which passeth all understanding" (Philippians 4:7). We will never get enough of what we don't need, but if we take time to ponder and seriously consider the Lord's priorities for our lives, we will know where to center our hearts and minds. "Write down the tasks you would like to accomplish each day," said Elder M. Russell Ballard. "Keep foremost in mind the sacred covenants you have made with the Lord as you write down your daily schedules" (*Ensign,* May 1987, 14). If we could tie together more closely our daily to-do lists with our eternal callings and sacred covenants, we would live more fully with an eternal perspective.

*It is glorious when you can lie down at night
with a clear conscience, knowing you have done your best
not to offend anyone and have injured no man.*

DAVID O. MCKAY
GOSPEL IDEALS, 502

A clear conscience is a precious endowment that comes to those who live with integrity and strive to walk uprightly before the Lord. Those who sleep in peace are not perfect, but they humbly strive to do their best. They know full well their foibles and short-comings, but they continue steadfastly on the path leading to eternal life. They understand that we are to have joy—not guilt or ego trips (2 Nephi 2:25). They live in the spirit of forgiveness and repentance, extending compassion and charity to others. President David O. McKay described how to obtain a clear conscience and what it feels like: "You have tried to cleanse your heart of all unrighteousness, and if you put forth precious effort, you can sense as you pray to God to keep you that night that he accepts your effort" (*Gospel Ideals,* 502). The peace of a clear conscience is one of life's most glorious joys.

*Every member of the Church
should be a missionary.*

DAVID O. MCKAY
TEACHINGS OF PRESIDENTS OF THE CHURCH, 53

President David O. McKay implored the Saints: "The world is hungry to hear the truth. . . . We have it. Are we equal to the . . . responsibility God has placed upon us?" (*Teachings of Presidents of the Church,* 52). We are to stand as witnesses of Jesus Christ in word and in deed. President McKay described the responsibility of every member: "He is authorized, by virtue of his membership, to set a proper example as a good neighbor. . . . He is a light, and it is his duty not to have that light hidden under a bushel, but it should be set up on a hill that all men may be guided thereby. . . . There's one responsibility which no man can evade, that's the responsibility of personal influence. . . . It's what you are, not what you pretend to be that will bring people to investigate" (ibid., 53).

I am confident that the hymns of Zion, when sung with the proper spirit, bring a peaceful and heavenly influence into our homes, and also aid in preaching the gospel of Jesus Christ.

HEBER J. GRANT
GOSPEL STANDARDS, 170

The hymns invite the Spirit into our homes and hearts and are a means of praising the Lord. The First Presidency stated: "Music has boundless powers for moving families toward greater spirituality and devotion to the gospel. Latter-day Saints should fill their homes with the sound of worthy music. . . . Sing as you work, as you play, and as you travel together. Sing hymns as lullabies to build faith and testimony in your young ones. . . . Hymns can lift our spirits, give us courage, and move us to righteous action. They can fill our souls with heavenly thoughts and bring us a spirit of peace. Hymns can also help us withstand the temptations of the adversary. . . . If unworthy thoughts enter your mind, sing a hymn to yourself, crowding out the evil with the good" (*Hymns*, ix–x).

Inside the temple a further sense of peace is experienced.
The world is left behind with its clamor and rush. In the house of
the Lord there is tranquillity. The temple is also a
place of personal inspiration and revelation.

GORDON B. HINCKLEY
TEACHINGS, 635–36

President Gordon B. Hinckley has said: "I urge our people everywhere . . . to live worthy to hold a temple recommend, to secure one and regard it as a precious asset, and to make a greater effort to go to the house of the Lord and partake of the spirit and the blessings to be had therein. I am satisfied that every man or woman who goes to the temple in a spirit of sincerity and faith leaves the house of the Lord a better man or woman. There is need for constant improvement in all of our lives. There is need occasionally to leave the noise and the tumult of the world and step within the walls of a sacred house of God, there to feel His spirit in an environment of holiness and peace" (*Ensign*, November 1995, 53).

OCTOBER 29

*Love is like a flower . . . and . . . cannot be expected to
last forever unless it is continually fed with portions of love, the
manifestation of esteem and admiration, the expressions of
gratitude, and the consideration of unselfishness.*

SPENCER W. KIMBALL
ENSIGN, MARCH 1977, 5

We live in a society that often seems designed to destroy marriage and family life. Our marriages need attention and care in order to thrive. "If one is forever seeking the interests, comforts, and happiness of the other, the love found in courtship and cemented in marriage will grow into mighty proportions," observed President Spencer W. Kimball. "Many couples permit their marriages to become stale and their love to grow cold like old bread or worn-out jokes or cold gravy. Certainly the foods most vital for love are consideration, kindness, thoughtfulness, concern, expressions of affection, [and] embraces of appreciation" (*Ensign,* March 1977, 5). We can nurture our marriages by making frequent deposits in our "marital account"—regular dates, empathetic listening, tokens of gratitude and love, support and help for one another, kind words and caring actions, and a hundred other ways.

Jesus Christ is the Redeemer of the world, the Son of the Living God. We cannot partly accept him—as a philosopher, as merely the most perfect man who ever lived. When we do that we reject . . . his sovereignty and his divinity.

GEORGE Q. MORRIS
IMPROVEMENT ERA, JUNE 1960, 430

George Q. Morris was eighty years old when he was called to the Quorum of the Twelve Apostles in 1954. Elder Morris served faithfully until his death eight years later. With his strong testimony of the Savior, he, like other apostles and prophets of the Lord, was a special witnesses of the name of Christ in all the world (D&C 107:23). These witnesses know that Jesus is more than a remarkable teacher, more than an impressive theorist, more than an eloquent sage. He is the Christ, the Son of God, our Savior and Redeemer. King Benjamin said, "There is no other name given whereby salvation cometh; therefore, I would that ye should take upon you the name of Christ, all you that have entered into the covenant with God that ye should be obedient unto the end of your lives" (Mosiah 5:8).

We must look out that we do not roll any manner of sin as a sweet morsel under our tongue, but strive with penitence day by day to put away from us everything that is contrary to godliness.

FRANKLIN D. RICHARDS
CONFERENCE REPORT, OCTOBER 1897, 28

We live in a world beset with sin and infused with the adversary's power. Our mortal sojourn is filled with temptation and trials. We are here to learn to put off the natural man, to resist the devil's power, to draw ever closer to the Infinite. We all make mistakes and sin, but in the strength of the Lord we can overcome the world. The Lord states clearly, "For I the Lord cannot look upon sin with the least degree of allowance; nevertheless, he that repents and does the commandments of the Lord shall be forgiven" (D&C 1:31–32). The power of righteousness—the power of God—is more potent than the worldly allurements that surround us. We have the comforting assurance that we will not be tempted beyond what we are capable of resisting (1 Corinthians 10:13).

NOVEMBER

*Be grateful. Every day is a new
canvas—a new opportunity. . . . Choice
blessings await those who live in thanksgiving daily. . . . Don't wait to start.
Open your eyes, open your hearts,
and open your arms.*

JOSEPH B. WIRTHLIN

*There is more built-in strength in
all of us than we sometimes suppose.*

RICHARD L. EVANS
MESSAGES FROM MUSIC AND THE SPOKEN WORD, 9

O n this date in 1971, Elder Richard L. Evans passed
away after serving for many decades as an apostle and
as the voice, writer, and producer of the Tabernacle
Choir's weekly broadcast. As he lay in his hospital bed,
ill with a viral infection, the prerecorded Sunday
morning broadcast of *Music and the Spoken Word* came on
the air. His own voice and words encouraged faith in
the future: "There are times when we feel that we can't
endure—that we can't face what's ahead of us. . . . But
these times come and go . . . and in the low times we
have to endure; we have to hold on until the shadows
brighten, until the load lifts. . . . There is more built-in
strength in all of us than we sometimes suppose"
(*Messages from Music and the Spoken Word,* 9).

None of us know what course our children will take.
We set good examples before them, and we strive to teach them
righteous principles; but when they come to years of accountabil-
ity they have their agency and they act for themselves.

WILFORD WOODRUFF
TEACHINGS OF PRESIDENTS OF THE CHURCH, 165

Y ou and I were among those who used their agency to accept the Father's plan to come to earth, gain a body, be tried and tested. Opportunities to exercise our agency abound, for here "there is an opposition in all things" (2 Nephi 2:11). We are accountable to God for how we use our agency: Will we grow in love and righteousness? Will we obey the commandments, serve others, and grasp the iron rod? Or will we yield to the influence of Satan and reject the good news of the gospel? Parents are responsible to teach the gospel to their children by precept and example (D&C 68:25); both children and parents will be held accountable for what they do with those sacred teachings and responsibilities. The perfect Judge will judge us perfectly, with fairness and mercy, justice and compassion.

I feel happy. "Mormonism" has made me all I am,
and the grace, the power, and the wisdom of God will make
me all that I ever will be, either in time or eternity.

BRIGHAM YOUNG
DISCOURSES, 451

The gospel can make of us better men and women.
It gives us knowledge and perspective, comfort and
reassurance; it gives us opportunities to serve and
work side by side with others, to grow in wisdom and
sociability, to associate with fellow citizens in the
household of faith. Along with those exceptional
blessings, it is the Spirit of the Lord that will transform our hearts, change our natures, and make of us
new creatures in Christ (2 Corinthians 5:17; Mosiah
27:26). At the same time we must remember that
while the fulness of the gospel of Christ has been
restored, this is no reason for anyone to feel superior.
It invokes in us a greater obligation to serve, love, and
bless others. As "Mormonism" changes us, we desire
to share that message of joy and peace with others.

All that we possess is the gift of God. We should acknowledge him in all things. . . . Our safety and happiness and our wealth depend upon our obedience to God and his laws.

JOHN TAYLOR
TEACHINGS OF PRESIDENTS OF THE CHURCH, 177

Every good gift and every perfect gift is from above, and cometh down from the Father of lights" (James 1:17). Indeed, the Giver of all that is good is God our Father. All that we are, all that we possess comes as a divine endowment, a bequest from above. President John Taylor said, "We ought always to remember that our strength is in God; we have nothing to boast of ourselves, we have no intelligence that God has not given unto us; we have nothing in life, or property, but what has been given unto us of the Lord. Everything we possess pertaining to time and eternity has been imparted to us by him" (*Teachings of Presidents of the Church,* 176–77). We feel, like the apostle Paul, to exclaim: "Thanks be unto God for his unspeakable gift" (2 Corinthians 9:15).

My hopes in reference to the future life are supremely grand and
glorious, and I try to keep these prospects bright continually; and
that is the privilege and the duty of every Latter-day Saint.

LORENZO SNOW
CONFERENCE REPORT, OCTOBER 1900, 4

The prophet of God is an optimist. He knows that while sin is pervasive and growing, so is the righteousness that comes of the light of the gospel. Although he deals with myriad problems and pressures, he knows that the gospel can bring us great joy and hope in spite of the realities of life. As a teacher of truth, he tells of the calamities that will befall the earth because of wickedness. As a preacher of righteousness, he denounces sin and foretells its consequences. His responsibility is to testify to the world as a special witness of Christ, make known God's will and true character, and buoy up the Saints of God in faith and testimony. Although the world grows ever darker, keep your eyes riveted on the prophet—he will guide us in the paths of safety and peace.

We may desire the wealth of the world,
but the most important treasures that we have are the
sons and daughters that God sends to our homes.

GEORGE ALBERT SMITH
TEACHINGS, 117

The parable is told of the husband and wife who focused so intently on the box that they missed the diamonds inside it. The box is our home, which of course we wish to make pleasant, comfortable, attractive, and well-maintained. But the diamonds, the treasures of greatest worth, are the people inside the home—the loving memories and family associations, the traditions and values that span generations and enrich the soul, the love and laughter of children and the quiet confidence of family members. And just as homes need maintenance, our greatest treasures—our loved ones—need care and concern, thought and time, nurturing and nourishment. These are the treasures that transcend time and space; these most important gifts from a loving Father are worthy of our most conscientious and loving attention.

NOVEMBER 7

*Spirituality, our true aim, is the consciousness
of victory over self and of communion with the Infinite.*

DAVID O. MCKAY
TEACHINGS OF PRESIDENTS OF THE CHURCH, 16

In this second act of a three-act play, we strive to draw closer to the Infinite, to develop the attributes of godliness, to become more Christlike. President David O. McKay observed: "Spirituality impels one to conquer difficulties and acquire more and more strength. To feel one's faculties unfolding and truth expanding the soul is one of life's sublimest experiences. Being true to self and being loyal to high ideals develops spirituality. The real test of any religion is the kind of man it makes" (*Teachings of Presidents of the Church,* 16). This life is about putting off the natural man and becoming true disciples of Christ. It's not what we *do* that matters most, but what we are *becoming* because of the atonement of Christ; it's not what we *say*, but how we strive to *live* each day.

339

*May we cling with the last thread of hope and prayer
to these precious souls that have strayed away from us and have
not received the full blessings of the gospel.*

HAROLD B. LEE
TEACHINGS, 472

These words reflect President Harold B. Lee's tender concern for those who have wandered from the path of righteousness: "If there be those who have slipped away from us, who have been led by forces which are evil, may we not despair either as parents or as teachers . . . , but put into our minds the feeling that the home or the church or a class is not a failure . . . so long as a teacher, [a] parent, or [a] class does not give up" (*Teachings*, 472). Undeniable power comes from the earnest faith and prayers of loved ones. The angel who appeared to Alma and the sons of Mosiah came not in response to any righteousness on their part; the angel came because of the hope and prayers of a faithful and loving parent who didn't give up (Mosiah 27:14, 22–23).

*This wondrous Restoration should make of us a people of
tolerance, of neighborliness, of appreciation and kindness toward
others. We cannot be boastful. We cannot be proud. We can be
thankful, as we must be. We can be humble, as we should be.*

GORDON B. HINCKLEY
DISCOURSES, 2:198

President Gordon B. Hinckley has repeatedly condemned pride and self-righteousness: "Let us as
Latter-day Saints reach out to others not of our faith.
Let us never act in a spirit of arrogance or with a
holier-than-thou attitude. Rather, may we show love
and respect and helpfulness toward them. . . . We can
be more tolerant, more neighborly, more friendly,
more of an example than we have been in the past. Let
us teach our children to treat others with friendship,
respect, love, and admiration" (*Ensign,* May 2000, 87).
There is no place for pride and haughtiness in the
work of the Lord. With the eternal perspective of the
gospel plan of happiness, we of all people ought to be
filled with charity and compassion, gentleness and
goodness, and humility toward all of humanity.

Search yourselves—the tongue is an unruly member—
hold your tongues about things of no moment—
a little tale will set the world on fire.

JOSEPH SMITH
HISTORY OF THE CHURCH, 5:20

In 1842, the Prophet Joseph exhorted the Relief Society sisters to hold their tongues and refrain from gossiping. The scriptures tell us that "every idle word that [we] shall speak, [we] shall give account thereof in the day of judgment" (Matthew 12:36). Few words are more idle than those spoken unkindly about others, especially since part of our covenant with Christ is to "love one another" (D&C 88:123) and to "succor the weak, lift up the hands which hang down, and strengthen the feeble knees" (D&C 81:5). When we refrain from repeating cutting or careless words—whether or not the words are true—we are able to love and serve more sincerely and build a foundation for friendship and trust. The well-known adage "if you can't say anything nice, don't say anything at all" is a timeless truth.

A grateful heart is a beginning of greatness.
It is an expression of humility. It is a foundation for the
development of such virtues as prayer, faith, courage,
contentment, happiness, love, and well-being.

JAMES E. FAUST
IN THE STRENGTH OF THE LORD, 327

Christ set an example in giving thanks at the Last Supper for the bread and wine (Mark 14:22–23). The scriptures are filled with references to praise and thanksgiving to the Lord. The Psalmist sang, "Know ye that the Lord he is God: . . . Enter into his gates with thanksgiving, and into his courts with praise: be thankful unto him, and bless his name" (Psalm 100:3–4.) King Benjamin admonished his people to render thanks and praise to God, our Heavenly King (Mosiah 2:19–21). Gratitude is a cardinal virtue from which other virtues flow; humility, faith, love, happiness, and generosity all have their roots in a grateful heart. Greatness of soul is manifest as we "thank the Lord [our] God in all things" (D&C 59:7).

NOVEMBER 12

*The Book of Mormon was written for us today.
God is the author of the book.*

EZRA TAFT BENSON
SERMONS AND WRITINGS, 72

The Book of Mormon is meant for us. President Ezra Taft Benson, who bore testimony so often of its power, said: "The Book of Mormon brings men to Christ. . . . It tells in plain manner of Christ and His gospel. It testifies of His divinity and of the necessity for a Redeemer and the need of our putting trust in Him. It bears witness of the Fall and the Atonement and the first principles of the gospel, including our need for a broken heart and a contrite spirit and a spiritual rebirth. It proclaims we must endure to the end in righteousness and live the moral life of a Saint. . . . It confounds false doctrines and lays down contention. It fortifies the humble followers of Christ against the evil designs, strategies, and doctrines of the devil in our day" (*Sermons and Writings*, 73).

*Men can only be saved and exalted in the
kingdom of God in righteousness, therefore we must repent
of our sins, and walk in the light as Christ is in the light,
that his blood may cleanse us from all sins.*

JOSEPH F. SMITH
GOSPEL DOCTRINE, 250

Jesus atoned for the sins and suffering of the world
and provided a rescue from spiritual and temporal
death. The Savior's atonement is the healing power
for all heartache and pain, all bitterness and infirmity,
all iniquity and anguish. He is mighty to forgive and
save. President Joseph F. Smith, who was born on this
day in 1838, said: "Men cannot forgive their own sins.
. . . Men can stop sinning and can do right in the
future, and so far their acts are acceptable before the
Lord and worthy of consideration. But who shall
repair the wrongs they have done to themselves and
to others, which it seems impossible for them to repair
themselves? By the atonement of Jesus Christ the sins
of the repentant shall be washed away. . . . This is the
promise given to you" (*Gospel Doctrine*, 98).

Let us follow the Son of God in all ways and in all walks of life.
Let us make him our exemplar and our guide.

HOWARD W. HUNTER
TEACHINGS, 43

Howard W. Hunter was born on this date in 1907. Throughout life he experienced many trials and adversities, but always bore strong testimony of the Lord, exhorting the Saints to follow Jesus: "We should at every opportunity ask ourselves, 'What would Jesus do?' and then be more courageous to act upon the answer. We must follow Christ" (*Teachings,* 43). Elder Jeffrey R. Holland, who was called by President Hunter to fill the vacancy in the Quorum of the Twelve Apostles, said: "Howard W. Hunter was fore-ordained in the councils of heaven before this world was, and he has been made, fashioned, molded into a prophet of God. . . . He has not . . . gone through what he has gone through by accident. He is a man of velvet and steel. He [was] called of God" (ibid., xiv).

If this Church were the work of man, it would fail,
but it is the work of the Lord, and he does not fail. If we
. . . are valiant in the testimony of Jesus, the Lord
will guide and direct us and his Church.

JOSEPH FIELDING SMITH
THE LORD NEEDED A PROPHET, 166

It may seem at times that wickedness will overwhelm the forces of good. But this is not the kingdom of a man or the church of a man—this is the Church of Jesus Christ, his kingdom and cause, and it will not, it cannot fail. "The keys of the kingdom of God are committed unto man on the earth, and from thence shall the gospel roll forth unto the ends of the earth, as the stone which is cut out of the mountain without hands shall roll forth, until it has filled the whole earth" (D&C 65:2). The prophets of this last and greatest of all dispensations have not felt fear—concern, yes; disquiet, yes; but they do not give in to fearfulness because they know that the work of the Lord will eventually and always triumph.

The fall had a twofold direction—downward,
yet forward. It brought man into the world and set his
feet upon progression's highway.

ORSON F. WHITNEY
SATURDAY NIGHT THOUGHTS, 287

The Creation, Fall, and Atonement have been called
the three pillars of eternity. Each is a necessary part of
the Father's plan of happiness for his children. We are
here to fulfill the measure of our creation and help
bring to pass the Father's purposes: "This is my work
and my glory—to bring to pass the immortality and
eternal life of man" (Moses 1:39). In this fallen world
we must overcome the natural man: "Adam fell that
men might be; and men are, that they might have joy"
(2 Nephi 2:25). We are here to repent and partake of
the marvelous gift of pure love: "It is expedient that
an atonement should be made; for according to the
great plan of the Eternal God there must be an atonement made, or else all mankind must unavoidably perish" (Alma 34:9).

*If ingratitude be numbered among the
serious sins, then gratitude takes its place
among the noblest of virtues.*

THOMAS S. MONSON
ENSIGN, FEBRUARY 2000, 2

Even when things seem bleak, we are blessed to live
in this beautiful world, to have limitless opportunities.
President Thomas S. Monson has noted: "While there
are some things wrong in the world today, there are
many things right, such as teachers who teach, minis-
ters who minister, marriages that make it, parents who
sacrifice, and friends who help. We can lift ourselves,
and others as well, when we refuse to remain in the
realm of negative thought and cultivate within our
hearts an attitude of gratitude" (*Ensign,* February
2000, 2). We would be wise to heed the counsel of
prophets and devote more of our prayers to expressions of gratitude and fewer to petitions and requests.
Let us "live in thanksgiving daily, for the many mercies
and blessings which [the Lord] doth bestow upon
[us]" (Alma 34:38).

As we approach this Thanksgiving,
we should be grateful for the goodness of the Lord to us.
Every day should be a day of thanksgiving.

HOWARD W. HUNTER
TEACHINGS, 94

Gratitude for the bounties of life should not be relegated to only one day of the year. Thankfulness flows daily from an abundant and humble heart. President Howard W. Hunter said, "When we celebrate Thanksgiving Day after the pattern of our Pilgrim Fathers, our thoughts should turn to the real reason why they were thankful. If we would make God first in our lives, freedom and prosperity would be added and Thanksgiving would become more than a day, or a season, but always" (*Teachings,* 93). Profound and sincere gratitude becomes a way of life, not just the way of a day or a weekend or a moment, as we turn to the Lord with full purpose of heart.

*If there is anything on earth I have tried to do as
much as anything else, it is to keep my word, my promises, my
integrity, to do what it was my duty to do.*

JOSEPH F. SMITH
TEACHINGS OF PRESIDENTS OF THE CHURCH, 416

On this date in 1918 President Joseph F. Smith
passed away at age eighty, after serving more than four
decades as a General Authority (seventeen years as the
President of the Church). He was beloved for his
dedicated service to the cause of Zion, and for his
steadfast commitment to the gospel. He said: "It is for
us to do our duty and live our religion on one day the
same as any other. Let us serve the Lord in righteousness all the day long" (*Teachings of Presidents of the
Church,* 417). We are to be true Saints of God every day
of the week. It could be said of Joseph F. Smith what
was said of his father, Hyrum Smith: "I, the Lord, love
him because of the integrity of his heart, and because
he loveth that which is right before me" (D&C
124:15).

To cease sinning is to begin living.

NEAL A. MAXWELL
QUOTE BOOK, 319

We read in the Book of Mormon of the change of heart Lamoni's father, the king, experienced as Aaron taught him of the plan of redemption. Desiring the great joy of eternal life, the king prayed mightily: "O God, Aaron hath told me that there is a God; and if there is a God, and if thou art God, wilt thou make thyself known unto me, and I will give away all my sins to know thee" (Alma 22:18). The king and all his household were converted. A latter-day apostle, Elder Neal A. Maxwell, testified: "Of all the stumbling blocks, personal sins are clearly the largest and most retarding. Before we can receive all that God has for us, we must first make room by giving away our sins" (*Quote Book,* 318). We become truly free as we humbly give away our sins.

*Men and women who are trying to make
themselves happy in the possession of wealth or power will
miss it, for nothing short of the Gospel of the Son of God can
make the inhabitants of the earth happy.*

BRIGHAM YOUNG
DISCOURSES, 314

The story is familiar: A person seeks fulfillment in the pursuit of treasure. He spends time acquiring the things of the world and climbing the ladder of success. The higher he climbs the more possessions he accumulates. Realizing his soul is still unsatisfied, he works harder to gain more wealth and status, finally giving up in despair. If he listens to the Spirit, however, he will instead "come to himself" (Luke 15:17) and realize that life is short and some things matter more than others. He will put family and faith first—where they should be. The Savior taught, "For what is a man profited, if he shall gain the whole world, and lose his own soul? or what shall a man give in exchange for his soul?" (Matthew 16:26). Eternal life and the everlasting things are of greatest worth.

*But, to the man of faith, death is but the taking up
again of the life he broke off when he came to the earth.*

HEBER J. GRANT
TEACHINGS OF PRESIDENTS OF THE CHURCH, 44

Heber J. Grant, seventh President of the Church, was born on this day in 1856. His father, Jedediah M. Grant, died nine days later. During his lifetime, President Grant lost numerous family members to death and spoke with empathy born of personal experience: "How bitter must be the suffering and grief of those who see nothing beyond the grave except the beginning of eternal night and oblivion. For them that thus believe, death hath its sting and the grave its victory. . . . I can never think of my loved ones . . . as being in the grave. I rejoice in the associations they are enjoying and in the pleasure they are having in meeting with their loved ones on the other side" (*Teachings of Presidents of the Church,* 44). Death is not the end, but a continuation of an eternal life.

The Lord has not quit talking
to his people. We do not just believe in the ancient
scripture. We have so much more.

LeGrand Richards
Improvement Era, December 1962, 952

LeGrand Richards served for fourteen years as presiding bishop of the Church, after which he was called to the Quorum of the Twelve Apostles, where he served for more than three decades. The author of *A Marvelous Work and a Wonder,* he was beloved worldwide for his stirring testimony and his indefatigable missionary zeal. Throughout his life he proclaimed that the heavens were open, that truth has been restored, that apostles and prophets again walk the earth, and that the Lord reveals his mind and will through them. Indeed, his clarion call was: "We believe all that God has revealed, all that He does now reveal, and we believe that He will yet reveal many great and important things pertaining to the Kingdom of God" (Article of Faith 9).

*When you are on your knees in prayer, there is
an overwhelming feeling of gratitude to the Lord for the
many blessings that he bestows on his children.*

L. TOM PERRY
ENSIGN, NOVEMBER 1983, 13

As we kneel in humble prayer, our hearts overflow with thanksgiving for the Lord and his goodness. "How blessed we are for our understanding of who [God] is. How blessed we are as a people for the gift of the gospel," said Elder L. Tom Perry. "I marvel at what He has created for our use and benefit and for the privilege of enjoying this earthly experience. My heart is especially filled with gratitude at this season of the harvest when I . . . pull off an ear of corn and see how those two or three kernels placed in the earth now yield a hundredfold. As I travel and see the beauty of His creations—the mountains, the fertile plains, the sparkling streams, or the mighty oceans—how grateful I am for His blessings to me" (*Ensign*, November 1983, 13).

Living the standards set in For the Strength of
Youth *will make you feel good about yourself. Write those
standards into your heart and mind, and live accordingly.*

DIETER F. UCHTDORF
ENSIGN, MAY 2006, 45

The principles in *For the Strength of Youth* apply to all
who seek to gain strength in the gospel, have power in
the Spirit, and more fully become the chosen generation, peculiar people, and royal priesthood the Lord
would have us be (1 Peter 2:9). Elder Dieter F.
Uchtdorf said: "Compare each of those standards with
where you are today. Listen to the Spirit, who will
teach you what you need to do to become more like
Jesus. If you recognize a need for change, make the
change; don't procrastinate. Use true repentance and
the gift and power of the Atonement of Jesus Christ
to clear up those things that are keeping you from
reaching your true potential. If this process appears
tough, hang in there; it is worth it" (*Ensign,* May 2006,
45).

*Be grateful. Every day is a new canvas—
a new opportunity. . . . Choice blessings await those who live in
thanksgiving daily. . . . Don't wait to start. Open your
eyes, open your hearts, and open your arms.*

JOSEPH B. WIRTHLIN
ENSIGN, SEPTEMBER 2001, 13

Elder Joseph B. Wirthlin has encouraged us to be people of gratitude: "It is simplicity itself to blame our unhappiness on the things we lack in life. . . . The problem is, the more we focus on the things we don't have, the more unhappy and more resentful we become. . . . One thing I can tell you with certainty is this: You cannot predict happiness by the amount of money, fame, or power a person has. External conditions do not necessarily make a person happy. . . . The fact is that the external things so valued by the world are often the cause of a great deal of misery in the world. Those who live in thanksgiving daily, however, are usually among the world's happiest people. And they make others happy as well" (*Ensign,* September 2001, 9).

Agency is strengthened by our faith and obedience.
Agency leads us to act: to seek that we may find, to ask that we
may receive guidance from the Spirit, to knock on that door that
leads to spiritual light and ultimately salvation.

ROBERT D. HALES
ENSIGN, MAY 2006, 8

Agency is an eternal principle and our greatest, most safeguarded endowment. Elder Robert D. Hales said: "Agency was manifested in the Council in Heaven as we chose to follow our Heavenly Father's plan and come to mortality for this probationary period. . . . Agency is the catalyst that leads us to express our inward spiritual desires in outward Christlike behavior. Agency permits us to make faithful, obedient choices that strengthen us so that we can lift and strengthen others. Agency used righteously allows light to dispel the darkness and enables us to live with joy and happiness in the present, look with faith to the future, even into the eternities, and not dwell on the things of the past. Our use of agency determines who we are and what we will be" (*Ensign,* May 2006, 7–8).

*The Lord will never permit me or
any other man who stands as President of this
Church to lead you astray.*

WILFORD WOODRUFF
TEACHINGS OF PRESIDENTS OF THE CHURCH, 199

God will see to it that his Church will not be led astray. This latter-day marvelous work and wonder is greater that any single individual or personality—this is the Lord's kingdom on earth, the system of salvation for all generations. While some will falter from time to time, we have the reassuring promise that the Lord's anointed prophet will not and cannot lead the Church away from its ordained course. President Wilford Woodruff said: "It is not in the programme. It is not in the mind of God. If I were to attempt that, the Lord would remove me out of my place" (*Teachings of Presidents of the Church,* 199). We too must do our part to remain faithful and stay the course.

Fasting is intended to be an affair of the heart rather than an outward manifestation, just as secret prayer is recommended by the Master in preference to the display of the Pharisees.

GEORGE Q. CANNON
GOSPEL TRUTH, 406

A certain kind of devil goes not out except by fasting and prayer (Matthew 17:14–21). That devil may be pride or self-righteousness or addiction. Fasting is a reflection of our willingness to submit to the Lord. Fasting can help clear the mind and strengthen the body and spirit; it can give us a sense of self-mastery and greater confidence in divine purposes. *How* we fast is also important. "One who fasts need not by a long face . . . give public notice in this manner of his observance of the fast," said President George Q. Cannon. "The main thing is to bring the heart and being into a condition receptive to the influences of the good Spirit and to approach in prayer the throne of the Father with a soul filled with praise, humility and faith" (*Gospel Truth,* 406).

Heed these warnings. Let us all improve our personal behavior and redouble our efforts to protect our loved ones and our environment from the onslaught of pornography that threatens our spirituality, our marriages, and our children.

DALLIN H. OAKS
ENSIGN, MAY 2005, 90

Elder Dallin H. Oaks gave us timely counsel to combat the scourge of our day: pornography. "Acknowledge the evil. Don't defend it or try to justify yourself. . . . Seek the help of the Lord and His servants. . . . Do all that you can to avoid pornography. If you ever find yourself in its presence—which can happen to anyone in the world in which we live—follow the example of Joseph of Egypt. When temptation caught him in her grip, he left temptation and 'got him out' (Gen. 39:12). Don't accommodate any degree of temptation. Prevent sin and avoid having to deal with its inevitable destruction. So, turn it off! Look away! Avoid it at all costs. Direct your thoughts in wholesome paths. Remember your covenants and be faithful in temple attendance" (*Ensign,* May 2005, 90).

December

Christmas and the holiday season
is a wonderful time to help us to forgive and
forget. We become our better selves and rise
above the shackles that seem to bind us.

James E. Faust

*I know that [Jesus Christ] lives, and that
in the last day he shall stand upon the earth, that he shall
come to the people who shall be prepared for him.*

JOSEPH F. SMITH
GOSPEL DOCTRINE, 506–7

The greatest comfort in life comes from the whisperings of the Spirit to the sincere seeker of truth and righteousness. We can receive sweet assurance that Christ is the Lord and that he shall come again to reign in glory if we truly seek him: "For every one that asketh, receiveth; and he that seeketh, findeth; and to him that knocketh, it shall be opened" (3 Nephi 14:8). The testimony of Jesus Christ is the spirit of prophecy, and no person can say that Jesus is the Christ unless inspired by the Holy Ghost (Revelation 19:10; 1 Corinthians 12:3). So, those who have a testimony of Jesus Christ have received revelation and partaken of the spirit of prophecy. The witness of the Spirit is more powerful and more transcendent than all other evidences and impels us to prepare for the Lord's triumphant return.

*The beauty of the gospel of Jesus Christ
is that it makes us all equal in as far as we keep
the commandments of the Lord.*

GEORGE ALBERT SMITH
TEACHINGS, 36

The Lord is no respecter of persons (D&C 1:35). He loves each of us with a perfect and constant love, and "all are alike unto [him]" (2 Nephi 26:33). His capacity to bless, however, is limited by our obedience to the commandments. Elder George Albert Smith said, "One of the beautiful things to me in the gospel of Jesus Christ is that it brings us all to a common level. . . . The humblest member of the Church, if he keeps the commandments of God, will obtain an exaltation just as much as any other man in the celestial kingdom. . . . In as far as we observe to keep the laws of the Church we have equal opportunities for exaltation" (*Teachings*, 35–36). We each have the prospect for everlasting joy hereafter if we do our part here and now.

*The gospel of Jesus Christ is the crucible in which hate, envy,
and greed are consumed, and good will, kindness, and love remain
as inner aspirations by which man truly lives and builds.*

DAVID O. MCKAY
TEACHINGS OF PRESIDENTS OF THE CHURCH, 3

A crucible is a severe test or trial that has the capacity to make us better—or bitter. We become stronger through the refining fires of life because of Christ. As we turn our hearts to him, hatred is burned away and love grows ever brighter. Experiencing Christ's refining influence changes everything: We can do and see and understand things that we could not do, see, or understand on our own. As our hearts are changed, our overriding desire is to help others experience the same joy. President David O. McKay said, "Let men and women everywhere keep their eyes upon him who ever shines as a Light to all the world—for Christ is the Way, the Truth, the Life, the only safe Guide to that haven of peace for which people the wide world over are earnestly praying" (*Teachings of Presidents of the Church,* 3).

Although not in every sense, everybody
is inactive; and to some degree everybody is active.

HAROLD B. LEE
TEACHINGS, 475

President Harold B. Lee wisely observed, "Each of us is, in one respect or more, partially inactive. We speak of activity and inactivity as though it were something that you could label and put in a pigeonhole and say, 'These are active, these are not.' But in some respects . . . each one of us is partially inactive. . . . We are not as activated into our priesthood offices and callings with all diligence as we should be. At the same time these we call inactive are to some extent partially active. It may be kind deeds, it may be a good home life, it may be various other factors, so that we must say, although not in every sense, everybody is inactive; and to some degree everybody is active" (*Teachings,* 474–75).

*If we make any little stumbles the Savior acts
not as a foolish, vindictive man, to knock another man down.
He is full of kindness, long suffering, and forbearance,
and treats everybody with kindness and courtesy.*

JOHN TAYLOR
TEACHINGS OF PRESIDENTS OF THE CHURCH, 27

Wise mothers and fathers teach their children that no one is perfect, that life is a schoolroom wherein we learn and grow and make mistakes. Even so, a parent's love can be close-to-perfect for their less-than-perfect child. Good parents don't tear down or mock their child; they don't denigrate or hold onto a grudge. Likewise, the Savior is quick to forgive, ready to extend compassion, eager to clasp us in his arms if we will repent and turn to him with full purpose of heart (Mormon 5:11). No vindictiveness or maliciousness, no anger or animosity is in him. The Savior *is* pure love, kindness, and long-suffering; he treats us ideally because of his perfect understanding of the plan of happiness and his perfect empathy for us. Life presents us with inevitable twists, turns, and trials, but our Savior's love is constant through them all.

*We are in the world for a purpose.
We are not here accidentally.*

LORENZO SNOW
TEACHINGS, 92

God has a plan for his children: "And we will prove them herewith, to see if they will do all things whatsoever the Lord their God shall command them; And they who keep their first estate shall be added upon" (Abraham 3:25–26). Without a plan of salvation, we would be lost: wanderers without purpose and strangers to truth. Our Father wants us to receive eternal joy, but he will never coerce. We are free to choose. "We came here because we were willing to come, and because it was the wish of our Father in Heaven that we should come," said President Lorenzo Snow. "We undoubtedly saw very clearly that there was no other way for us to secure what the Father had in store for us" (*Teachings*, 92). We are here as part of our Father's great plan of happiness.

*Each of us is an innkeeper who
decides if there is room for Jesus!*

NEAL A. MAXWELL
QUOTE BOOK, 175

Long ago, in the little town of Bethlehem, new Life came into the world—and the world would forever be changed. Mary and Joseph had traveled from Nazareth to their ancestral home of Bethlehem, but there was no room for them in the inns. So, in a stable, Mary "brought forth her firstborn son, and wrapped him in swaddling clothes, and laid him in a manger" (Luke 2:7). Emmanuel, meaning "God with us," was born in what would otherwise be considered an insignificant Judean town. *Bethlehem* in Hebrew means "house of bread," and Jesus came as the Bread of Life to a hungry world. He came as Living Water to quench the thirst of all honest seekers. He came to lift souls and spread joy. As the Prince of Peace, he still reigns in the hearts of all who make room for him.

Jesus Christ was the greatest teacher who ever taught.
He made known the greatest truths ever learned. He revealed the
meaning of life, the way to success, and the secret of happiness.

SPENCER W. KIMBALL
TEACHINGS, 11

Jesus Christ is the pattern for living, the pathway to perfection. Indeed, he is the perfect way, truth, and life, and we seek to emulate him (John 14:6). Elder Spencer W. Kimball said, "To be like Christ! What an ambitious goal! What a lofty ideal! The Savior had a pleasing personality, he was kind, he was pleasant, he was understanding, he never went off on tangents, he was perfectly balanced. No eccentricities could be found in his life. Here was no ostentation and show, but he was real and humble and genuine. He made no play for popularity. He made no compromises to gain favor. He did the right thing always, regardless of how it might appeal to men. He drew all good people to him as a magnet" (*Teachings*, 13). In truth and testimony, in personality and perfection, we desire to become more like him.

The Spirit of the Lord can be our guide. . . . We invite the Holy Ghost into our lives through meaningful personal and family prayer, feasting upon the words of Christ, diligent and exacting obedience, faithfulness and honoring of covenants.

DAVID A. BEDNAR
ENSIGN, MAY 2006, 31

Elder David A. Bednar has given us a clear standard: "If something we think, see, hear, or do distances us from the Holy Ghost, then we should stop thinking, seeing, hearing, or doing that thing. . . . I recognize we are fallen men and women living in a mortal world and that we might not have the presence of the Holy Ghost with us every second of every minute of every hour of every day. However, the Holy Ghost can tarry with us much, if not most, of the time—and certainly the Spirit can be with us more than it is not with us" (*Ensign,* May 2006, 30). When we feel the Spirit withdraw, we would do well to ask ourselves *why* and then do all in our power to reclaim its influence.

*We are full of selfishness; the devil
flatters us that we are very righteous, when we
are feeding on the faults of others.*

JOSEPH SMITH
HISTORY OF THE CHURCH, 5:24

One of Satan's great deceptions is to lead the righteous astray by persuading them to feel superior. In their delusion, the self-righteous deny the power of the Atonement, the need for a Redeemer, and the marvelous transforming power of the gospel. They make themselves miserable with their dependence upon external markers of righteousness and neglect the inner workings of their soul. In such a state of comparison, they become prey to jealousy, enmity, false witness, and gossip as they struggle to maintain their "superiority." If, however, they realize their errors and humbly recognize their own weaknesses, a generosity of soul will replace the selfishness. Love and meekness will overcome animosity and haughtiness. And they will feel a compelling desire to serve others and demonstrate compassion toward them. In so doing, they will see the great potential for good in all of God's children.

However much faith to obey God we now have,
we will need to strengthen it continually and keep it refreshed
constantly. We can do that by deciding now to be more
quick to obey and more determined to endure.

HENRY B. EYRING
ENSIGN, NOVEMBER 2005, 38

Spiritual preparedness is as vital today as ever. To survive the increasing flood of immorality, we need to strengthen our faith in God and tighten our grip on the iron rod. Some of the enemies of spiritual preparedness are procrastination, sloth, and inconsistency. With a humble attitude of obedience and faithfulness, we will be able to withstand the tempests ahead. Elder Henry B. Eyring has wisely counseled: "Let me suggest to you four settings in which to practice quick and steady obedience. One is the command to feast upon the word of God. A second is to pray always. A third is the commandment to be a full-tithe payer. And the fourth is to escape from sin and its terrible effects. Each takes faith to start and then to persevere. And all can strengthen your capacity to know and obey the Lord's commands" (*Ensign,* November 2005, 38).

*What the prophet says is what the
Lord would say if he were here, and it is scripture.
It should be studied, understood, and followed.*

MARION G. ROMNEY
LEARNING FOR THE ETERNITIES, 107–8

The Lord said, "My word shall not pass away, but shall all be fulfilled, whether by mine own voice or by the voice of my servants, it is the same" (D&C 1:38). When the authorized servants of the Lord speak, it is the Lord speaking. Elder Marion G. Romney said, "Those who [understand this] will not interpret what he says as being inspired by political bias or selfishness; . . . nor that his counsels cannot be accepted because they are not prefaced by the quotation, 'Thus saith the Lord.' Those who will through mighty prayer and earnest study inform themselves as to what the living prophets say and who will act upon it will be visited by the Spirit of the Lord and know by the spirit of revelation that they speak the mind and will of the Father" (*Learning for the Eternities,* 108).

*When you as husband and wife recognize
the divine design in your union—when you feel deeply that
God has brought you to each other—your vision will be
expanded and your understanding enhanced.*

RUSSELL M. NELSON
ENSIGN, MAY 2006, 38

Elder Russell M. Nelson has given us some suggestions to strengthen our marriages: "Expressions of love and appreciation do more than acknowledge a kind thought or deed. . . . As grateful partners look for the good in each other and sincerely pay compliments to one another, wives and husbands will strive to become the persons described in those compliments. . . . To communicate well with your spouse—is also important. Good communication includes taking time to plan together. Couples need private time to observe, to talk, and really listen to each other. They need to cooperate—helping each other as equal partners. . . . If couples contemplate often—with each other in the temple—sacred covenants will be better remembered and kept. Frequent participation in temple service and regular family scripture study nourish a marriage and strengthen faith within a family" (*Ensign,* May 2006, 37–38).

DECEMBER 14

*Those born under the covenant, throughout all eternity,
are the children of their parents. Nothing except the unpardon-
able sin, or sin unto death, can break this tie.*

JOSEPH FIELDING SMITH
DOCTRINES OF SALVATION, 2:90

Covenants made in holy temples bless families for
generations, linking loved ones in an eternal chain.
Our gracious Father has provided a plan in which the
making and keeping of sacred covenants by couples,
sealed for time and eternity, can assure not only their
own eternal destiny, but that of their offspring as well.
Eternal family bonds give us the hope and strength to
persevere as we face the realities of life—as individuals, as couples, as parents. Like links in a chain,
covenant promises and blessings connect us in an
everlasting string of generations. Our children are forever ours, in a sacred stewardship that is bound in
righteousness. The holy covenants and ordinances
received in the temple allow couples and families to
be united forever. These covenants bring sweet assurances to those who exercise faith in the gospel plan
and prove themselves worthy through obedience.

DECEMBER 15

*Christmas and the holiday season is a wonderful time
to help us to forgive and forget. We become our better selves
and rise above the shackles that seem to bind us.*

JAMES E. FAUST
IN THE STRENGTH OF THE LORD, 270

Christmas has its own special spirit. During these days we focus more on others, more on the treasures of family and friends, more on the birth and life of the Savior of the world. Elder James E. Faust said, "The holiday season is a wonderful time to find peace. It is a time to make new resolves and to hope for better days. The holiday season is a special time because we make time for family, loved ones, and friends. We seem to turn outward rather than inward. We think more of others, including strangers. We have the spirit of giving. The heavenly hosts who proclaimed the birth of Jesus declared, 'Glory to God in the highest, and on earth peace, good will toward men' (Luke 2:14)" (*In the Strength of the Lord,* 270–71). Christmas is a season of renewal for the soul and of hope for all people.

It is Christ's love which suffereth long and is kind. It is Christ's love which is not puffed up nor easily provoked. Only His pure love enables Him—and us—to bear all things, believe all things, hope all things, and endure all things.

JEFFREY R. HOLLAND
TRUSTING JESUS, 81

With all the ups and downs of life we can sometimes feel like there is little that can be counted on to stand the test of time. Elder Jeffrey R. Holland reassured us: "Life has its share of some fear and some failure. Sometimes things fall short, don't quite measure up. Sometimes in both personal and public life, we are seemingly left without strength to go on. Sometimes people fail us, or economies and circumstance fail us, and life with its hardship and heartache can leave us feeling very alone. But when such difficult moments come to us, I testify that there is one thing which will never, ever fail us. One thing alone will stand the test of all time, of all tribulation, all trouble, and all transgression. One thing only never faileth—and that is the pure love of Christ" (*Trusting Jesus,* 80).

I testify that Jesus is the Christ, the Savior and Redeemer of the world; I have obeyed his sayings, and realized his promise, and the knowledge I have of him, the wisdom of this world cannot give, neither can it take away.

BRIGHAM YOUNG
DISCOURSES, 26

Coming to know Jesus as our Savior is not for the spiritually slothful: "The natural man receiveth not the things of the Spirit of God: for they are foolishness unto him: neither can he know them, because they are spiritually discerned" (1 Corinthians 2:14). We come to know that Jesus is the Christ through the gift of revelation (Revelation 19:10). Our testimony deepens as we obey his words and realize his sustaining promise of forgiveness. As we cast our burdens upon him, we feel of his matchless power (Psalm 55:22). Our awareness and appreciation for his life and infinite sacrifice grow as we learn of him, feast upon the words of eternal life, and embrace his loving grace. If we are humble and true, steadfast and immovable, the world cannot take from us our sure knowledge that Jesus is the Christ, our Savior and Redeemer.

DECEMBER 18

We must take advantage of everyday teaching moments. These moments are priceless. They come when we are working, playing, and struggling together. When they come, the Spirit of the Lord can help us know what to say and help our children accept our teaching.

ROBERT D. HALES
ENSIGN, MAY 2004, 90

As parents, we can build a bond with our children by taking advantage of everyday teaching moments. Our best teaching flows from a loving relationship and from a humble desire to exemplify in our lives the principles we teach. It is often done with few words, but emerges in both the carefully chosen and serendipitous moments of daily life. Our children won't care what we *say* if we are not striving to *live* what we teach. Elder Robert D. Hales gives us this advice: "Are we likening all of our children's gospel experiences to the real needs in their lives? Are we teaching them about the gift of the Holy Ghost, repentance, the Atonement, the sacrament, and the blessing of sacrament meeting as they meet the challenges in their lives?" (*Ensign,* May 2004, 90). The Spirit will help us to *become* the kind of teachers our children need.

Christmas is more than trees and twinkling lights,
more than toys and gifts and baubles of a hundred varieties. It is
love. It is the love of the Son of God for all mankind.

GORDON B. HINCKLEY
TEACHINGS, 61

The Christmas season is like none other. President Gordon B. Hinckley has spoken of the transformative power of this marvelous time of the year: "What a glorious and wonderful season of year this is. Our hearts change. Our attitudes change. Our way of thinking changes. There is a little more forgiveness in us. A little more of kindness. A little more of love. A little more of patience. A little more of understanding at the Christmas season of the year. What a glorious thing it is that at least once in twelve months we can become a little better than we have been during the remainder of the year. Thanks be to God for the gift of His Son, and thanks be to His Son for the gift of His life" (*Teachings,* 60–61). Reverence and gratitude for the Son of God will transform our souls.

DECEMBER 20

God's gifts, unlike seasonal gifts, are eternal and unperishable,
constituting a continual Christmas which is never over! These
infinite gifts are made possible by the "infinite atonement."

NEAL A. MAXWELL
QUOTE BOOK, 44

We each have been given a gift (D&C 46:11–12).
Some are given to know that Jesus Christ is the Son
of God; to others it is given to believe on their words;
to some it is given by the Holy Ghost to know the differences of administration, the diversities of opera-
tions, and the word of wisdom and knowledge; to
some it is given to have faith to be healed and to others to have faith to heal; to some is given the working
of miracles; to others it is given to prophesy; to others
the discerning of spirits; to some to speak with
tongues; to another is given the interpretation of
tongues (D&C 46:13–25). While we seek earnestly the
best gifts (D&C 46:8), we always remember that "all
these gifts come from God, for the benefit of the children of God" (D&C 46:26).

The birth of Christ the Lord was more than an incident,
it was an epoch in the history of the world to which prophets had
looked forward, of which poets had sung, and in which angels
joined their voices with mortals in praise to God.

HEBER J. GRANT
TEACHINGS OF PRESIDENTS OF THE CHURCH, 223

Prophets foretold the birth of Christ since the beginning. Adam and his posterity were taught to believe in the Only Begotten Son who "should come in the meridian of time, who was prepared from before the foundation of the world" (Moses 5:57). Isaiah prophesied: "Behold, a virgin shall conceive, and bear a son, and shall call his name Immanuel" (Isaiah 7:14). Nephi and his father, Lehi, similarly saw "a virgin, most beautiful and fair above all other virgins" who an angel said was "the mother of the Son of God, after the manner of the flesh" (1 Nephi 11:15, 18). The angel Gabriel appeared to Mary and foretold the birth of Christ: "Thou shalt conceive in thy womb, and bring forth a son, and shalt call his name Jesus" (Luke 1:31). And so the way was prepared for the advent of the Son of God.

The real Christmas comes to him who has taken Christ into his life as a moving, dynamic, vitalizing force. The real spirit of Christmas lies in the life and mission of the Master.

HOWARD W. HUNTER
TEACHINGS, 269

Christmas is about Christ, his birth and life, his love and mercy, his atonement and resurrection. "For God so loved the world, that he gave his only begotten Son, that whosoever believeth in him should not perish, but have everlasting life" (John 3:16). Elder Howard W. Hunter said, "If you desire to find the true spirit of Christmas and partake of the sweetness of it, let me make this suggestion to you. During the hurry of the festive occasion of this Christmas season, find time to turn your heart to God. Perhaps in the quiet hours, and in a quiet place, and on your knees . . . give thanks for the good things that have come to you, and ask that his Spirit might dwell in you" (*Teachings*, 271). By cherishing the gift of a Savior, we invite the real spirit of Christmas into our lives.

If we would secure and cultivate the love of others,
we must love others, even our enemies as well as friends.

JOSEPH SMITH
HISTORY OF THE CHURCH, 5:498

Joseph Smith was born on this day in 1805. When he was asked why he gained so many followers and retained them, he answered: "It is because I possess the principle of love. All I can offer the world is a good heart and a good hand" (*History of the Church,* 5:498). The Prophet's ability to bring others to the truth came from the purity of his heart, not necessarily from the strength of his intellect. Though he was not well educated, he was blessed with that intelligence which flows from God, and people gathered from far and wide to be taught by him. He was so full of the Spirit of God that people could not help but feel his love—as well as God's (Galatians 5:22). And Joseph Smith could not withhold that love from anyone, including his enemies. Love is the defining characteristic of a servant of God.

*Without Christ there would be no Christmas,
and without Christ there would be no fulness of joy.*

EZRA TAFT BENSON
TEACHINGS, 12

Christmas is another word for *joy*. Children and adults alike feel an extra measure of joy as they celebrate the birth of Christ. Carols proclaim *joy* to the world, and Christmas festivities usher in a season of joyful celebration. The feelings of joy are not reserved for a select group. The Savior came to the *whole* world. "Glad tidings of great joy" were pronounced to all. In Christ's own words: "I am come that they might have life, and that they might have it more abundantly" (John 10:10). Learning to "have life" and to "have it more abundantly" accounts for much of the joy we feel during Christmastime as we remember that night in Bethlehem, when angels sang and a bright star shone in the heavens. Each carol, every sparkling light, recall the majesty of that birth—and, with them, the promise of a more abundant life.

*We rejoice with you in this glorious season commemorating
the birth of our Savior, the Prince of Peace.*

THE FIRST PRESIDENCY
CHURCH NEWS, DECEMBER 4, 2004, 1

Every year the First Presidency issues a statement regarding the glorious birth of Jesus and the joy of the Christmas season. They speak as prophets, seers, and revelators—special witnesses of Christ: "As His servants, we testify that Jesus Christ is the Son of the Almighty. He left His Father's royal courts on high and condescended to come to earth as a babe born in the most humble of circumstances. Angels announced His birth, bringing 'good tidings of great joy' (Luke 2:10). After His incomparable mortal ministry and Atonement, angels again declared good tidings: 'He is not here, but is risen' (Luke 24:6). We testify that as we follow His divine example and teachings, our lives will be blessed and we will find that peace that 'passeth all understanding' (Philippians 4:7)" ("First Presidency Christmas Message, *Church News,* December 4, 2004, 1).

We bear testimony, as His duly ordained Apostles—that Jesus is the Living Christ, the immortal Son of God. He is the great King Immanuel, who stands today on the right hand of His Father.

THE FIRST PRESIDENCY AND QUORUM
OF THE TWELVE APOSTLES
ENSIGN, APRIL 2000, 3

The First Presidency and Quorum of the Twelve Apostles issued a statement to the world proclaiming the divinity of Jesus Christ: "As we commemorate the birth of Jesus Christ two millennia ago, we offer our testimony of the reality of His matchless life and the infinite virtue of His great atoning sacrifice. None other has had so profound an influence upon all who have lived and will yet live upon the earth" (*Ensign*, April 2000, 3). This document, "The Living Christ: The Testimony of the Apostles," stands as an enduring witness to the world that Jesus is the Christ, the Son of God: "He is the light, the life, and the hope of the world. His way is the path that leads to happiness in this life and eternal life in the world to come. God be thanked for the matchless gift of His divine Son" (*Ensign*, April 2000, 3).

There is a spirit attending the administration of the sacrament that warms the soul from head to foot; you feel the wounds of the spirit being healed, and the load is lifted. Comfort and happiness come to the soul that is worthy . . . of partaking of this spiritual food.

MELVIN J. BALLARD
IMPROVEMENT ERA, OCTOBER 1919, 1027

The sacrament can strengthen our commitment to the everlasting things. To partake of the sacrament worthily is to remember the sacrifice of our Lord and Savior; that he offered his life as a ransom for our sins and took upon himself the iniquity of the world so that we may receive the blessings of the Atonement. As we partake of the sacrament, we take upon ourselves anew the name of Christ and promise to always remember him and keep his commandments. We also promise to stand as witnesses of Christ at all times, in all places. We promise to keep sacred our covenant relationship with the Lord by being "willing to bear one another's burdens, that they may be light; Yea, and . . . mourn with those that mourn; yea, and comfort those that stand in need of comfort" (Mosiah 18:8–9).

The purpose of [the Church] is to help all of the children of God understand their potential and achieve their highest destiny. This church exists to provide the sons and daughters of God with the means of entrance into and exaltation in the celestial kingdom.

DALLIN H. OAKS
ENSIGN, MAY 1995, 87

The great plan of happiness is a family plan. Our Heavenly Father wants for us, his beloved children, the quality of life that he himself enjoys. Elder Dallin H. Oaks has taught, "This is a family-centered church in doctrine and practices. . . . Our theology begins with heavenly parents. Our highest aspiration is to be like them. Under the merciful plan of the Father, all of this is possible through the atonement of . . . Jesus Christ. . . . The fulness of eternal salvation is a family matter" (*Ensign,* May 1995, 87). The gospel plan gives us both a reassuring knowledge and clarity of purpose. We are not here by accident or chance, without reason or purpose or ultimate aim. We are children of God whose reason for being is to learn and grow, become like God, and enjoy exaltation in the celestial kingdom.

Do you want peace in your families? . . . If you do,
live your religion, and the very peace of God will dwell and
abide with you, for that is where peace comes from.

JOHN TAYLOR
GOSPEL KINGDOM, 340

Many people long for peace in their lives but don't know where to find it. Some search for peace on the dead-end streets of selfishness or take unsatisfying detours through empty fields of pleasure—only to discover more unrest, more uneasiness. Peace is a gift of God; it comes to those who strive to live righteously, those who sincerely submit to the Lord's will in their lives. When our trust rests in the Lord and our lives reflect his teachings, we are blessed with peace of mind and courage in the face of adversity. What blessing is greater, what peace more lasting, than the peace of God! His promise is certain: "Peace I leave with you, my peace I give unto you: not as the world giveth, give I unto you. Let not your heart be troubled, neither let it be afraid" (John 14:27).

Trust in God. Do your duty. Remember
your prayers. Get faith in the Lord, and take hold
and build up Zion. All will be right.

WILFORD WOODRUFF
TEACHINGS OF PRESIDENTS OF THE CHURCH, 258

We have been promised that if we are prepared we need not fear (D&C 38:30). Fear and worry are weapons in Satan's arsenal designed to paralyze us with anxiety. If we give in to fear, we will find it harder to go forward with faith, trust God and his purposes, and do our part to build Zion. We need strong conviction to prepare for the Lord's triumphant return. Elder Wilford Woodruff said, "Who is going to be prepared for the coming of the Messiah? [Those] who enjoy the Holy Ghost and live under the inspiration of the Almighty, who abide in Jesus Christ and bring forth fruit to the honor and glory of God" (*Teachings of Presidents of the Church,* 258). These are the last moments of the last days. Let us be steadfast, immovable, faithful, and prepared for that which assuredly is to come.

Let us ever bear in mind that in train travel and in life,
there are stations, there are departures, calls, schedules, and
opportunities for being side-tracked and diverted. . . . Safety and
joy belong to those who will come and follow [the Savior].

MARVIN J. ASHTON
ENSIGN, JULY 1972, 63

Throughout life we have occasion to ponder the
path of our feet (Proverbs 4:26). We ask ourselves
questions like *What is my destination?* and *Where will the
road I am traveling lead?* Each turn of the calendar is a new
beginning, a time to pause to review the past and look
forward to the future. We celebrate the new year as a
commencement, a chance to renew, an opportunity to
do better. It is a time to mend fences, build bridges,
and strengthen friendships. This year we can more
fully strive to do as the apostle Paul admonished: "Put
on charity. . . . And let the peace of God rule in your
hearts" (Colossians 3:14–15). Now is the time to
soften hearts, forgive, forget, and move on. It is the
time to recommit ourselves to primary causes—faith
and family, love and compassion.

SOURCES

Ballard, Melvin J. *Crusader for Righteousness.* Salt Lake City: Bookcraft, 1966.

Benson, Ezra Taft. *Sermons and Writings of President Ezra Taft Benson.* Salt Lake City: The Church of Jesus Christ of Latter-day Saints, 2003.

———. *Teachings of Ezra Taft Benson.* Salt Lake City: Bookcraft, 1988.

———. *A Witness and a Warning.* Salt Lake City: Deseret Book, 1988.

Brickey, Wayne E. *101 Powerful Promises from Latter-day Prophets.* Salt Lake City: Deseret Book, 2004.

Brown, Hugh B. *Vision and Valor.* Salt Lake City: Bookcraft, 1971.

Cannon, George Q. *Gospel Truth.* Edited by Jerreld L. Newquist. Salt Lake City: Deseret Book, 1987.

Church News. Salt Lake City: Deseret News, 1943–2006.

Collected Discourses. Edited by Brian H. Stuy. Burbank, California: B. H. S. Publishing, 1987–1992.

Conference Reports. Salt Lake City: The Church of Jesus Christ of Latter-day Saints. 1880–2006.

Cowley, Matthias F. *Cowley's Talks on Doctrine.* Chattanooga, Tenn.: Ben E. Rich, 1902.

Dew, Sheri L. *Go Forward with Faith: The Biography of Gordon B. Hinckley.* Salt Lake City: Deseret Book, 1996.

Ensign. Salt Lake City: The Church of Jesus Christ of Latter-day Saints. 1971–2006.

Evans, Richard L. *Messages from Music and the Spoken Word.* Compiled by Lloyd D. Newell. Salt Lake City: Shadow Mountain, 2003.

Eyring, Henry B. *To Draw Closer to God.* Salt Lake City: Deseret Book, 1997.

"Family, The: A Proclamation to the World." *Ensign.* November 1995, 102.

Faust, James E. and James P. Bell. *In the Strength of the Lord: The Life and Teachings of James E. Faust.* Salt Lake City: Deseret Book, 1999.

Flake, Lawrence. *Prophets and Apostles of the Last Dispensation.* Provo: Religious Studies Center, Brigham Young University, 2001.

Garr, Arnold, Donald Q. Cannon, and Richard O. Cowan. *Encyclopedia of Latter-day Saint History.* Salt Lake City: Deseret Book, 2000.

Grant, Heber J. *Gospel Standards.* Salt Lake City: Deseret Book, 1976.

———. *Teachings of Presidents of the Church: Heber J. Grant.* Salt Lake City: The Church of Jesus Christ of Latter-day Saints, 2002.

Hinckley, Gordon B. *Church News.* November 16, 1996, 4.

———. *Discourses of President Gordon B. Hinckley.* 2 vols. Salt Lake City: Deseret Book, 2004–2005.

———. *Stand a Little Taller.* Salt Lake City: Deseret Book, 2001.

———. *Teachings of Gordon B. Hinckley.* Salt Lake City: Deseret Book, 1997.

Holland, Jeffrey R. *Trusting Jesus.* Salt Lake City: Deseret Book, 2003.

Hunter, Howard W. *The Teachings of Howard W. Hunter.* Edited by Clyde J. Williams. Salt Lake City: Bookcraft, 1997.

Hymns of The Church of Jesus Christ of Latter-day Saints. Salt Lake City: The Church of Jesus Christ of Latter-day Saints, 1985.

Improvement Era. Salt Lake City: The Church of Jesus Christ of Latter-day Saints. 1897–1970.

Journal of Discourses. 26 vols. London: Latter-day Saints' Book Depot, 1854–86.

Kimball, Spencer W. *Teachings of Spencer W. Kimball.* Edited by Edward L. Kimball. Salt Lake City: Bookcraft, 1982.

Lee, Harold B. *The Teachings of Harold B. Lee.* Edited by Clyde J. Williams. Salt Lake City: Bookcraft, 1996.

———. *Teachings of Presidents of the Church: Harold B. Lee.* Salt Lake City: The Church of Jesus Christ of Latter-day Saints, 2000.

Lewis, C. S. *Mere Christianity.* Anniversary Edition. New York: Macmillan, 1981.

"Living Christ, The." *Ensign.* April 2000.

Madsen, Susan Arrington. *The Lord Needed a Prophet.* 2d ed. Salt Lake City: Deseret Book, 1996.

Maxwell, Neal A. *The Neal A. Maxwell Quote Book*. Edited by Cory H. Maxwell. Salt Lake City: Bookcraft, 1997.

McConkie, Bruce R. *The Millennial Messiah*. Salt Lake City: Deseret Book, 1982.

———. "The Probationary Test of Mortality." Address delivered at institute of religion. Salt Lake City: January 10, 1982.

———. "Spare Time's Rare to Apostle." *Church News*. January 24, 1976, 4.

McKay, David O. *Gospel Ideals*. Salt Lake City: Improvement Era, 1953.

———. *Teachings of Presidents of the Church: David O. McKay*. Salt Lake City: The Church of Jesus Christ of Latter-day Saints, 2003.

Monson, Thomas S. *Live the Good Life*. Salt Lake City: Deseret Book, 1988.

Oaks, Dallin H. *The Lord's Way*. Salt Lake City: Deseret Book, 1991.

Packer, Boyd K. *That All May Be Edified*. Salt Lake City: Bookcraft, 1982.

———. *Things of the Soul*. Salt Lake City: Bookcraft, 1996.

Perry, L. Tom. *Living with Enthusiasm*. Salt Lake City: Deseret Book, 1996.

Petersen, Mark E. *Faith Works*. Salt Lake City: Bookcraft, 1963.

Pratt, Parley P. *Key to the Science of Theology*. Classics in Mormon Literature. Salt Lake City: Deseret Book, 1978.

SOURCES

Richards, Stephen L. *Where Is Wisdom?* Salt Lake City: Deseret Book, 1955.

Romney, Marion G. *Learning for the Eternities.* Salt Lake City: Deseret Book, 1977.

———. *Look to God and Live.* Compiled by George J. Romney. Salt Lake City: Deseret Book, 1971.

Smith, George Albert. *The Teachings of George Albert Smith.* Edited by Robert and Susan McIntosh. Salt Lake City: Bookcraft, 1996.

Smith, Joseph Jr. *Encyclopedia of Joseph Smith's Teachings.* Edited by Larry E. Dahl and Donald Q. Cannon. Salt Lake City: Bookcraft, 1997.

———. *History of The Church of Jesus Christ of Latter-day Saints.* Edited by B. H. Roberts. 2d ed. rev., 7 vols. Salt Lake City: The Church of Jesus Christ of Latter-day Saints, 1932–51.

———. *Teachings of the Prophet Joseph Smith.* Selected by Joseph Fielding Smith. Salt Lake City: Deseret Book, 1976.

Smith, Joseph F. *Gospel Doctrine.* 5th ed. Salt Lake City: Deseret Book, 1939.

———. *Teachings of Presidents of the Church: Joseph F. Smith.* Salt Lake City: The Church of Jesus Christ of Latter-day Saints, 1998.

Smith, Joseph Fielding. *Doctrines of Salvation.* Compiled by Bruce R. McConkie. 3 vols. Salt Lake City: Bookcraft, 1954–56.

Snow, Lorenzo. *The Teachings of Lorenzo Snow.* Edited by Clyde J. Williams. Salt Lake City: Bookcraft, 1984.

Talmage, James E. *Jesus the Christ.* Salt Lake City: Deseret Book, 1983.

Taylor, John. *The Gospel Kingdom.* Edited by G. Homer Durham. Salt Lake City: Improvement Era, 1941.

——. *Teachings of Presidents of the Church: John Taylor.* Salt Lake City: The Church of Jesus Christ of Latter-day Saints, 2001.

Whitney, Orson F. *Life of Heber C. Kimball.* Salt Lake City: Kimball Family, 1888.

——. *Saturday Night Thoughts.* Salt Lake City: Deseret News, 1921.

Widtsoe, John A. *Evidences and Reconciliations.* Salt Lake City: Bookcraft, 1960.

Woodruff, Wilford. *The Discourses of Wilford Woodruff.* Edited by G. Homer Durham. Salt Lake City: Bookcraft, 1969.

——. *Teachings of Presidents of the Church: Wilford Woodruff.* Salt Lake City: The Church of Jesus Christ of Latter-day Saints, 2004.

Young, Brigham. *Discourses of Brigham Young.* Selected by John A. Widtsoe. Salt Lake City: Deseret Book, 1954.

——. *Teachings of Presidents of the Church: Brigham Young.* Salt Lake City: The Church of Jesus Christ of Latter-day Saints, 1997.

PROPHETS AND
APOSTLES QUOTED
IN THIS BOOK

Marvin J. Ashton—Born May 16, 1915, in Salt Lake City, Utah. He was ordained an apostle in 1971. He died on February 25, 1994, in Salt Lake City, Utah.

M. Russell Ballard—Born October 8, 1928, in Salt Lake City, Utah. He was ordained an apostle in 1985.

Melvin J. Ballard—Born February 9, 1873, in Logan, Utah. He was ordained an apostle in 1919. He died on July 30, 1939, in Salt Lake City, Utah.

David A. Bednar—Born on June 15, 1952, in Oakland, California. He was ordained an apostle in 2004.

Ezra Taft Benson—Born August 4, 1899, in Whitney, Idaho. He was ordained an apostle in 1943 and became the thirteenth president of the Church on November 10, 1985. He died May 30, 1994, in Salt Lake City, Utah.

Hugh B. Brown—Born October 24, 1883, in Granger, Utah. He was ordained an apostle in 1958 and was called to serve in the First Presidency in 1961, serving with President David O. McKay. He died December 2, 1975, in Salt Lake City, Utah.

Charles A. Callis—Born May 4, 1865, in Dublin, Ireland. He was ordained an apostle in 1933. He died on January 21, 1947, in Jacksonville, Florida.

George Q. Cannon—Born January 11, 1827, in Liverpool, England. He was ordained an apostle in 1860 and was called to serve in the First Presidency in 1873, serving as a counselor to four Presidents of the Church. He died on April 12, 1901, in Monterey, California.

J. Reuben Clark Jr.—Born September 1, 1871, in Grantsville, Utah. He was called to serve in the First Presidency in 1933 and was ordained an apostle in 1934. He served as a counselor to three Presidents of the Church. He died October 6, 1961, in Salt Lake City, Utah.

Matthias F. Cowley—Born August 25, 1858, in Salt Lake City, Utah. He was ordained an apostle in 1897, and resigned in 1905. He died on June 16, 1940, in Salt Lake City, Utah.

Richard L. Evans—Born March 23, 1906, in Salt Lake City, Utah. He was ordained an apostle in 1953. He died on November 1, 1971, in Salt Lake City, Utah.

Henry B. Eyring—Born May 31, 1933, in Princeton, New Jersey. He was ordained an apostle in 1995.

James E. Faust—Born July 31, 1920, in Delta, Utah. He was ordained an apostle in 1978 and was set apart as second counselor to President Gordon B. Hinckley on March 12, 1995.

Heber J. Grant—Born November 22, 1856, in Salt Lake City, Utah. He was ordained an apostle in 1882 and became the seventh president of the Church on November 23, 1918. He died May 14, 1945, in Salt Lake City, Utah.

David B. Haight—Born September 2, 1906, in Oakley,

Idaho. He was ordained an apostle in 1976. He died July 31, 2004, in Salt Lake City, Utah.

Robert D. Hales—Born August 24, 1932, in New York City, New York. He was ordained an apostle in 1994.

Gordon B. Hinckley—Born June 23, 1910, in Salt Lake City, Utah. He was ordained an apostle in 1961 and became the fifteenth president of the Church on March 12, 1995.

Jeffrey R. Holland—Born December 3, 1940, in St. George, Utah. He was ordained an apostle in 1994.

Howard W. Hunter—Born November 14, 1907, in Boise, Idaho. He was ordained an apostle in 1959 and became the fourteenth president of the Church on June 5, 1994. He died on March 3, 1995, in Salt Lake City, Utah.

Heber C. Kimball—Born June 14, 1801, in Sheldon, Vermont. He was ordained an apostle in 1935 and became first counselor to Brigham Young in 1847. He died on June 22, 1868, in Salt Lake City, Utah.

Spencer W. Kimball—Born March 28, 1895, in Salt Lake City, Utah. He was ordained an apostle in 1943 and became the twelfth president of the Church on December 30, 1973. He died November 5, 1985, in Salt Lake City, Utah.

Harold B. Lee—Born March 28, 1899, in Clifton, Idaho. He was ordained an apostle in 1941 and became the eleventh president of the Church on July 7, 1972. He died December 26, 1973.

Neal A. Maxwell—Born July 6, 1926, in Salt Lake City,

Utah. He was ordained an apostle in 1981. He died on July 21, 2004, in Salt Lake City, Utah.

Bruce R. McConkie—Born July 29, 1915, in Ann Arbor, Michigan. He was ordained an apostle in 1972. He died on April 19, 1985, in Salt Lake City, Utah.

David O. McKay—Born September 8, 1873, in Huntsville, Utah. He was ordained an apostle in 1906 and became the ninth president of the Church on April 9, 1951. He died on January 18, 1970, in Salt Lake City.

Marriner W. Merrill—Born September 25, 1835, in Sackville, New Brunswick. He was ordained an apostle in 1889. He died on February 6, 1906, in Richmond, Utah.

Thomas S. Monson—Born August 21, 1927, in Salt Lake City, Utah. He was ordained an apostle in 1963 and was called to serve in the First Presidency in 1985. He has served as a counselor to three Presidents of the Church.

George Q. Morris—Born February 20, 1874, in Salt Lake City, Utah. He was ordained an apostle in 1954. He died on April 23, 1962, in Salt Lake City, Utah.

Henry D. Moyle—Born April 22, 1889, in Salt Lake City, Utah. He was ordained an apostle in 1947 and was called to serve in the First Presidency in 1959, serving with President David O. McKay. He died on September 18, 1963, in Deer Park, Florida.

Russell M. Nelson—Born September 9, 1924, in Salt Lake City, Utah. He was ordained an apostle in 1984.

Dallin H. Oaks—Born August 12, 1932, in Provo, Utah. He was ordained an apostle in 1984.

Boyd K. Packer—Born September 10, 1924, in Brigham City, Utah. He was ordained an apostle in 1970 and was set apart as the acting president of the Quorum of the Twelve Apostles on June 5, 1994, and again on March 12, 1995.

L. Tom Perry—Born August 5, 1922, in Logan, Utah. He was ordained an apostle in 1974.

Mark E. Petersen—Born November 7, 1900, in Salt Lake City, Utah. He was ordained an apostle in 1944. He died on January 11, 1984, in Salt Lake City, Utah.

Orson Pratt—Born September 19, 1811, in Hartford, New York. He was ordained an apostle in 1835. He was excommunicated in 1842, then was rebaptized and reinstated as an apostle in 1843. He died October 3, 1881, in Salt Lake City, Utah.

Parley P. Pratt—Born April 12, 1807, in Burlington, New York. He was ordained an apostle in 1835. He was assassinated on May 13, 1857, near Van Buren, Arkansas.

Franklin D. Richards—Born April 2, 1821, in Richmond, Massachusetts. He was ordained an apostle in 1849. He died December 9, 1899, in Ogden, Utah.

LeGrand Richards—Born February 6, 1886, in Farmington, Utah. He was ordained an apostle in 1952. He died on January 11, 1983, in Salt Lake City, Utah.

Stephen L Richards—Born June 18, 1879, in Mendon, Utah. He was ordained an apostle in 1917 and was called to serve in the First Presidency in 1951, serving with President David O. McKay. He died on May 19, 1959, in Salt Lake City, Utah.

Marion G. Romney—Born September 19, 1897, in Colonia Juarez, Mexico. He was ordained an apostle in 1951 and was called to serve in the First Presidency in 1972, serving first with President Harold B. Lee and then with President Spencer W. Kimball. He died May 20, 1988, in Salt Lake City, Utah.

Richard G. Scott—Born November 7, 1928, in Pocatello, Idaho. He was ordained an apostle in 1988.

George Albert Smith—Born April 4, 1870, in Salt Lake City, Utah. He was ordained an apostle in 1903 and became the eighth President of the Church on May 21, 1945. He died April 4, 1951, in Salt Lake City, Utah.

Joseph Smith—Born December 23, 1805, in Sharon, Vermont. He became the first President of the Church when it was organized in 1830. He was martyred June 27, 1844, in Carthage, Illinois.

Joseph F. Smith—Born November 13, 1838, in Far West, Missouri. He was ordained an apostle in 1866 and became the sixth President of the Church on October 17, 1901. He died November 19, 1918, in Salt Lake City, Utah.

Joseph Fielding Smith—Born July 19, 1876, in Salt Lake City, Utah. He was ordained an apostle in 1910 and became the tenth President of the Church on January 23, 1970. He died on July 2, 1972, in Salt Lake City, Utah.

Lorenzo Snow—Born April 3, 1814, in Mantua, Ohio. He

was ordained an apostle in 1849 and became the fifth president of the Church on September 13, 1898. He died October 10, 1901, in Salt Lake City, Utah.

Delbert L. Stapley—Born December 11, 1896, in Mesa, Arizona. He was ordained an apostle in 1950. He died on August 19, 1978, in Salt Lake City, Utah.

James E. Talmage—Born September 21, 1862, in Hungerford, England. He was ordained an apostle in 1911. He died on July 27, 1933, in Salt Lake City, Utah.

John Taylor—Born November 1, 1808, in Milnthorpe, England. He became the third President of the Church on October 10, 1880. He died on July 25, 1887, in Kaysville, Utah.

N. Eldon Tanner—Born May 9, 1898, in Salt Lake City, Utah. He was ordained an apostle in 1962 and was called to serve in the First Presidency in 1963. He served as a counselor to four Presidents of the Church. He died November 27, 1982.

Dieter F. Uchtdorf—Born November 6, 1940, in Ostrava, Czechoslovakia. He was ordained an apostle in 2004.

Daniel H. Wells—Born October 27, 1814, in Trenton, New Jersey. He became second counselor to Brigham Young in 1857 and was released on President Young's death. He was then called to serve as a counselor to the Twelve Apostles. He died on March 24, 1891, in Salt Lake City, Utah.

Orson F. Whitney—Born July 1, 1855, in Salt Lake City, Utah. He was ordained an apostle in 1906. He died on May 16, 1931, in Salt Lake City, Utah.

John A. Widtsoe—Born January 31, 1872, in Daloe, Norway. He was ordained an apostle in 1921. He died on November 29, 1952, in Salt Lake City, Utah.

Joseph B. Wirthlin—Born June 11, 1917, in Salt Lake City, Utah. He was ordained an apostle in 1986.

Abraham O. Woodruff—Born November 23, 1872, in Salt Lake City, Utah. He was ordained an apostle in 1897. He died June 20, 1904, in El Paso, Texas.

Wilford Woodruff—Born March 1, 1807, in Avon, Connecticut. He was ordained an apostle in 1839 and became the fourth president of the Church on April 7, 1889. He died on September 2, 1898, in San Francisco, California.

Brigham Young—Born June 1, 1801, in Whitingham, Vermont. He was ordained an apostle in 1835 and became the second president of the Church on December 27, 1847. He died August 29, 1877, in Salt Lake City, Utah.

ABOUT THE AUTHOR

Lloyd D. Newell has a Ph.D. from Brigham Young University, where he is on the faculties of Religious Education and the School of Family Life. He has addressed audiences in forty-five states and more than a dozen countries through his seminars and keynote-speaking engagements, and has worked as a television news anchor and news magazine host. He has served as announcer and writer for the Mormon Tabernacle Choir broadcast "Music and the Spoken Word" since 1990 and is the author of several books. He has co-authored, with Robert L. Millet, four previous daily devotionals: *Jesus, the Very Thought of Thee, When Ye Shall Receive These Things, Draw Near Unto Me,* and *A Lamp Unto My Feet.* He and his wife, Karmel, are the parents of four children.